FOOD & WINE BEST OF THE BEST VOL. 15

EXECUTIVE EDITOR **Kate Heddings**
DESIGNER **Michelle Leong**
EDITOR **Susan Choung**
FEATURES EDITOR **Michael Endelman**
ASSOCIATE FOOD EDITOR **Justin Chapple**
ASSOCIATE WINE EDITOR **Megan Krigbaum**
COPY EDITOR **Lisa Leventer**
PRODUCTION MANAGER **Matt Carson**
DEPUTY PHOTO EDITOR **Anthony LaSala**
REPORTERS **Justin Chapple, Maggie Mariolis,
  Chelsea Morse, M. Elizabeth Sheldon**

FOOD & WINE MAGAZINE

SVP / EDITOR IN CHIEF **Dana Cowin**
CREATIVE DIRECTOR **Stephen Scoble**
MANAGING EDITOR **Mary Ellen Ward**
EXECUTIVE EDITOR **Pamela Kaufman**
EXECUTIVE FOOD EDITOR **Tina Ujlaki**
EXECUTIVE WINE EDITOR **Ray Isle**
EXECUTIVE DIGITAL EDITOR **Rebecca Bauer**
DEPUTY EDITOR **Christine Quinlan**
ART DIRECTOR **Courtney Waddell Eckersley**

ISBN 10: 1-932624-42-2
ISBN 13: 978-1-932624-42-7
ISSN 1524-2862

Published by American Express Publishing Corporation
1120 Avenue of the Americas, New York, New York 10036

Manufactured in the United States of America

AMERICAN EXPRESS PUBLISHING CORPORATION

PRESIDENT / CEO **Ed Kelly**
CHIEF MARKETING OFFICER / PRESIDENT,
  DIGITAL MEDIA **Mark V. Stanich**
SVP / CHIEF FINANCIAL OFFICER **Paul B. Francis**
VPs / GENERAL MANAGERS **Frank Bland, Keith Strohmeier**

VP, BOOKS & PRODUCTS / PUBLISHER **Marshall Corey**
DIRECTOR, BOOK PROGRAMS **Bruce Spanier**
SENIOR MARKETING MANAGER, BRANDED BOOKS **Eric Lucie**
ASSISTANT MARKETING MANAGER **Stacy Mallis**
DIRECTOR OF FULFILLMENT & PREMIUM VALUE **Philip Black**
MANAGER OF CUSTOMER EXPERIENCE
  & PRODUCT DEVELOPMENT **Betsy Wilson**
DIRECTOR OF FINANCE **Thomas Noonan**
ASSOCIATE BUSINESS MANAGER **Uma Mahabir**
OPERATIONS DIRECTOR (PREPRESS) **Rosalie Abatemarco Samat**
OPERATIONS DIRECTOR (MANUFACTURING) **Anthony White**
SENIOR MANAGER, CONTRACTS & RIGHTS **Jeniqua Moore**

FRONT & BACK COVERS & PAGE 10

PHOTOGRAPHER **Lucas Allen**
FOOD STYLIST **Simon Andrews**
STYLIST **Suzie Myers**

FLAP PHOTOGRAPHS

DANA COWIN **Sylvain Gaboury**
KATE HEDDINGS **Andrew French**

BEST OF THE BEST

the BEST RECIPES *from the* 25 BEST COOKBOOKS *of the year*

FOOD&WINE
BOOKS

American Express Publishing Corporation, New York

CONTENTS

PAGE 12

MOLTO BATALI
mario batali

Summer Beans with a Spicy Lime Spritz
Manicotti Baresi al Forno
Lamb Shanks with Leeks & Grapes
Ziti with Tuna & Salame Piccante
Braised Chicken Thighs with Saffron, Green Olives & Mint

PAGE 22

THE COOK & THE BUTCHER
brigit binns

Lamb & Pita Salad
Roasted Beef Tenderloin with Mushroom Ragout
Korean-Style Short Ribs
Oven-Browned Spareribs with Lemongrass, Honey & Soy
Israeli Couscous Salad

PAGE 32

AMERICAN FLAVOR
andrew carmellini & gwen hyman

Scallops with Grapefruit Butter
Black-Eyed Pea & Kale Chili with Monterey Jack Cheese
Duck with Peaches, Ginger & Lemon Thyme
Korean Steak
Smoky Eggplant Dip

PAGE 44

COOK THIS NOW
melissa clark

Cumin Seed Roasted Cauliflower with Salted Yogurt, Mint & Pomegranate Seeds
Shrimp Scampi with Pernod & Fennel Fronds
Vietnamese Grilled Steak & Cabbage Salad with Peanuts, Cilantro & Chiles
Mallobars
Sweet Potato Tea Cake with Brown Sugar–Rum Glaze

PAGE 58

MY GRILL
pete evans

Fish with Crispy Garlic & Almond Salad
Grilled Fish with an Italian Garden Salsa of Artichokes & Tomato
Grilled Gözlemes
Quick Steaks with Green Olive Dressing & Tomato Salad

PAGE 68

RIVER COTTAGE EVERY DAY
hugh fearnley-whittingstall

Warm Leek & White Bean Salad with Mustard Dressing
Roast Jerusalem Artichoke, Hazelnut & Goat Cheese Salad
Thrifty Fish Soup with Cheaty Rouille
Baked Chicken Curry
Leek & Goat Cheese Speltotto

Recipe titles in **bold** are brand-new dishes appearing exclusively in *Best of the Best*.

PAGE 78

BOBBY FLAY'S BAR AMERICAIN COOKBOOK
bobby flay with stephanie banyas & sally jackson

Smoked Chile Collard Greens

Chicken Cutlet with American Triple Cream Cheese, Southern Ham & Arugula

Deep-Dish Chocolate Cream Pie

Smoked Tomatoes with Ancho Bread Crumbs & Creamy Cilantro Vinaigrette

PAGE 86

A SOUTHERLY COURSE
martha hall foose

Deviled Tomatoes

Hominy Salad

Sausage Dinner

Gulf Coast–Style Crab Rolls

PAGE 92

THE MEATBALL SHOP COOKBOOK
daniel holzman & michael chernow with lauren deen

Mini Buffalo Chicken Balls

Smashed Turnips with Fresh Horseradish

Bolognese Balls

Chicken Cordon Bleu Meatballs

PAGE 100

DESSERTS FROM THE FAMOUS LOVELESS CAFE
alisa huntsman

Southern Belle Raspberry Pie

Chocolate Cookie–Peanut Butter Pie

Chocolate Mashed Potato Cake

One-Bowl Brownie Drops

Red Velvet Cheesecake Bars

PAGE 112

BOCCA COOKBOOK
jacob kenedy

Orecchiette with 'Nduja

Pappardelle with Chicken Liver Ragù

Gorgonzola, Asparagus & Hazelnut Risotto

Burned Ricotta Pie

Young Swiss Chard, Fennel & Parmesan Salad

PAGE 122

MOURAD: NEW MOROCCAN
mourad lahlou with susie heller, steve siegelman & amy vogler

Spiced Almonds

Salt-Roasted Potatoes

Roast Chicken with Preserved Lemons & Root Vegetables

Chicken Skewers

Piquillo Pepper Jam

CONTENTS *continued*

PAGE 134

BI-RITE MARKET'S EAT GOOD FOOD
sam mogannam & dabney gough

Seared Saffron Albacore Tuna with Fennel-Olive Tapenade

Romesco Chicken Salad

Sicilian Meatballs with Fresh Basil Marinara

Lemony Kale Caesar Salad

Crispy Fresh Salmon Cakes

PAGE 144

THE ART OF LIVING ACCORDING TO JOE BEEF
frédéric morin, david mcmillan & meredith erickson

Baked Mushrooms with New (or Old!) Garlic

Petits Farcis

Mouclade

Chicken Skin Tacos

Schnitzel of Pork

Yukon Gold Soup with Smoked Fish & Pumpernickel Croutons

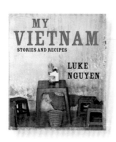

PAGE 156

MY VIETNAM
luke nguyen

Sautéed Jumbo Shrimp

Wok-Tossed Beef with Kohlrabi

Silken Tofu & Pork Soup

Hanoi Chicken & Vermicelli Noodle Soup

Grilled Eggplant Salad with Prawns

PAGE 166

THE JAPANESE GRILL
tadashi ono & harris salat

Bone-In Chicken Breast with Soy Sauce

Turkey Burger with Quick Barbecue Sauce

Salmon with Shiso Pesto

Pork Chops with Yuzu-Miso Marinade

Yuan Yaki–Style Grilled Spanish Mackerel

PAGE 174

PLENTY
yotam ottolenghi

Marinated Pepper Salad with Pecorino

Green Bean Salad with Mustard Seeds & Tarragon

Crusted Pumpkin Wedges with Sour Cream

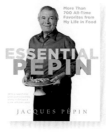

PAGE 182

ESSENTIAL PEPIN
jacques pépin

Broccoli Velvet Puree

Halibut Steaks Grenoble-Style

Spicy Ginger & Lemon Chicken

My Mother's Chicken Ragout

PAGE 188

MIETTE
meg ray with leslie jonath

Buttermilk Panna Cotta

Fleur de Sel Caramels

English Toffee

Banana Bread with Nutty Streusel

Lemon Cloud Cake

Recipe titles in **bold** are brand-new dishes appearing exclusively in *Best of the Best*.

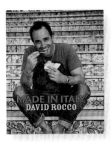

PAGE 200
MADE IN ITALY
david rocco

Cavolfiori Stufati al Pomodoro
The Best Cauliflower Ever

Penne alla Trapanese
Penne Trapani Style

Polpette di Zucchine
Zucchini Balls

Spaghetti alla Ravellese

PAGE 208
TRULY MEXICAN
*roberto santibañez with jj goode
& shelley wiseman*

Blue Cheese Guacamole
Guacamole con Queso Azul

Mexican-Style Noodles
Fideos Secos

Chicken in Chunky Tomatillo Sauce
Pollo Entomatado

Pork in Adobo
Cerdo en Adobo

Stewed Frankfurter Tortas

PAGE 222
MICHAEL'S GENUINE FOOD
michael schwartz & joann cianciulli

Chile Chicken Wings with
Creamy Cucumbers

Pan-Roasted Striped Bass with
Tunisian Chickpea Salad & Yogurt Sauce

Roasted Sweet Onions Stuffed with
Ground Lamb & Apricots

Apricot-Bourbon-Glazed Grilled Chicken

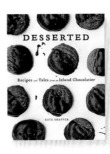

PAGE 230
DESSERTED
kate shaffer

Ricotta Doughnut Holes with
Orange-Scented Dipping Chocolate

Bittersweet Chocolate Chunk
& Cream Cheese Scones

Black Dinah Chocolate Tiramisu

Pumpkin Cheesecake with Elderberry Glaze
& Chocolate Walnut Crumb Crust

Persian Love Caramel Sauce

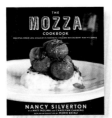

PAGE 242
THE MOZZA COOKBOOK
*nancy silverton with matt molina
& carolynn carreño*

Nancy's Chopped Salad

Fiorentini with Guanciale, Tomato
& Spicy Pickled Peppers

Garganelli with Ragù Bolognese

PAGE 256
BAKING STYLE
lisa yockelson

Molasses Crinkles

Apple Cake, Maple Butter Glaze

Craggy-Top Sour Cream Buns,
Vanilla Streusel

Butter + Cinnamon + Sugar = Cake

Bacon, Onion & Gruyère Scones

RECIPES

starters

43 Smoky Eggplant Dip

64 Grilled Gözlemes

70 Warm Leek & White Bean Salad with Mustard Dressing

72 Roast Jerusalem Artichoke, Hazelnut & Goat Cheese Salad

85 Smoked Tomatoes with Ancho Bread Crumbs & Creamy Cilantro Vinaigrette

88 Deviled Tomatoes

89 Hominy Salad

94 Mini Buffalo Chicken Balls

99 Chicken Cordon Bleu Meatballs

121 Young Swiss Chard, Fennel & Parmesan Salad

124 Spiced Almonds

132 Chicken Skewers

133 Piquillo Pepper Jam

142 Lemony Kale Caesar Salad

148 Petits Farcis

155 Yukon Gold Soup with Smoked Fish & Pumpernickel Croutons

176 Marinated Pepper Salad with Pecorino

206 Polpette di Zucchine

210 Blue Cheese Guacamole

224 Chile Chicken Wings with Creamy Cucumbers

244 Nancy's Chopped Salad

pasta, grains & beans

16 Manicotti Baresi al Forno

20 Ziti with Tuna & Salame Piccante

31 Israeli Couscous Salad

36 Black-Eyed Pea & Kale Chili with Monterey Jack Cheese

77 Leek & Goat Cheese Speltotto

114 Orecchiette with 'Nduja

116 Pappardelle with Chicken Liver Ragù

117 Gorgonzola, Asparagus & Hazelnut Risotto

204 Penne alla Trapanese

207 Spaghetti alla Ravellese

212 Mexican-Style Noodles

247 Fiorentini with Guanciale, Tomato & Spicy Pickled Peppers

250 Garganelli with Ragù Bolognese

fish & shellfish

34 Scallops with Grapefruit Butter

48 Shrimp Scampi with Pernod & Fennel Fronds

60 Fish with Crispy Garlic & Almond Salad

62 Grilled Fish with an Italian Garden Salsa of Artichokes & Tomato

74 Thrifty Fish Soup with Cheaty Rouille

91 Gulf Coast–Style Crab Rolls

136 Seared Saffron Albacore Tuna with Fennel-Olive Tapenade

143 Crispy Fresh Salmon Cakes

150 Mouclade

158 Sautéed Jumbo Shrimp

170 Salmon with Shiso Pesto

173 Yuan Yaki–Style Grilled Spanish Mackerel

185 Halibut Steaks Grenoble-Style

226 Pan-Roasted Striped Bass with Tunisian Chickpea Salad & Yogurt Sauce

poultry

21 Braised Chicken Thighs with Saffron, Green Olives & Mint

38 Duck with Peaches, Ginger & Lemon Thyme

76 Baked Chicken Curry

82 Chicken Cutlet with American Triple Cream Cheese, Southern Ham & Arugula

128 Roast Chicken with Preserved Lemons & Root Vegetables

138 Romesco Chicken Salad

152 Chicken Skin Tacos

162 Hanoi Chicken & Vermicelli Noodle Soup

168 Bone-In Chicken Breast with Soy Sauce

169 Turkey Burger with Quick Barbecue Sauce

186 Spicy Ginger & Lemon Chicken

187 My Mother's Chicken Ragout

216 Chicken in Chunky Tomatillo Sauce

229 Apricot-Bourbon-Glazed Grilled Chicken

meat

18 Lamb Shanks with Leeks & Grapes

24 Lamb & Pita Salad

26 Roasted Beef Tenderloin with Mushroom Ragout

28 Korean-Style Short Ribs

30 Oven-Browned Spareribs with Lemongrass, Honey & Soy

40 Korean Steak

51 Vietnamese Grilled Steak & Cabbage Salad with Peanuts, Cilantro & Chiles

66 Quick Steaks with Green Olive Dressing & Tomato Salad

90 Sausage Dinner

98 Bolognese Balls

140 Sicilian Meatballs with Fresh Basil Marinara

154 Schnitzel of Pork

160 Wok-Tossed Beef with Kohlrabi

161 Silken Tofu & Pork Soup

172 Pork Chops with Yuzu-Miso Marinade

218 Pork in Adobo

221 Stewed Frankfurter Tortas

vegetables & sides

14 Summer Beans with a Spicy Lime Spritz

46 Cumin Seed Roasted Cauliflower with Salted Yogurt, Mint & Pomegranate Seeds

80 Smoked Chile Collard Greens

96 Smashed Turnips with Fresh Horseradish

126 Salt-Roasted Potatoes

146 Baked Mushrooms with New (or Old!) Garlic

165 Grilled Eggplant Salad with Prawns

178 Green Bean Salad with Mustard Seeds & Tarragon

180 Crusted Pumpkin Wedges with Sour Cream

184 Broccoli Velvet Puree

202 Cavolfiori Stufati al Pomodoro

228 Roasted Sweet Onions Stuffed with Ground Lamb & Apricots

brunch

57 Sweet Potato Tea Cake with Brown Sugar–Rum Glaze

197 Banana Bread with Nutty Streusel

232 Ricotta Doughnut Holes with Orange-Scented Dipping Chocolate

234 Bittersweet Chocolate Chunk & Cream Cheese Scones

264 Craggy-Top Sour Cream Buns, Vanilla Streusel

269 Bacon, Onion & Gruyère Scones

desserts

54 Mallobars

84 Deep-Dish Chocolate Cream Pie

102 Southern Belle Raspberry Pie

105 Chocolate Cookie–Peanut Butter Pie

108 Chocolate Mashed Potato Cake

110 One-Bowl Brownie Drops

111 Red Velvet Cheesecake Bars

118 Burned Ricotta Pie

190 Buttermilk Panna Cotta

191 Fleur de Sel Caramels

194 English Toffee

199 Lemon Cloud Cake

236 Black Dinah Chocolate Tiramisu

238 Pumpkin Cheesecake with Elderberry Glaze & Chocolate Walnut Crumb Crust

241 Persian Love Caramel Sauce

258 Molasses Crinkles

261 Apple Cake, Maple Butter Glaze

268 Butter + Cinnamon + Sugar = Cake

Israeli couscous salad (page 31),
exclusive recipe from Brigit Binns,
author of The Cook & the Butcher

FOREWORD

when we select recipes to try out for our annual collection *Best of the Best,* we get excited about the potential of each and every one. Unfortunately, there are always more than a few clunkers in the batch, though the let-downs can be as funny as they are sad. One time, we were counting the minutes until Justin Chapple, our terrific recipe tester, finished baking a mile-high lemon meringue pie. Finally it emerged from the oven and we gathered around the table in our kitchen to taste it. The pie was gorgeous! Justin cut into it: lemon soup.

A much happier day of testing ends with the editors photocopying our favorite recipes and making them at home that very night. One such hit was the pork schnitzel from *The Art of Living According to Joe Beef.* We loved the smart trick of mixing a little sour cream into the egg wash that coats the pork. The result was a succulent, tender and slightly tangy piece of meat that we couldn't stop eating. And the recipe of the year was from *The Meatball Shop Cookbook;* chef Daniel Holzman took one of America's most beloved dishes, Buffalo chicken wings, and reimagined it as spicy, juicy little meatballs, with blue cheese dipping sauce on the side. Every editor here has since gone home and made it.

Because we've tested all the recipes in *Best of the Best,* you won't find a goose egg in the bunch. We loved each one, and hope you do too.

Dana Cowin
Editor in Chief
FOOD & WINE Magazine

Kate Heddings
Executive Editor
FOOD & WINE Cookbooks

Ziti with tuna and salame piccante, page 20

MOLTO BATALI

mario batali

why we love this book

Mario Batali isn't just a culinary superstar; he's the father of two teenage boys (Benno and Leo) who makes a point of eating dinner at home with his family. In his ninth cookbook, he offers 12 menus—each with a main dish, several pastas and sides, a soup and a dessert— designed for simple, family-style eating. By suggesting shortcuts (such as jarred tomato sauce) in dishes like Ziti with Tuna and Salame Piccante (page 20), he makes it easy to re-create his signature big flavors.

quick dinner

"A lot of my family's favorite weeknight dishes are Mexican, like tacos. But in a pinch, you can't go wrong with spaghetti *aglio e olio* [with garlic, oil and chiles]."

pantry staple

"I love hot sauce. At my house we always have an arsenal of hot sauces in our pantry. Some are vinegar-based, some are spicy, some are aged."

on molto batali

"Each of my cookbooks has a different concept. *Babbo* records recipes from my New York City restaurant Babbo. *Holiday Food* features the meals I eat with my family on special occasions. I was starting to cook more large-format, family-style dishes for suppers at home, so *Molto Batali* is a compilation of those meals—old standards as well as new dishes I tested with my kids."

his culinary mentor

"The infamous British phenom Marco Pierre White was my first mentor. He showed me how to run a kitchen with brilliance, poise and rock-and-roll style."

secret to cooking like an italian

"It's all about learning proportions and the best balance of flavors and ingredients. The perfect risotto is the ultimate test of a cook's command of this balance."

PUBLISHED BY ECCO, $30

SUMMER BEANS WITH A SPICY LIME SPRITZ

SERVES 8 TO 10 AS A SIDE DISH

- 2 pounds romano, green, or wax beans (a mix is best)

Salt

- ¼ cup extra-virgin olive oil
- 2 medium red onions, chopped into ⅛-inch dice
- 6 garlic cloves, thinly sliced
- 1 tablespoon hot red pepper flakes
- ¼ cup anchovy paste

Kosher salt and freshly ground black pepper, to taste

- 4 limes, halved

Bring 8 quarts of water to a boil in a large pasta pot. Set up a large ice bath nearby.

Trim the beans and cut them into 3-inch lengths.

When the water comes to a boil, add 2 tablespoons salt. Drop the beans into the water and cook until just tender, 4 to 5 minutes. Using a spider or a slotted spoon, transfer the beans to the ice bath. When they have cooled, drain the beans and set them aside in a colander.

In a 14-inch sauté pan, heat the olive oil over high heat until just smoking. Add the onions, garlic, red pepper flakes, and anchovy paste. Reduce the heat to medium-high, and stir until the onions have begun to brown, about 5 minutes. Add the beans and cook until they are hot and coated with the anchovy sauce, 3 to 4 minutes. Season with salt and black pepper. Squeeze the limes over the beans, place them on a warmed platter, and serve (or let them cool to room temperature and then serve).

Lots of
crushed red
pepper makes
these beans
fiery.

MANICOTTI BARESI AL FORNO

SERVES 8 TO 10 AS A FIRST
COURSE, 6 AS A MAIN

- 2 tablespoons plus ¼ cup extra-
  virgin olive oil
- 2 pounds ground veal
- 2 pounds ground lamb

Salt

Two 16-ounce packages manicotti pasta

- 1 pound prosciutto cotto, cut into
  ¼-inch dice (see Editor's Note)
- 2 large eggs
- 1 cup plus ¼ cup plus ¼ cup
  grated Pecorino Romano
- ½ cup finely chopped fresh Italian
  parsley
- 2 cups fresh ricotta, drained
- 2 cups fresh breadcrumbs

Freshly ground black pepper

- 3 cups tomato alla vodka sauce
  (for quick results, try my Mario
  Batali pasta sauces by Gia Russa)

EDITOR'S NOTE
Prosciutto cotto ("cooked ham") is
Italian ham that has been boiled or
roasted rather than cured. It resembles American-style baked ham.

EDITOR'S WINE CHOICE
Bright, earthy Sangiovese: 2009
Querciabella Chianti Classico

Bring 8 quarts of water to a boil in a large pasta pot. Set up an ice
bath nearby.

Preheat the oven to 400°F. Brush the sides and bottom of a 9-by-13-
inch lasagne pan with 2 tablespoons of the olive oil.

In a 14-inch sauté pan, heat the remaining ¼ cup oil over medium
heat. Add the veal and lamb, and cook until lightly browned, carefully
separating the meat with a wooden spoon so it crumbles evenly. Remove
the pan from the heat, drain off the fat, and allow the meat to cool.

Add 2 tablespoons salt to the boiling water. Carefully add the manicotti
tubes to the water and cook for 2 minutes less than the package
instructions indicate. Drain, and submerge the pasta in the ice bath.
When it has cooled, drain again and set aside.

Place the cooled meat mixture in a large mixing bowl, and add the
prosciutto cotto, eggs, 1 cup of the grated cheese, the parsley, ricotta,
and breadcrumbs. Mix gently but thoroughly. Season with salt and
pepper to taste. Using a piping bag or a small spoon, carefully stuff the
filling into the pasta tubes. Place half of the stuffed pasta tubes in the
oiled lasagne pan, arranging them in an even layer across the bottom.
Spread 1½ cups of the vodka sauce over the tubes, and sprinkle with
¼ cup of the remaining grated cheese. Place the remaining stuffed pasta
tubes over the first layer, like a pile of logs, and spread the remaining
sauce over them. Sprinkle with the remaining ¼ cup cheese.

Bake in the oven for 20 to 25 minutes, until golden brown and crispy on
top. Remove, and allow the manicotti to rest for 5 minutes before serving.

There's a secret second layer of manicotti in here.

LAMB SHANKS WITH LEEKS & GRAPES

SERVES 8 TO 10 AS A
MAIN COURSE

- 10 large, meaty lamb shanks
- Salt and freshly ground black pepper
- 6 tablespoons extra-virgin olive oil
- 2 Spanish onions,
  chopped into ¼-inch dice
- 18 garlic cloves
- 5 carrots, peeled and cut into
  1-inch pieces
- 6 leeks, white and light green parts
  only, trimmed, halved lengthwise,
  cut crosswise into thin half-moons,
  rinsed thoroughly, and drained
- 2 cups dry white wine
- 1 cup basic tomato sauce
  (for quick results, try my Mario
  Batali pasta sauces by Gia Russa)
- 3 cups Brown Chicken Stock
  (recipe follows)
- 2 cups red grapes, wine grapes
  such as Sangiovese, or, even
  better, Concord grapes, halved
  and seeded

MAKES 2 QUARTS

- 2 tablespoons extra-virgin olive oil
- 1 whole capon or chicken
  (3 to 4 pounds), cut into pieces,
  excess fat removed
- 3 carrots, peeled and coarsely
  chopped
- 2 onions, coarsely chopped
- 4 celery stalks, coarsely chopped
- 1 tablespoon tomato paste
- 1 tablespoon black peppercorns
- Stems from 1 bunch of flat-leaf parsley

Preheat the oven to 375°F.

Rinse and dry the lamb shanks, and season them liberally with salt and pepper. In a very large heavy-bottomed Dutch oven, heat the olive oil over medium-high heat until smoking. Add the lamb shanks, 5 at a time, and sear until dark golden brown all over, 10 to 12 minutes per batch. Remove the shanks and set them aside.

Add the onions, garlic, carrots, and leeks to the pot and cook until softened, 8 to 10 minutes.

Add the wine, tomato sauce, and stock to the vegetables and bring to a boil. Return the lamb shanks to the pot and bring back to a boil. Cover the pot tightly, place it in the oven, and bake for about 1½ hours, until the meat is fork-tender.

Remove the pot from the oven, check the sauce for seasoning, and then add the grapes. Stir them in gently, and serve directly from the pot.

BROWN CHICKEN STOCK

In a large, heavy-bottomed saucepan, heat the oil over medium-high heat until smoking. Add the capon or chicken pieces and brown them all over, stirring to avoid burning. Transfer the browned pieces to a bowl.

Add the carrots, onions, and celery to the pan and cook until soft and browned. Return the browned poultry to the pan and add 4 quarts of water, the tomato paste, peppercorns, and parsley, stirring to dislodge the browned bits from the bottom of the pan. Bring almost to a boil. Then reduce the heat and cook at a low simmer for 2 hours, until reduced by half, occasionally skimming off the fat.

Strain the stock, pressing the solids with the bottom of a ladle to extract all the liquid. Cool; then refrigerate or freeze until ready to use.

The subtle sweetness here comes from fresh grapes.

ZITI WITH TUNA & SALAME PICCANTE

SERVES 8 TO 10 AS A FIRST
COURSE, 6 AS A MAIN

- 4 ounces thinly sliced *salame piccante* (see Editor's Note)
- ¼ cup extra-virgin olive oil
- 2 medium red onions, halved and thinly sliced
- 1 tablespoon hot red pepper flakes
- 2 cups basic tomato sauce (for quick results, try my Mario Batali pasta sauces by Gia Russa)

Two 6-ounce cans oil-packed Italian or Spanish tuna, drained and crumbled
- 2 tablespoons salt
- 1½ pounds ziti pasta
- 6 scallions, whites and about 2 inches of greens thinly sliced

EDITOR'S NOTE
Salame piccante is a spicy salami similar to what is known as pepperoni in the United States.

EDITOR'S WINE CHOICE
Lively, full-bodied white:
2011 Fontanafredda Pradalupo Roero Arneis

Bring 8 quarts of water to a boil in a large pasta pot.

Cut the *salame* into thin julienne. Heat the oil in a 14-inch sauté pan over medium heat. Add the *salame* and onions, and cook until the onions have softened, about 7 minutes. Add the red pepper flakes and the tomato sauce, and bring to a boil. Then remove from the heat and stir in the tuna. Set aside.

Add the salt to the boiling water. Drop the ziti into the water and cook for 1 minute less than the package instructions indicate. Just before it is done, carefully ladle ¼ cup of the cooking water into the tuna mixture.

Drain the pasta in a colander and add it to the sauce. Toss over medium heat for about 30 seconds, until the pasta is nicely coated. Add the scallions and toss again. Pour into a warmed serving bowl and serve immediately.

BRAISED CHICKEN THIGHS

with saffron, green olives & mint

SERVES 6 AS A MAIN COURSE

- ¼ cup extra-virgin olive oil
- All-purpose flour, for dredging
- 12 bone-in chicken thighs with skin (about 2½ pounds)
- Kosher salt and freshly ground pepper
- 2 large red onions, halved lengthwise and thinly sliced crosswise
- Small pinch of saffron
- 1 cup small pitted green olives (about 4 ounces)
- 1 medium carrot, finely diced
- 3 cups chicken stock or low-sodium broth
- ½ cup lightly packed mint leaves, chopped

EDITOR'S WINE CHOICE
Full-bodied Rhône white: 2010
Kermit Lynch Sunflower Cuvée
Côtes du Rhône Blanc

The flavors in this juicy chicken dish from Batali evoke North Africa. It's delicious spooned over egg noodles, rice or couscous.

1. In a large enameled cast-iron casserole, heat the olive oil until shimmering. Spread some flour in a shallow bowl. Season the chicken with salt and pepper, then dredge in the flour. Add half of the thighs to the casserole, skin side down. Cook over moderately high heat, turning once, until golden brown, about 8 minutes. Transfer to a platter. Repeat with the remaining chicken.

2. Spoon off all but 2 tablespoons of the fat in the casserole. Add the onions and saffron and cook over moderate heat, stirring, until the onions are softened, about 10 minutes. Add the olives, carrot and chicken stock and bring to a boil, scraping up any browned bits from the bottom of the pot. Nestle the chicken thighs in the casserole, cover and simmer over low heat until the chicken is cooked through, about 45 minutes.

3. Uncover the casserole and simmer over moderately low heat until the sauce is reduced slightly, about 15 minutes longer. Arrange the chicken thighs on a platter. Season the sauce with salt and pepper and stir in the mint. Spoon the sauce over the chicken and serve.

MARIO BATALI ONLINE

mariobatali.com

f Mario Batali

t @Mariobatali

Roasted beef tenderloin with mushroom ragout, page 26

THE COOK & THE BUTCHER

brigit binns

why we love this book

Food writer Brigit Binns has collected insider's advice from some of America's top meat experts—outstanding butchers and steak-house chefs—to create this guide to sourcing, buying and cooking beef, pork, lamb and veal. Recipes like Roasted Beef Tenderloin (page 26), Asian-inspired ribs (pages 28 and 30) and even meat-heavy salads come with valuable tips directly from the butchers, such as how to choose the most flavorful chops and the best way to grind your own meat.

on butchers

"The butchers in the book are part of a new breed in a profession that was all but lost until just a couple of years ago. I have a tremendous amount of respect for them, because it's not a pretty business. It's dangerous, you need a ton of physical stamina and you really have to learn what you're doing. Among my favorite butchers are the two tattooed girls at Lindy & Grundy in Los Angeles, but I love them all."

her favorite value cuts

"I used to be super-snobby about the round, because it's so lean that it tends to dry out. But then a fireman in upstate New York taught me that you need to cook it really, really slowly at a low temperature so the meat doesn't get tough. The round is ideal in salads and sandwiches. The flatiron steak is also very reasonably priced but harder to find—not a lot of butchers cut it. You can cook flatiron steak hot and dry in a cast-iron pan or on the grill and it'll be great."

when meat meets salad

"I like to add some kind of meat to a salad. I love how the acidity of the dressing cuts the fat of the meat, so it doesn't feel so heavy and you don't get palate fatigue. I use lemon juice and pomegranate molasses in the dressing for my Lamb and Pita Salad (page 24)—the brightness of those flavors lightens the dish."

PUBLISHED BY WELDON OWEN, $30

LAMB & PITA SALAD

MAKES 4 TO 6 SERVINGS

1¼ pounds (625 grams) boneless lamb leg steaks, each about ½ inch (12 millimeters) thick, or 1½ pounds (750 grams) bone-in lamb leg steaks

2 tablespoons olive oil

½ teaspoon ground cumin

Kosher salt and freshly ground pepper

FOR THE PITA SALAD

2 pita breads, split horizontally

2 cloves garlic

2 tablespoons fresh lemon juice

2 teaspoons pomegranate molasses

2 to 3 teaspoons honey

¼ cup (2 fluid ounces/60 milliliters) extra-virgin olive oil

Kosher salt

2 large tomatoes, halved crosswise, seeded, and diced

4 green onions, white and light green parts, thinly sliced

1 English cucumber, seeded and cut into small dice

4 to 6 radishes, coarsely chopped

1 head romaine lettuce, pale inner leaves only, cut crosswise into ½-inch (12-millimeter) pieces

½ cup (½ ounce/15 grams) coarsely chopped fresh flat-leaf parsley

½ cup (¾ ounce/20 grams) coarsely chopped fresh mint

1 tablespoon ground sumac or *za'atar*

EDITOR'S WINE CHOICE
Juicy, light-bodied red:
2010 Georges Duboeuf Jean Descombes Morgon

This salad is similar to fattoush, *a Middle Eastern favorite that uses a sweet-and-savory combination of flavors. It is worth seeking out sumac (an aromatic spice) and za'atar (a spice blend) at a well-stocked supermarket or Middle Eastern store to impart an authentic flavor to the salad. Pomegranate molasses varies in sweetness; taste the dressing first and add honey until the sourness of the molasses is tamed.*

Brush both sides of the lamb steaks with oil and season with the cumin and generously with salt and pepper. Let stand at room temperature for about 1 hour.

To make the pita salad, preheat the oven to 350°F (180°C). Arrange the pita breads on a baking sheet and bake until lightly crisped and golden, about 10 minutes. Let cool, then break into 1-inch (2.5-centimeter) pieces. In a mini food processor, process the garlic until minced. Add the lemon juice, molasses, honey, oil, and 1 teaspoon salt. Pulse to combine. Set the pita pieces and dressing aside. In a large serving bowl, combine the tomatoes, green onions, cucumber, radishes, romaine, parsley, and mint. Toss to combine. Refrigerate while you cook the lamb.

Prepare a charcoal or gas grill for direct-heat grilling over high heat, or preheat a cast-iron stove-top grill pan over high heat. Place the steaks on the grill rack over the hottest part of the fire or in the grill pan, and cook, turning once, until an instant-read thermometer inserted into a steak registers 135°F (57°C) for medium-rare, 2 to 2½ minutes per side, or to your desired doneness. Transfer to a cutting board and let rest for 5 minutes. Cut the steaks crosswise into strips 1 inch (2.5 centimeters) wide, working around the bone if necessary.

Add the pita pieces to the salad, drizzle with the dressing, and toss to mix. Arrange the lamb on top, sprinkle with the sumac, and serve at once.

This grilled lamb salad is a superb one-bowl meal.

ROASTED BEEF TENDERLOIN
with mushroom ragout

MAKES 6 TO 8 SERVINGS

- 1 beef tenderloin, 3½ to 4 pounds (1.75 to 2 kilograms), silverskin removed or snipped in several places
- 2 tablespoons whole-grain mustard
- 1½ tablespoons olive oil, plus more for searing
- 1½ teaspoons dried thyme

Kosher salt and freshly ground pepper

FOR THE RAGOUT

- 2 tablespoons unsalted butter
- 2 large shallots, finely chopped
- 1 pound (500 grams) mixed mushrooms, such as oyster and cremini, brushed clean and thickly sliced
- ¼ cup (2 fluid ounces/60 milliliters) Madeira or medium-dry sherry
- ¼ cup (2 fluid ounces/60 milliliters) heavy cream
- 2 teaspoons finely snipped fresh chives

EDITOR'S WINE CHOICE
Earthy, inky Syrah: 2009
Lagier Meredith

Tenderloin, a tender, special-occasion cut, is quite mild—not as beefy as rib roast. So here I add an earthy contrast of sherry-flavored woodsy mushrooms to serve alongside the meat. If you don't ask your butcher to trim the roast of silverskin, just make sure to snip through the sinewy layer every 3 to 4 inches (7.5 to 10 centimeters) to prevent the roast from curling. Serve hot or cold with Horseradish Crème Fraîche (recipe follows).

Remove the tenderloin from the refrigerator and let stand at room temperature for 2 hours.

Preheat the oven to 425°F (220°C).

Whisk together the mustard, 1½ tablespoons oil, and the thyme. Set aside. Using kitchen string, tie the tenderloin firmly at 1½-inch (4-centimeter) intervals, to keep it plump and round during cooking. Pat thoroughly dry and season all sides generously with salt. Heat a large roasting pan over medium-high heat until it is very hot, about 3 minutes. Add enough oil to the pan to coat the bottom. When the oil is shimmering, add the tenderloin and sear without moving for 2½ minutes. Turn and continue to sear until the tenderloin has an even, dark brown crust on all sides. Transfer to a cutting board, brush with the mustard mixture, and season generously with pepper.

Set a rack in the roasting pan and transfer the tenderloin to the rack. Place in the oven and cook until an instant-read thermometer inserted into the center of the roast registers 125° to 130°F (52° to 54°C), 15 to 20 minutes. The temperature will range from rare to medium-rare in different parts of the tenderloin. Transfer the tenderloin to a platter, tent loosely with aluminum foil, and let rest for at least 15 minutes or up to 30 minutes.

While the meat is resting, prepare the ragout: In a large frying pan over medium heat, melt the butter. Add the shallots and cook until softened, about 5 minutes. Add the mushrooms and cook, stirring occasionally, until they release their liquid, about 10 minutes. Add the Madeira and simmer until almost completely evaporated. Stir in the cream, chives, ¼ teaspoon salt, and pepper to taste. Continue to cook, stirring, until the ragout is thick, creamy, and bubbling, 1 to 2 minutes more.

Snip the strings and cut the tenderloin into slices about ½ inch (12 millimeters) thick. Arrange on plates with the ragout. Serve at once.

A NOTE FROM THE BUTCHER Purchase a whole 6- to 7-pound (3- to 3.5-kilogram) tenderloin; it is a better value than a center-cut roast. Ask your butcher to prepare it "chef ready," with the gristly side muscle and the silverskin removed and the roast tied.
—*Michael Milazo, Alexander's Prime Meats & Catering, San Gabriel, CA*

HORSERADISH CRÈME FRAÎCHE

In a bowl, whisk together all the ingredients. Cover and refrigerate for 30 minutes before serving.

MAKES 1¼ CUPS
(9 OUNCES/250 GRAMS)

- 3 tablespoons freshly grated horseradish
- 1 cup (8 ounces/220 grams) crème fraîche
- 1 tablespoon plus 2 teaspoons finely snipped fresh chives
- ½ teaspoon ground white pepper

KOREAN-STYLE SHORT RIBS

MAKES 6 SERVINGS

- ½ cup (4 fluid ounces/125 milliliters) sake or dry white wine
- ¾ cup (6 fluid ounces/180 milliliters) reduced-sodium soy sauce
- ¼ cup (2 fluid ounces/60 milliliters) Thai or Vietnamese fish sauce
- ¼ cup (3 fluid ounces/90 grams) honey
- 2 tablespoons peanut oil
- 1 teaspoon Asian sesame oil
- 7 large cloves garlic, minced
- 1 tablespoon peeled and minced fresh ginger
- 5 green onions, white and light green parts, minced
- 5 pounds (2.5 kilograms) flanken-cut beef short ribs, cut ½ inch (12 millimeters) thick, patted dry

Freshly ground pepper
- ½ teaspoon five-spice powder

EDITOR'S WINE CHOICE
Lively, fruit-forward Grenache-based wine: 2010 Dusted Valley Squirrel Tooth Alice

The classic flavors of soy sauce and fish sauce provide a satisfying balance to the deep and beefy character of the short ribs in this recipe. Fish sauce, an excellent complement to generously marbled meat, stands in for salt, so you don't need to salt. If you want to broil the ribs on the baking sheet in which they are drained and allowed to dry, be sure to line the pan with aluminum foil to avoid burnt-on caramelized juices.

Combine the sake, soy sauce, fish sauce, honey, peanut oil, sesame oil, garlic, ginger, half of the green onions, and 1 cup (8 fluid ounces/250 milliliters) water in a large baking dish and mix well. Add the ribs to the dish and rub all sides of the ribs with the mixture. Let stand for at least 2 hours at room temperature or preferably overnight in the refrigerator, turning ribs once or twice.

Remove the ribs from the dish and discard the marinade. Place the ribs on a rack on a baking sheet. Let come to room temperature and air-dry for about 30 minutes.

Preheat the broiler. Season the ribs all over with about ¾ teaspoon pepper and the five-spice powder. Transfer the rack to a roasting pan. Place under the broiler about 3 inches (7.5 centimeters) from the heat source and cook the ribs, turning once, until nicely browned and sizzling on all sides, about 6 minutes per side.

Leave the ribs whole or, if desired, cut the ribs between the bones into smaller pieces. Garnish with the remaining green onions and serve at once.

A NOTE FROM THE BUTCHER Short ribs can be cut between the ribs (English cut) or across the ribs (flanken cut). Each slab of short ribs has a thick end, which has more meat, and a smaller end, which has less meat. Ask for your short ribs to be cut from the thick end and for the excess surface fat to be trimmed.
—*Tanya Cauthen, Belmont Butchery, Richmond, VA*

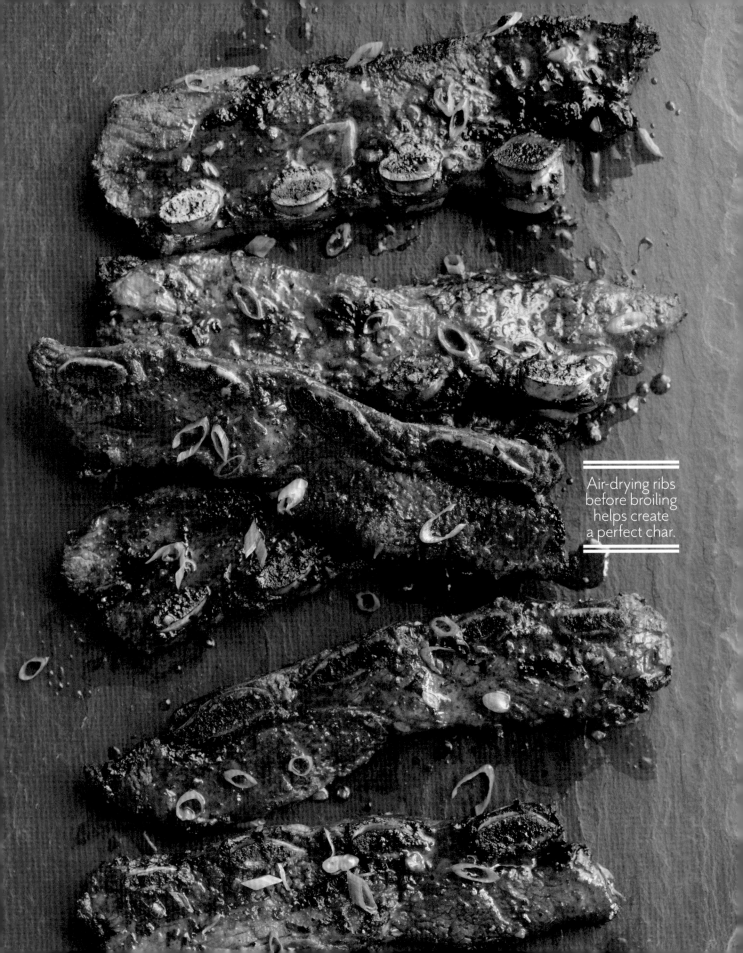

Air-drying ribs before broiling helps create a perfect char.

OVEN-BROWNED SPARERIBS
with lemongrass, honey & soy

MAKES 6 TO 8 SERVINGS

- 4 lemongrass stalks, pale inner parts only, finely chopped
- ⅓ cup (2 ounces/60 grams) pickled red ginger, minced
- 6 large cloves garlic, minced
- ⅓ cup (4 ounces/125 grams) honey
- ⅓ cup (3 fluid ounces/80 milliliters) reduced-sodium soy sauce
- 3 tablespoons Thai or Vietnamese fish sauce
- 3 tablespoons peanut oil
- Juice of 1 large lime
- Kosher salt and freshly ground pepper
- 2 racks pork spareribs, about 6 pounds (3 kilograms) total weight
- 1 lime, quartered
- ¼ cup (⅓ ounce/10 grams) coarsely chopped fresh basil, preferably Thai

EDITOR'S WINE CHOICE
Medium-bodied, berry-rich Côtes du Rhône: 2010 M. Chapoutier Belleruche Rouge

Some of the classic elements of Asian cuisine are showcased in this chunky lemongrass-perfumed marinade. The final browning of the ribs is done in the broiler, but if yours cannot achieve high heat, you may want to finish the ribs in a 500°F (260°C) oven or on a hot grill. They will be cooked at that point—the goal is to create a crispy crust quickly.

In a large roasting pan or baking dish, whisk together the lemongrass, ginger, garlic, honey, soy sauce, fish sauce, oil, and lime juice. Whisk in ½ teaspoon salt and season with pepper. Poke the ribs with a small, sharp knife every 3 to 4 inches (7.5 to 10 centimeters), to allow the marinade to penetrate the meat. Place the ribs in the pan and turn to coat evenly, rubbing the marinade into the nooks and crannies. Cover and refrigerate for at least 6 hours or up to overnight, turning the ribs occasionally.

Remove the ribs from the refrigerator and let stand at room temperature for 30 minutes. Preheat the oven to 250°F (120°C) and position one rack in the middle and another rack in the lower third.

Line 2 rimmed baking sheets with aluminum foil and place a wire rack in each pan. Arrange the ribs on the racks, meaty side up, and spoon the remaining marinade over the tops. Bake without moving the ribs for 3½ hours, switching the positions of the pans halfway through.

Remove the ribs from the oven and let rest for at least 10 minutes or up to 1 hour. Discard the greasy foil lining the pans, replace with clean foil, and return the ribs to the racks in the pans, meaty side up.

Preheat the broiler and place an oven rack about 4 inches (10 centimeters) from the heat source. Broil each rack of ribs just until the fat starts to sizzle and crisp, 3 to 4 minutes. Turn and broil for 2 to 3 minutes more. Let cool for 5 minutes, then cut between the ribs to separate them. Squeeze the lime wedges over the ribs, garnish with the basil, and serve at once.

A NOTE FROM THE BUTCHER Ask the butcher to remove the membrane from the bone side of a rack of spareribs. It is very tough, even when cooked for a long time.
—*Larry Jobin, The Meat Shop, Phoenix, AZ*

ISRAELI COUSCOUS SALAD

**MAKES 4 FIRST-COURSE
OR SIDE-DISH SERVINGS**

- ¼ cup plus 2 tablespoons extra-virgin olive oil
- ¾ cup slivered almonds
- 1 red onion, finely diced
- 2 garlic cloves, minced
- 1½ cups Israeli couscous
- 2 cups vegetable stock or low-sodium broth

Sea salt and freshly ground pepper

- 2 blood oranges
- ⅓ cup pitted brine-cured olives, such as kalamata, finely chopped
- 2 tablespoons fresh lemon juice
- 2 tablespoons finely chopped mint
- ¼ cup finely chopped flat-leaf parsley

EDITOR'S WINE CHOICE
Light-bodied, fruity Beaujolais:
2010 Nicole Chanrion Domaine de la
Voûte des Crozes Côte de Brouilly

This couscous salad (pictured on page 10) from Binns has great Middle Eastern flavors: juicy blood orange, briny olives, fresh mint and wonderfully crisp fried almonds.

1. In a small skillet, heat 1 tablespoon of the olive oil. Add the almonds and cook over moderate heat, stirring, until golden brown, about 5 minutes. Transfer to a paper towel–lined plate.

2. In a medium saucepan, heat 1 tablespoon of the olive oil. Add the onion and garlic and cook over moderate heat, stirring occasionally, until softened, about 5 minutes. Add the couscous and cook, stirring, until lightly toasted, about 5 minutes. Add the stock, season with salt and pepper and bring to a boil. Cover and simmer over low heat until the couscous is tender and all the liquid is absorbed, about 8 minutes. Transfer the couscous to a large bowl and stir in the remaining ¼ cup of olive oil; let cool slightly.

3. Meanwhile, using a sharp knife, peel the oranges, removing all of the bitter white pith. Working over a bowl, cut in between the membranes to release the sections into the bowl. Fluff the couscous with a fork and fold in the orange segments, olives, lemon juice, mint, toasted almonds and half of the parsley; season with salt and pepper. Garnish the salad with the remaining parsley and serve.

MAKE AHEAD The couscous salad can be refrigerated overnight. Toss with the almonds, parsley and mint just before serving.

BRIGIT BINNS ONLINE

brigitbinns.com

[f] Brigit Binns

[t] @BrigitBinns

AMERICAN FLAVOR

andrew carmellini & gwen hyman

why we love this book

New York City star chef Andrew Carmellini is dedicated to American food, but not blindly: He picks and chooses only his favorites—from Southern dishes like a smoky, bacon-studded Black-Eyed Pea and Kale Chili (page 36) to multi-culti entries like the Korean Steak marinated in soy sauce, Coca-Cola and garlic (page 40). Mostly taken from his hit restaurant The Dutch, recipes are streamlined for the home cook but include chef-y refinements, like the bitter orange juice in his Scallops with Grapefruit Butter (page 34).

on gaining perspective

"Some of the French chefs I worked for earlier in my career just had no perspective outside French cooking. On their days off, they'd go eat steak tartare and *boeuf à l'anglaise* and drink wine from the Loire Valley, as opposed to discovering new things and flavors. I was always more interested in what grandmothers were cooking, the traditional foods of all ethnicities."

writing clear recipes

"My wife, Gwen, and I worked on the cookbook together. I do all the cooking at our apartment. I just start making a dish and telling stories and she sits next to me with her laptop, putting it all together so it makes sense. She's not a professional cook; she's the one who gets me to simplify. She wants everything to be written in a way that she can make it. She'll say, 'I don't know how to cut a butternut squash, so you need to explain it so that the average person who picks up the book can make this recipe.'"

his dream trips

"You never really stop learning. When it comes to cooking, I would travel more through Mexico, because I love the cuisine. I'd also really like to go back to Thailand. It's good to visit the countries before you start messing around with their food."

PUBLISHED BY ECCO, $35

SCALLOPS WITH GRAPEFRUIT BUTTER

SERVES 4

FOR THE GRAPEFRUIT BUTTER

- 1 cup white wine
- 1 large shallot, diced (2 tablespoons)
- Juice of 3 ruby red grapefruits (about 1 cup)
- ¼ cup bitter orange juice (Goya has one called Naranja Agria/Bitter Orange Marinade, see Author's Note); or juice of 1 orange and juice of 1 lime, mixed together
- ¾ stick (6 tablespoons) salted butter

FOR THE SCALLOPS

- 16 sea scallops
- ½ teaspoon salt
- ½ teaspoon fresh-ground black pepper
- 2 tablespoons extra-virgin olive oil (or 1 tablespoon for each batch of scallops)
- 2 tablespoons unsalted butter
- 2 fresh thyme sprigs
- Juice of 1 lime (2 tablespoons)

TO FINISH THE DISH

- 2 ruby red grapefruits, segmented (about 1 cup segments)
- 2 tablespoons chopped fresh parsley

EDITOR'S WINE CHOICE
Citrusy, minerally Sauvignon Blanc: 2010 Alphonse Mellot La Moussière Sancerre

This dish is an ode to Miami, circa 1982. When I was a kid, my family used to drive down to Florida a couple of times every winter, to see my grandma and to get out of the Cleveland weather. We always stopped at a citrus grove in Fort Pierce called Boudrias Groves. They sold amazing Indian River citrus: we'd buy navels, Honeybells, temples, and this unbelievable red orange juice, crazy-good stuff. When we got to Miami, we'd get to go out to a fancy restaurant as a treat—one of those places that served amazing fresh seafood, stuff you just couldn't get in Cleveland back then. So this dish brings together two of my favorite Florida things. And it's got a little bit of retro going on: the butter sauce is definitely old-school.

You can serve this citrus sauce with just about any fish or seafood—lobster, mahi mahi, anything that makes you think of the beach. (You can prep the fish any way you like, too: grilled, broiled, sautéed, whatever.)

TO MAKE THE GRAPEFRUIT BUTTER Heat the white wine in a large saucepan over medium-high heat. Add the shallots, stir to coat them in the wine, and let them cook for about 5 minutes, until the wine has evaporated completely—there should be no more liquid left in the pan at all.

Add the grapefruit juice and bitter orange juice, and cook for about 5 to 6 minutes, until the mixture thickens up and reduces to about ¼ cup.

Pull the pan off the heat and whisk in the butter a tablespoon at a time, whisking continuously until each pat is melted, then adding the next one.

TO COOK THE SCALLOPS Preheat the oven to 175°F.

Season the scallops with the salt and pepper on both sides.

Heat 1 tablespoon of the olive oil in a saucepan over medium-high heat until it starts to smoke; then add half of the scallops. (If you put a scallop in and it sticks, the oil isn't hot enough.)

Let the scallops cook for about a minute and a half, until they brown up on the bottom, then flip them over and keep cooking for another minute and a half, until the tops and bottoms are brown but the sides are still white.

Add half the butter and half the thyme. Shake the pan around as the butter melts, so it gets everywhere, then squeeze half the lime juice. Tilt the pan so the juice slides to one side, and use a deep spoon to catch the sauce and spoon it over the scallops so they're shining and glazed.

Pull the pan off the heat and slide the scallops onto a plate. Hold them in the oven while you do the same with the second batch, heating another tablespoon of olive oil in the saucepan to brown the scallops, then adding another tablespoon of butter, another thyme sprig, plus another tablespoon of lime juice.

TO FINISH THE DISH If the sauce has cooled down, heat it up again.

Add the grapefruit segments to the sauce and mix everything together well, so the grapefruit is coated.

Add the parsley, mix again, and then pour the grapefruit butter over the scallops. Serve right away.

AUTHOR'S NOTE You can find frozen sour orange concentrate online, but it's almost impossible to find fresh sour orange juice north of the Mason-Dixon Line. I found sour orange juice at Kalustyan's, an amazing specialty store in Manhattan. If you can't get your hands on any of the real stuff, you can substitute the orange/lime juice mix. It will be just as good.

BLACK-EYED PEA & KALE CHILI
with monterey jack cheese

SERVES 6 TO 8
AS A MAIN DISH

- 2 tablespoons extra-virgin olive oil
- 8 slices bacon, diced (1 cup)
- 1 small onion, diced (1 cup)
- 2 celery stalks, diced (1 cup)
- 1 clove garlic, crushed
- One 28-ounce can diced tomatoes, with their juice
- One 15-ounce can black-eyed peas, drained
- 2 cups chicken broth
- 1 or 2 canned chipotle peppers in adobo sauce, depending on how spicy you like your chili (I like La Morena brand), including seeds, chopped fine (1 to 2 tablespoons)
- ¼ teaspoon ground cumin
- ¼ teaspoon ground coriander
- 1 tablespoon honey
- 1 tablespoon Dijon mustard
- 1 bunch Tuscan or green kale (about ½ pound), stems removed, leaves washed and cut into 1-inch pieces
- ½ cup grated Monterey Jack cheese

EDITOR'S WINE CHOICE
Juicy, spicy Malbec: 2010 Recuerdo

This might read like a dish that belongs on the menu of some vegetarian restaurant in California—but actually, it's a secret carnivore special: hidden inside is a whole cup of bacon. (If you want it veg, you can always just leave the bacon out: the chili will still have lots of flavor and smokiness from the peppers.) The black-eyed peas and kale both have a really good earthiness that makes this what you might call an umami chili. Toss a piece of cornbread on the side and you've got a perfect winter-day dish.

Don't go to the cheesemonger for fancy high-quality Monterey Jack for this one: believe it or not, the regular supermarket stuff gives you the best melting texture.

Heat the olive oil in a large soup pot over a medium flame. Add the bacon, and allow it to render a bit (about 2 minutes), stirring regularly to stop it from sticking.

Add the onions, celery, and garlic. Stir well to coat everything in the fat, and keep cooking for about 2 minutes, until the vegetables start to soften.

Add the tomatoes, black-eyed peas, chicken broth, 1 cup of water, and the chipotle peppers, cumin, and coriander. Stir to mix everything together well; then let the chili cook, uncovered, over medium heat for about 10 minutes, until the flavors come together.

Stir in the honey and mustard.

Stir in the kale and cook for 10 minutes or so, until the kale is soft.

Serve the chili in large bowls, with the Monterey Jack cheese grated right on top.

Make a double
batch; this chili
freezes well.

DUCK WITH PEACHES, GINGER & LEMON THYME

SERVES 4

FOR THE DUCK BREASTS

4 boned duck breasts
(about 3 pounds total)
1½ teaspoons salt
1½ teaspoons fresh-ground
black pepper

FOR THE PEACH SYRUP

1 tablespoon butter
One 2-inch piece of fresh ginger, peeled
and chopped fine (2 tablespoons)
1 shallot, chopped fine
(about 2 tablespoons)
3 tablespoons peach schnapps
⅓ cup peach preserves
Juice of 3 lemons (6 tablespoons)

TO FINISH THE DISH

4 to 6 ripe medium-sized peaches
2 tablespoons fresh lemon
thyme leaves

EDITOR'S WINE CHOICE
Ripe peach–inflected white blend:
2011 Planeta La Segreta Bianco

This is a shout-out to John D'Amico, chef-owner of Chez François in Vermilion, Ohio, the first serious restaurant I ever got the chance to cook at. Chez François is an old-school French restaurant to the core, but John could teach the locavore kids a thing or two: he's been cooking local and seasonal since way before anybody thought about pig tattoos and backyard bee-keeping. In the summertime, there was always some kind of roast bird with fruit on his menu, and, this being Ohio, summer peaches were often his inspiration. This is my home version of a dish you might have seen on John's menu.

If you can't find lemon thyme, regular thyme will work fine here. Timing, on the other hand, is important. Make the peach syrup while the duck is cooking; cut the peaches and bake them while the duck is resting. Kitchen control is also important: watch out for the flame when you add the peach schnapps to the syrup, and keep long hair, kids, and pets out of the way!

TO PREPARE THE DUCK BREAST Preheat the oven to 450°F.

Use a small sharp knife to score the fatty skin of the duck in a cross-hatch pattern, scoring about 5 times in one direction, 5 in the other. (This will stop the skin from supercontracting, so it cooks right and protects the meat.)

Season the duck breasts well with the salt and pepper on all sides.

Put the duck breasts, skin side down, in a large ovenproof saucepan and render the fat over medium-high heat. (You'll want to open a window, and maybe disable your smoke alarm: this will definitely be smoky.) Use a pair of tongs to shake the duck breasts around every so often, so they don't stick. (If you don't have a big enough pan, you can do this in two pans at the same time.) The ducks will give off a lot of liquefied fat; it's a good idea to drain it off every so often by taking the pan over to the sink and tipping it out, holding the duck breasts back with a pair of tongs.

When the skin has crisped and turned a deep golden brown (about 8 to 10 minutes), turn the duck breasts over so they're skin side up, and put the pan on the middle oven rack. Roast the duck for 5 to 7 minutes, until the flesh springs back a little when you poke it. (You want your duck nice and medium-rare: if the skin is very loose, it's not cooked enough, but if it's completely taut, it's overcooked.) The internal temperature should be about 115°F.

TO MAKE THE PEACH SYRUP While the duck is in the oven, melt the butter in a medium-sized saucepan over medium heat.

Add the ginger and shallots, and stir everything together. Cook for a minute or two, until the ginger aroma has come out and the ginger and shallots have softened.

Add the peach schnapps. Be careful! The alcohol is likely to flame up pretty high. Let it cook, stirring it (carefully) for about 30 seconds or so until the alcohol has burned off and the mixture has thickened up.

Stir in the peach preserves and squeeze the lemon juice into the saucepan, using a strainer to catch the seeds.

Bring the syrup up to a simmer, and let it cook for about 5 minutes, until it reduces a little and the flavors are blended into a sweet-and-sour mix.

TO FINISH THE DISH Pull the pan out of the oven (leave the oven on) and move the duck breasts to a plate to rest.

While the duck is resting, cut the peaches in half, remove the pits, and lay the peaches, skin side down, in the same pan that you cooked the duck in.

Bake the peaches on the middle oven rack for about 5 minutes, until they start to soften and roast a little on the bottom.

Pull the peaches out of the oven and pour the glaze over them right in the pan. Sprinkle on the lemon thyme, and drizzle the resting liquid (the drippings) from the ducks over them.

Slice the duck into 1-inch-thick slices. Lay each breast, in slices, on an individual plate. Lay a couple of peaches next to each breast, and then spoon the glaze mixture over everything. Serve right away.

KOREAN STEAK

SERVES 4 TO 6

- 1 cup soy sauce
- 1 cup Coca-Cola
- ¼ cup sesame oil
- ¼ cup hoisin sauce
- 4 cloves garlic, chopped
- 4 green onions, minced
- 2 bone-in rib-eye steaks (2½ pounds each)
- ½ cup kimchee (from a jar), for serving (optional)
- ½ cup peeled, grated daikon radish (from a 3-inch piece), for serving (optional)

EDITOR'S WINE CHOICE
Dark fruited, full-bodied
Tempranillo: 2009 Bodegas Volver

Here's what I've learned from all the Korean cooks who've worked with us over the years: at the end of a long service, there's nothing better than Korean barbecue. We like to go to Hahm Ji Bach in Flushing, Queens (I like Park's in Los Angeles, too), but I wanted to learn how to make it myself. When I started asking Korean cooks about it, I learned that in every family recipe, there's always one key ingredient in the overnight marinade for sweetening and tenderizing. Sometimes it's ground-up Asian pears; sometimes it's kiwi. But the most popular ingredient? The ultimate American flavor: Coca-Cola.

This recipe is definitely not authentic bulgogi: it's my backyard version of that sweet-salty late-night flavor. I like rib-eyes for my version, but you can use any kind of steak that you grill—and you don't need a grill to do it. Even if you're using the broiler in your apartment oven, I guarantee it will come out seriously succulent and flavorful.

In a small bowl, whisk together the soy sauce, Coke, sesame oil, and hoisin sauce. Add the garlic and green onions, and whisk well.

There are two ways to get the marinade on the steak. Do whichever of these floats your boat: (a) Put the steaks in a large deep dish and pour the marinade over them. Cover the dish tightly with tin foil and put it in the fridge. Or (b) pour the marinade into a gallon plastic bag, put in the steaks, seal the bag, and shake them around till they're coated in the marinade. Either way, the steaks should marinate in the fridge for 12 hours. (But don't let them marinate for longer than that: you don't want the meat to break down too much.)

Pull the steaks out of the marinade, pile them on a plate, and let them come up to room temperature (about 20 to 30 minutes).

Either fire up the grill or turn the broiler on high. If you're using the grill, you should also preheat the oven to 400°F.

continued on page 42

Coca-Cola is the secret ingredient in the marinade.

KOREAN STEAK *continued*

IF YOU'RE USING THE BROILER, put the steaks on a rack set over a rimmed baking sheet, place the baking sheet on the middle or middle-high rack, and broil the steaks for about 6 minutes per side. **IF YOU'RE USING THE GRILL,** lay the meat right on the rack so it gets a nice char, and let it grill for 4 to 6 minutes a side, depending on the thickness of the meat: you just want to get a nice char going. Then bring the meat back inside and finish it on a rack in a roasting pan in the oven at 400°F for 6 minutes, turning it over once so it cooks more evenly.

No matter how you're cooking the steak, it's done when the meat springs back to the touch (if you have a meat thermometer, the internal temperature should be 115°F).

Let the meat rest for 5 minutes; then slice it thin. If you want the full Korean experience, serve up a bowl of kimchee on the side. And even though it's not Korean at all, I really love to serve this with grated daikon, too.

SMOKY EGGPLANT DIP

MAKES ABOUT 3¼ CUPS

- 1 small head of garlic
- 3 tablespoons extra-virgin olive oil, plus more for drizzling
- Three 1-pound eggplants, 1 cut into ⅓-inch dice
- Kosher salt and freshly ground black pepper
- ¼ cup plain yogurt
- ¼ cup mayonnaise
- 2 tablespoons fresh lemon juice
- 2 tablespoons finely chopped parsley
- 2 tablespoons finely chopped mint, plus more for garnish
- ¼ teaspoon cayenne pepper
- Za'atar, for garnish (see Editor's Note)
- Potato chips, for serving

EDITOR'S NOTE
Za'atar is available at Middle Eastern markets and *penzeys.com.*

Carmellini's silky, rich eggplant dip is sprinkled with za'atar, a pungent mix of herbs, sesame seeds and sumac.

1. Preheat the oven to 375°F. Drizzle the garlic with olive oil and wrap tightly in foil. Roast for 40 minutes, until very tender. Let cool, then squeeze out the cloves.

2. Meanwhile, light a grill or preheat a grill pan. Grill the 2 whole eggplants over moderately high heat, turning frequently, until the skin is blistered and the flesh is just tender, about 12 minutes. Transfer to a plate and let cool. Cut off the stems, then peel and coarsely chop the eggplants.

3. In a large skillet, heat 2 tablespoons of the olive oil until shimmering. Add the diced eggplant and a generous pinch of salt and black pepper and cook over moderately high heat, stirring occasionally, until tender, about 6 minutes. Transfer the eggplant to a plate and let cool completely.

4. In a medium bowl, whisk the yogurt with the mayonnaise, lemon juice, parsley, 2 tablespoons of mint, the cayenne, roasted garlic and 1 tablespoon of olive oil. Fold in all of the eggplant and season with salt and black pepper. Drizzle with olive oil and garnish with za'atar and mint. Serve with potato chips.

MAKE AHEAD The dip can be refrigerated for up to 3 days. Bring to room temperature and garnish just before serving.

ANDREW CARMELLINI ONLINE

andrewcarmellini.com

 @andrecarmellini

Clark's daughter, Dahlia, reaching for mallobars, page 54

COOK THIS NOW

melissa clark

why we love this book

Prolific cookbook author and *New York Times* columnist Melissa Clark has mastered recipes that walk the line between accessibility and, as she says, "not the same old boring food you've made a million times before." In this incredibly user-friendly cookbook—each recipe includes suggestions for substitutions, additions and variations—she provides a year's worth of dishes that are satisfying and inventive, like her Shrimp Scampi with Pernod and Fennel Fronds (page 48).

three key cooking techniques

"High-heat roasting will make almost any vegetable taste good—even just with a bit of oil, salt and pepper. If you can show someone how to make a really easy salad dressing, it can change their entire relationship to vegetables. And learning how to properly sauté—first heat the pan, then add the oil, then let the oil get hot and then add the food—makes a huge difference in the way that the food cooks and tastes."

top party dishes

"If there's baked Brie at a party, I'll just stand over the cheese and forget about the guests. I will fight off everyone with my cracker. I love any kind of dish with molten cheese; if there's *queso fundido,* I'm there and not talking to anyone else."

her inspiration

"Most dishes start at the market, with what's in season or what I'm excited about. But sometimes I'm just trying to use up stuff before it gets wilty, so I start pulling things out of the fridge and then combine them with ingredients I have in the pantry. (I have an extensive condiment collection.) Like the cabbage salad I pair with Vietnamese Grilled Steak (page 51); by mixing shredded cabbage with what I have in the house—soy sauce, rice wine vinegar, fish sauce, lime and garlic—it becomes really flavorful."

PUBLISHED BY HYPERION, $30

CUMIN SEED ROASTED CAULIFLOWER
with salted yogurt, mint & pomegranate seeds

SERVES 2

1	large head cauliflower, cut into bite-size florets
2	tablespoons extra-virgin olive oil
1	teaspoon whole cumin seeds
½	teaspoon kosher salt, plus additional
½	teaspoon freshly ground black pepper

Plain yogurt, for serving
Chopped fresh mint leaves, for serving
Pomegranate seeds, for serving

When the nights turn blustery and the temperature drops, I know that roasted vegetable season has arrived, and I embrace it with reckless abandon. I'll roast any kind of sturdy vegetable that I can cut up and fit into my oven, but one of my favorites is cauliflower, preferably tossed with whole cumin seeds. Not only does the cumin act as a natural remedy to help reduce the dreaded intestinal gas factor (or so I've been told), but it also adds a pleasant earthy flavor to balance the assertive tang of the vegetable.

Roasted cauliflower with cumin makes a nice and simple side dish. Even Dahlia will eat it if she's distracted enough. But recently I made it into lunch. I roasted up a small head all for myself, and added a topping of salted yogurt (which is simply a good, full-fat yogurt with a little kosher salt mixed in), a few leftover pomegranate seeds (which I can buy at my local market already picked out of the husk), and a smattering of bright green chopped fresh mint. It was a perfect light lunch. It could even be dinner, served over brown rice, bulgur, or some other filling, toasty grain, for a warming meal to start out roasting season right.

1. Preheat the oven to 425°F. Toss the cauliflower with the oil, cumin seeds, salt, and pepper. Spread the mixture in an even layer on a large baking sheet. Roast, tossing occasionally, until the cauliflower is tender and its edges are toasty, 20 to 30 minutes.

2. Whisk a pinch of salt into the yogurt. Dollop the yogurt on top of the cauliflower and strew the mint and pomegranate seeds over the yogurt.

WHAT ELSE? Don't worry if your florets seem unevenly cut. The bigger pieces will get tender and golden, while the little bits get crispy-caramelized all over. I think it makes for an excellent contrast of textures.

I abhor the chalky texture of low-fat yogurts, so please use full-fat for this dish. The only exception I've found is 2 percent plain Greek yogurt, which tastes more or less like the real deal.

If you don't have pomegranate seeds, just leave them off. The dish is lovely enough without them.

SHRIMP SCAMPI
with pernod & fennel fronds

SERVES 4 TO 6

- 3 tablespoons unsalted butter
- 2 garlic cloves, minced
- ⅓ cup dry white wine
- 2 tablespoons Pernod
- ¾ teaspoon kosher salt, or to taste
- Pinch crushed red pepper flakes
- 2 pounds large shrimp, shelled
- 2 tablespoons fresh, finely minced fennel fronds (save the bulbs for snacking)
- Freshly squeezed juice of ½ lemon

EDITOR'S WINE CHOICE
Floral, berry-scented Provençal rosé:
2011 Commanderie de Peyrassol

I've gotten complacent when it comes to shrimp cookery. Out of the dozens of methods possible for cooking the crustacean, I've reduced it to two, which fall along a seasonal divide.

In winter, I roast them until caramelized and golden; in summer, I sauté them with garlic, scampi style.

Not that I make the same two dishes over and over. I keep the techniques consistent, and change up the flavorings to match my mood and the contents of my fridge.

For example, this licorice-scented scampi is the love child of a bag of shrimp and a shock of wandering, feathery fennel fronds that met in the fridge while waiting for me to figure out what to make for dinner. When I opened the fridge and noticed their intimate proximity, the dish seemed destined to be.

So I married them in the pan, anointing the union with butter for creaminess, crushed red pepper for heat, and Pernod to play up the anise flavor of the fennel. I have to say, it's one of the happiest pairings to ever end up on my dinner plate.

You'll notice I don't use the fennel bulbs here. I could have, slicing them thinly and caramelizing them in butter before adding the shrimp. But in the end I decided to keep things simple and pure between fronds and seafood. After all, three's a crowd, even in a sauté pan.

1. In a large skillet over medium heat, melt the butter. Add the garlic and cook, stirring, until fragrant, about 1 minute. Add the wine and Pernod, salt, and red pepper flakes. Bring to a simmer. Let the mixture reduce by half, about 2 minutes.

2. Add the shrimp and cook, stirring, until they just turn pink, 2 to 4 minutes depending on their size. Stir in the fennel fronds and lemon juice. Serve with crusty bread.

continued on page 50

This dish
cooks in under
10 minutes.

SHRIMP SCAMPI *continued*

WHAT ELSE? Scampi is such an adaptable recipe because the combination of butter, garlic, and wine makes anything taste good. So, to that end, here are a few of my favorite variations:

Skip the Pernod and use Cognac or more white wine.

Any fresh, floppy, soft herb can step into the fennel fronds' shoes. Parsley is classic, mint is refreshing, sage is musky, basil is summery, cilantro is citrusy, anise hyssop is exotic, chervil is licorice-ish, and a combination might just blow your mind.

Chunks of fish or scallops or even chicken can replace the shrimp if you're not feeling shrimpy.

A pinch of Turkish or Aleppo red pepper is a nice substitute for the more pedestrian red pepper flakes, adding a fruity, smoky note.

Lime juice is nice sometimes instead of the lemon. To bump up the citrus flavor of either lemon or lime, you can also grate in some fresh zest, which zips things up nicely, especially given the butter quotient here.

If you like it aromatic, try adding a pinch of garam masala or ground cumin to the butter.

Sometimes I throw some cubed tomatoes into the pan along with the shrimp. If you do this, you'll need more salt and pepper to season everything properly.

VIETNAMESE GRILLED STEAK & CABBAGE SALAD

with peanuts, cilantro & chiles

SERVES 4

- ¼ cup soy sauce
- Freshly squeezed juice and finely grated zest of 1 lime
- 2 tablespoons grated fresh gingerroot
- 2 teaspoons toasted (Asian) sesame oil
- 2 garlic cloves, finely chopped
- 1¼-pound flank steak, rinsed and patted dry
- 2 carrots, peeled and trimmed
- 10 cups shredded napa or regular cabbage (about ½ head)
- ¼ cup chopped fresh cilantro (or use mint or basil)
- Kosher salt and freshly ground black pepper
- 2 tablespoons chopped peanuts (optional)

FOR THE SPICY VINAIGRETTE

- 2 tablespoons soy sauce
- 1 tablespoon rice wine vinegar
- 2 tablespoons extra-virgin olive or peanut oil
- 1 teaspoon Thai or Vietnamese fish sauce, such as nam pla or nuoc mam
- Freshly squeezed juice of 1 lime
- Pinch cayenne
- 1 garlic clove, finely chopped

EDITOR'S WINE CHOICE
Juicy, light-bodied red: 2010 Vietti Tre Vigne Dolcetto d'Alba

By the time April rolls around, I'm ready to be done with cabbage. It's not that I don't appreciate its stalwart, pale presence at the otherwise near-depleted farmers' market of winter. I do. But after months and months of the stuff, you can bet I've sautéed, stewed, fried, and roasted the orb to the outer limits of my cruciferous desires.

That's when I know it's time for a new recipe, something slightly out of my Eastern European comfort zone, to whet my appetite and get me back into a cabbage groove.

Whenever I start to get that winter palate fatigue, my best cure is usually a dish inspired by more temperate climes, places rich with spunky spice and heat and plenty of lively citrus.

My first thought was to take a mental trip to Mexico and whip up some fish tacos piled high with a cilantro-spiked cabbage slaw. I kept daydreaming, and the combination of cilantro, cabbage, and lime juice made my mind skip over to a place I've been to in restaurants only: Vietnam. I remembered a cabbage salad spiked with chile, garlic, fish sauce, limes, and herbs that I often order, and immediately sat down to scour the Internet trying to find it.

There were hundreds of renditions, some with meat, some without. Since I was looking for dinner, I cherry-picked from the selections, adding and subtracting ingredients to match what I had in the fridge and freezer (namely, a flank steak), and what I could easily pick up at the store around the corner (ginger, lime, cilantro, but not lemongrass).

I made a pungent marinade for the steak, and while it marinated I whisked together a vibrant soy sauce–based vinaigrette and tossed it with the shredded cabbage. The dressing was so bright and flavorful it immediately made me overcome any cabbage inhibitions, and I inhaled half the bowl before I remembered that there were also some nice slices of bloody steak on my plate, too.

It was a perfect winter-doldrums meal that made spring seem not so very far away after all.

continued on page 52

GRILLED STEAK & CABBAGE SALAD *continued*

1. Whisk together the soy sauce, lime juice and zest, gingerroot, and sesame oil. With a mortar and pestle or with the flat side of a knife, mash the garlic into a paste. Whisk into the marinade. Place the steak in a shallow dish and cover with the marinade, turning completely to coat. Cover the dish with plastic wrap and refrigerate for at least 1 hour and up to 12. Remove the steak from the refrigerator 30 minutes prior to cooking.

2. In a food processor fitted with the large grating attachment, shred the carrots. Turn them out into a large bowl. Add the cabbage and cilantro. Toss well. Cover tightly with plastic wrap and refrigerate for up to 3 hours.

3. To make the vinaigrette, in a small bowl, whisk together the soy sauce, vinegar, olive or peanut oil, fish sauce, lime juice, and cayenne. Using a mortar and pestle or with the back of a knife, mash the garlic to a paste; whisk into the vinaigrette.

4. Preheat the broiler and position a rack in the top third of the oven. Remove the steak from the marinade, scraping off any excess, and season with salt and pepper. Transfer the steak to a baking sheet. Broil, turning once halfway through, until browned, about 3 minutes per side for medium-rare. Transfer the steak to a cutting board and let rest for 5 minutes. Thinly slice the steak against the grain.

5. To assemble, add just enough of the vinaigrette to the salad to coat it and toss well. Taste and add more dressing or salt or lime juice if desired. Place the salad onto the center of a platter and top with the steak. Sprinkle with the chopped peanuts, if desired, drizzle with more vinaigrette, and serve.

WHAT ELSE? If you're absolutely done with cabbage but crave a tangy, meaty hunk of flesh, make the steak and marinade part of this dish and serve it by itself, or on a bed of watercress or arugula.

The steak is a great recipe for summer grilling season, too. Serve it with sliced heirloom tomatoes and/or cucumbers if you can get nice ones.

If you love mango, add some ripe cubes to the cabbage salad; it gives it an amazing sweet burst of flavor.

This makes a light meal; if you want to add a hefty carb, I would recommend either plain rice or coconut brown rice, which isn't traditional but the flavors work nicely together.

Bring the
meat to room
temperature
before grilling
to ensure
even cooking.

MALLOBARS

MAKES ABOUT 18 (2-INCH) SQUARES

FOR THE GRAHAM CRACKER BASE

1	cup (2 sticks) unsalted butter
¼	cup firmly packed dark brown sugar
¼	cup granulated sugar
¼	cup honey
1½	cups whole wheat flour
1	cup all-purpose flour
1	teaspoon kosher salt
½	teaspoon ground cinnamon

FOR THE HONEY MARSHMALLOW

3	envelopes unflavored gelatin (about 3 tablespoons)
1	cup cold water
2	cups granulated sugar
¼	cup honey
2	large egg whites
¼	teaspoon kosher salt
1	tablespoon vanilla extract

FOR THE CHOCOLATE GLAZE

9	ounces bittersweet chocolate, chopped
¾	cup heavy cream

This is my version of homemade Mallomars. But instead of painstakingly forming individual cookies, I use the bar cookie method, spreading everything in one large pan. I end up with a crisp, homemade graham cracker crust topped by honey marshmallow and a thick layer of chocolate. Though they are easier than the original recipe, I wouldn't call them a super-quick dessert. You still need to devote a good part of an afternoon to their confection. Or try to make the components over several days if it's easier to carve that out of your schedule.

However you manage it, the payoff is big: They are truly scrumptious, and I guarantee that if you bring them to a potluck or party, no one else will have brought anything remotely like them. They are unusual, crowd pleasing, fancy looking, and even slightly good for you (okay, just slightly) from the whole wheat flour.

1. First, make the graham cracker base. In the bowl of an electric mixer, cream the butter, sugars, and honey until smooth. In a medium bowl, combine the flours, salt, and cinnamon. Add the dry ingredients to the mixer and beat until the dough just comes together.

2. Wrap the dough in plastic and pat into a disc. Chill the dough for at least 1 hour and up to 2 days.

3. When ready to bake, preheat the oven to 325°F. Line a 9-by-13-inch baking pan with foil or parchment paper. On a lightly floured surface, or in between two sheets of parchment paper, roll out the dough into a rectangle that just fits the prepared pan. Carefully transfer the dough to the prepared pan. Squish it to fit if it starts to tear (the dough is soft). Prick the dough all over with a fork. Bake the graham cracker base until golden brown, 18 to 20 minutes. Allow the crust to cool completely before topping with the marshmallow. (The graham cracker base can be made a few days ahead; store, covered in foil, at room temperature.)

continued on page 56

MALLOBARS *continued*

4. While the graham cracker base cools, prepare the honey marshmallow. Place the gelatin in the cold water to bloom. In a saucepan over medium heat, cook the sugar, honey, and ½ cup water, stirring until the sugar dissolves, until the mixture reaches 240°F on a candy thermometer.

5. In the bowl of an electric mixer, whisk the egg whites and salt until soft peaks form. When the sugar mixture has come up to temperature, carefully pour it into the egg whites while whisking. Continue whisking until the mixture has cooled slightly, about 1 minute, and add the gelatin and water mixture and the vanilla. Continue whisking until the mixture begins to thicken and quadruples in volume, 5 to 7 minutes. Scrape the marshmallow onto the graham cracker base and smooth the top with a spatula. Allow the marshmallow to set for 4 hours or overnight at room temperature.

6. To prepare the chocolate glaze, place the chocolate pieces in a bowl. In a saucepan over medium-high heat, bring the cream just to a boil. Pour the cream over the chocolate and whisk until the chocolate has melted and the glaze is smooth and shiny. Pour the glaze onto the set marshmallow and smooth with a spatula. Allow the glaze to set, about 30 minutes, before cutting into squares.

WHAT ELSE? What else can I tell you? If these seem like too much trouble, you can always just go out and buy some Mallomars. And, being a seasonal product themselves (they are only available in the colder months), they arguably fit into a seasonal kitchen if you don't think about it all too deeply.

The graham cracker dough also makes fantastic cookies all by itself. Just bake as directed above, but as soon as you take the pan out of the oven, while still hot, score the dough into 2-inch squares. Cool and break up into cookies.

SWEET POTATO TEA CAKE

with brown sugar–rum glaze

SERVES 6 TO 8

- 1 large sweet potato (about 1 pound)
- ½ cup safflower or vegetable oil, plus more for greasing
- 1 cup dark brown sugar
- 1¾ cups plus 2 tablespoons all-purpose flour
- ¾ teaspoon baking soda
- ¼ teaspoon freshly grated nutmeg
- ⅛ teaspoon ground cardamom

Fine sea salt

- 2 large eggs
- ⅓ cup milk
- 1½ teaspoons pure vanilla extract
- 2 tablespoons confectioners' sugar
- 2 tablespoons dark rum
- 2 tablespoons unsalted butter

A sweet and boozy brown sugar–rum glaze tops this moist, lightly spiced tea cake from Clark.

1. Preheat the oven to 350°F. Prick the sweet potato all over with a fork and wrap in aluminum foil. Roast on a baking sheet for about 1 hour and 15 minutes, until tender. Let cool completely. Peel the sweet potato and pass the flesh through a ricer or coarse sieve into a small bowl.

2. Grease an 8-inch round cake pan. In a medium bowl, whisk ¾ cup plus 2 tablespoons of the brown sugar with the flour, baking soda, nutmeg, cardamom and ½ teaspoon of salt. In a large bowl, whisk ¾ cup of the sweet potato with the eggs, milk, vanilla and ½ cup of oil. Whisk in the dry ingredients. Scrape the batter into the prepared pan and bake for about 1 hour, until a toothpick inserted in the center comes out clean. Transfer to a rack and let the cake cool completely in the pan.

3. In a small saucepan, combine the remaining 2 tablespoons of brown sugar with the confectioners' sugar, rum and a pinch of salt. Cook over moderately low heat until the sugar is dissolved. Add the butter and cook over low heat, stirring, until melted. Turn the cake out onto a rack, then set it right side up. Drizzle the glaze over the top, cut the cake into wedges and serve.

MAKE AHEAD The cake can be stored in an airtight container at room temperature for up to 2 days.

MY GRILL

pete evans

why we love this book

Australian TV chef and restaurateur Pete Evans exports his can't-mess-it-up style of food to America. His delicious, doable recipes, designed to be cooked on a grill or over a campfire—though many could easily be made on a stove or in an oven—epitomize the cool diversity of Australian cuisine. There are plenty of flavors from all over Asia (as in his fish and crispy garlic salad with a Japanese-style dressing, page 60) and the Mediterranean (Turkish-style flatbreads stuffed with ground beef, spinach and feta, page 64), plus lots of superfresh seafood.

his grill mentor

"It was actually my mum who taught me the art of outdoor grilling when I was growing up. She'd make the most amazing steak sandwiches for me when I came back from surfing. She also loved to experiment with marinating meat in Asian flavors—Japanese, Chinese, Indian—and that was really influential."

easiest protein to grill

"Seafood is so quick to cook on a hot grill; I think it's the easiest thing to make at the last minute. For example, in my grilled fish with artichoke-tomato salsa (page 62), the thin fillets cook in five minutes and you can put together the salsa with just a few ingredients."

favorite vegetable to grill

"Corn on the cob, served Mexican-style, is a great crowd-pleaser. You just grill the corn in its husk, slather it with a chipotle mayonnaise made with lots of lime, cilantro and chipotle chiles, then finish it with lashings of lime juice. It's simply gorgeous."

go-to dish for friends

"I might be a clichéd Australian, but you can't go wrong with shrimp on the grill. Flavored with oregano, lemon and chile flakes, it's one of the yummiest dishes."

PUBLISHED BY WELDON OWEN, $30

FISH WITH CRISPY GARLIC & ALMOND SALAD

SERVES 4

- 1 tablespoon peanut oil
- 6 garlic cloves, thinly sliced

Four 6-ounce white-fleshed fish fillets or steaks

- 2 large handfuls of baby arugula
- 2 large handfuls of baby mizuna leaves
- 2 large handfuls of frisée lettuce leaves
- 1 small handful of fresh mint
- 1 handful of fresh cilantro leaves
- 3 tablespoons julienned leek
- 1 banana chile, cut into thin strips
- 4 tablespoons toasted chopped almonds

JAPANESE SALAD DRESSING

- ½ cup grapeseed oil
- ⅓ cup Japanese rice vinegar
- 2 teaspoons sliced green onion, white part only
- 2 teaspoons English mustard
- 2 teaspoons light soy sauce
- 2 teaspoons mirin (Japanese cooking wine)

Few drops of Asian fish sauce

Pinch of pure chile powder

EDITOR'S WINE CHOICE
Vibrant, citrusy Sauvignon Blanc:
2011 Cadaretta SBS

It's nice to make something a little out of the ordinary, especially when it's this easy. Try using wild kingfish steaks if you can as you get some of the belly, which is my favorite part of this fish. You could also use salmon for this and, alternatively, you could serve the fish as a whole portion rather than flaking it. The crispy garlic and almonds add a great texture.

To make the Japanese dressing, combine all the ingredients in a nonreactive bowl and set aside.

Heat a little peanut oil in a skillet over medium-high heat. Add the garlic and cook for a few minutes or until golden and crispy. Remove and drain on paper towels.

Set up the outdoor grill for direct-heat cooking over medium-high heat. Coat the fish fillets with a little more of the oil. Season with salt and pepper and place, skin side down, on the grill. Cook for a few minutes until golden, then turn over and cook for another 1 to 2 minutes or until just cooked through.

In a bowl combine the arugula, mizuna, frisée, mint and cilantro, leek and chile and pour over the salad dressing. Toss to combine.

Flake the fish over the salad, discarding the bones if using steaks, and serve scattered with the crispy garlic and almonds.

The fish
here can also
be kept as
whole fillets
to serve
alongside the
salad.

GRILLED FISH
with an italian garden salsa of artichokes & tomato

SERVES 4

- 4 vine-ripened tomatoes
- 1 jar (5½ ounces) marinated artichokes, drained
- 1 cup pitted kalamata olives
- 1 handful of fresh Italian parsley, chopped
- ¼ cup pine nuts, toasted
- ⅔ cup extra-virgin olive oil

Juice of 1 lemon

Four 6-ounce pieces of fish such as snapper, sea bass or halibut

Olive oil, for cooking

EDITOR'S WINE CHOICE
Zippy, fresh Grüner Veltliner:
2011 H.u.M. Höfer

This is a style of food I so love to eat and also cook—a beautiful piece of fish that you have either caught or bought, married with a light flavorful salsa that only takes a matter of minutes to put together. And the best thing of all is that you know you are doing yourself and your guests a favor by cooking it as it's delicious and healthy.

To make the salsa, cut the tomatoes into quarters and discard the seeds. Finely dice the tomato flesh and artichokes and place in a bowl. Add the olives, parsley and pine nuts, then add the oil and lemon juice, and season with salt and pepper.

Set up the outdoor grill for direct-heat cooking over high heat. Place a griddle, *plancha* or *piastra* suitable for use on an outdoor grill on the grill to preheat. Brush the fish with some oil and cook on the griddle for a few minutes on each side, or until cooked through, depending on how thick the fish is. Serve with the salsa.

GRILLED GÖZLEMES

SERVES 4

Scant 1 cup plain yogurt
Pinch of salt
2   cups self-rising flour
6   ounces ground beef
2   tablespoons olive oil, plus
    extra for cooking
1   garlic clove, minced
Pinch of ground cumin
Pinch of red pepper flakes
4   tablespoons tomato juice
1¾ cups baby spinach or Swiss chard
4   ounces feta cheese, crumbled
¼   cup butter, melted (optional)
Lemon wedges, to serve

EDITOR'S WINE CHOICE
Bright, spiced Oregon Pinot Noir:
2010 A to Z

Turkish-style stuffed flatbreads, gözlemes are great fun to make (well, I think so) and everyone loves them. This version is made with ground beef and finished with feta cheese and spinach leaves and lashings of lemon juice. I have tried it with lamb, chicken, beef and vegetarian options and they all taste delicious. I'll let you decide which is your favorite variation.

Beat the yogurt and salt together in large bowl until smooth. Gradually stir in the flour until you have a stiff dough. Tip onto a lightly floured work surface and gradually knead the dough, incorporating any remaining flour until the dough is soft and only slightly sticky. Transfer to a clean bowl and let stand, covered, for 30 minutes.

Cook the ground beef with the olive oil in a skillet over medium-high heat for about 2 minutes, or until browned all over. Add the garlic, cumin, pepper flakes and tomato juice and cook for another 1 to 2 minutes or until the mixture is dry. Remove from the heat, place the mixture in a colander and leave to cool and drain.

On a floured work surface, split the dough into 4 equal balls. Roll each piece of dough into a 12-inch circle.

Place a quarter of the spinach over half of each circle, sprinkle a quarter of the feta cheese over, then add a quarter of the beef mixture and season with salt and pepper. Fold the dough over and seal the edges with a fork. Repeat with the remaining dough and ingredients.

Set up the outdoor grill for direct-heat cooking over medium heat. Place a griddle, *plancha* or *piastra* suitable for use on an outoor grill on the grill to preheat. Brush one side of each gözleme with olive oil and cook on the griddle until the base is golden. Brush the top side with olive oil, then turn over and cook until golden. Brush with the butter, if using, cut into 4 pieces and serve with lemon wedges.

QUICK STEAKS
with green olive dressing & tomato salad

SERVES 4

Four 6-ounce sirloin steaks, pounded
     to flatten slightly
  4 lemon wedges, to serve (optional)

TOMATO SALAD
  30 cherry tomatoes, cut into quarters
    2 garlic cloves, thinly sliced
  10 fresh basil leaves, torn
  ½ cup sparkling mineral water
    4 tablespoons extra-virgin olive oil

GREEN OLIVE DRESSING
    3 teaspoons finely chopped onion
  ½ cup olive oil
  ½ cup roughly chopped green
    Sicilian olives
    3 tablespoons lemon juice
  ½ celery rib, finely chopped
    3 tablespoons chopped fresh
    Italian parsley

EDITOR'S WINE CHOICE
Fresh, cherry-rich Barbera d'Alba:
2010 Elio Altare

It is so hard to cook something to everyone's taste. Take my brother Dave for instance, he has an aversion to fennel and also to any meat with fat running through it (I, on the other hand, love it). Now I am not having a go at him, he doesn't like it and that's fine, but when your brother is your business partner and toughest critic it can be hard coming up with dishes that he likes. That is where this dish comes in—Dave loves filet mignon and sirloin (if the fat is taken off) so this was designed as a no-nonsense dish that would please him, as well as the customers, and also the cooks in the kitchen. We have had this on and off at my restaurant, Hugo's Bar Pizza in Kings Cross, Sydney, for years. Quick to cook and a wonderful grilled dish for the warmer months . . .

To make the tomato salad, place the tomatoes, garlic, basil leaves, mineral water and olive oil into a bowl, season to taste with sea salt and cracked black pepper, then squeeze with your hand. Let stand for 10 minutes for the flavors to develop.

Set up the outdoor grill for direct-heat cooking over medium heat. To make the green olive dressing, sauté the onion with a little olive oil in a skillet for a minute, then add them to a bowl with the olives, lemon juice, celery, olive oil, sea salt, pepper and chopped parsley.

Brush the steaks with a little oil and season with salt and pepper. Then cook on the grill for 1 to 2 minutes on each side or until cooked to your liking.

Serve the steaks topped with some of the olive dressing, and the tomato salad on the side.

PETE EVANS ONLINE
peterevanschef.com.au

 Pete Evans

 @PeterEvansChef

RIVER COTTAGE EVERY DAY

hugh fearnley-whittingstall

why we love this book

In his seventh River Cottage title, British celebrity chef and sustainable food champion Hugh Fearnley-Whittingstall tackles a familiar modern-day dilemma: how to stay true to ethical eating principles when time and money are limited. His recipes are economical, wholesome and simple to prepare, reflecting what he feeds his own family. His Thrifty Fish Soup with Cheaty Rouille (page 74), for example, uses inexpensive fish and potatoes, and leftover bread for croutons.

passing ideas on to his kids

"My own kids have been drenched in the culture of growing your own food and eating the animals that you've raised yourself. When I was butchering our pigs, my then three-year-old son Oscar was running around with an ear in one hand and an eyeball in the other. Making that connection between food in the field and food on the plate is something that I learned at a later age, but my kids have grown up with it."

favorite thrifty ingredient

"Stinging nettles are the single most prolific weed in the UK, yet they're such a fabulous green vegetable— like spinach with extra oomph. The acid in them adds a bit of edge to nettle soup. It's a frugal dish associated with the war years, but it's really wonderful."

one way to eat better

"I try to persuade people to change how they shop and cook, at the very least to be a little more skeptical of anonymous, prepackaged food. Instead of buying a jar of curry sauce, for instance, you could make a simple curry sauce to bake with chicken (page 76)."

his start in the kitchen

"By the age of eight, I was making desserts for my mother's dinner parties—classics of the seventies like profiteroles, rum gâteau and lemon mousse."

PUBLISHED BY TEN SPEED PRESS, $32.50

WARM LEEK & WHITE BEAN SALAD
with mustard dressing

SERVES 4

- 2 tablespoons canola or olive oil
- 2 large leeks, white part only, finely sliced

Sea salt and freshly ground black pepper

One 14-ounce can white beans such as cannellini, drained and rinsed

- 1 heaping tablespoon chopped fresh flat-leaf parsley

Lettuce leaves, to serve

FOR THE DRESSING

- 1 tablespoon Dijon mustard
- 1 teaspoon whole-grain mustard (optional)
- 3 tablespoons canola or extra-virgin olive oil
- 2 teaspoons cider vinegar

A pinch each of sea salt, freshly ground black pepper, and superfine sugar

This simple little dish works very well as a vegetarian starter, but can also function as a side dish to something robust, such as pork chops or sausages. It's all about the sweetness of the leeks and the creaminess of the beans. Put the extra whole-grain mustard into the dressing if you like real bite.

Heat the oil in a large frying pan over medium heat, then add the leeks and a good pinch of salt. As soon as the leeks begin to soften, turn the heat down fairly low and continue to cook, stirring from time to time, for 6 to 7 minutes, until they are soft; don't let them color. Add the beans and toss together until heated through. Remove from the heat and stir in the parsley and plenty of black pepper.

For the dressing, whisk all the ingredients together to combine. Add to the pan of warm leeks and beans and stir well.

Divide the salad leaves among 4 plates and spoon the warm bean and leek mixture on top. Serve right away, accompanied by toasted sourdough bread. Alternatively, forget the leaves and just serve the dressed beans on toast.

Mix a little whole-grain mustard into the dressing for added kick.

ROAST JERUSALEM ARTICHOKE, HAZELNUT & GOAT CHEESE SALAD

SERVES 4 TO 6

- ⅓ cup hazelnuts
- 1 pound Jerusalem artichokes
- 4 tablespoons canola or olive oil
- 2 sprigs of thyme
- 1 to 2 bay leaves
- Sea salt and freshly ground black pepper
- 1 teaspoon hazelnut oil
- ½ lemon
- A couple of handfuls of peppery salad greens (optional)
- 2 ounces hard goat cheese, crumbled or shaved into strips with a vegetable peeler, according to texture

EDITOR'S WINE CHOICE
Nutty, minerally Italian white:
2010 Barberani Castagnolo Orvieto
Classico Superiore

The earthy flavor of roasted artichokes is delicious with toasted hazelnuts. Jerusalem artichokes have a tendency to collapse into fluffiness when roasted, but keeping the skin on keeps them from breaking up too much when you toss them into the salad.

First, toast the hazelnuts. Preheat the oven to 350°F. Spread the nuts out on a baking sheet in a single layer and toast in the oven for about 5 minutes, until they are lightly colored and the skins are blistered and cracked. Wrap them in a clean tea towel for a minute and then rub them vigorously with the towel until the skins fall off. Let cool and chop very coarsely or leave whole.

Turn the oven up to 375°F and put a large roasting pan in to heat up. Scrub the artichokes well and cut into halves or quarters lengthwise, depending on size—you need chunks about ½ inch thick. Put the artichokes in a bowl and turn over in 3 tablespoons of the canola or olive oil with the thyme, bay, and a little salt. Add to the hot roasting pan and roast for about 35 minutes, until tender and lightly golden, taking the pan out after 15 minutes to turn the artichokes over. Allow to cool slightly.

Whisk the remaining tablespoon of oil with the hazelnut oil, drizzle it over the warm artichokes, squeeze on a good spritz of lemon juice, and season with salt and a few grinds of black pepper. Turn the artichokes over gently with your hands so that everything is well combined. Add the hazelnuts and the salad greens if you're using them, toss gently, then divide among serving plates. Scatter over the crumbled or shaved goat cheese and serve right away.

THRIFTY FISH SOUP
with cheaty rouille

SERVES 4

1 firm-fleshed fish, 1½ to 2 pounds, filleted and skinned, skin, head, and bones saved

FOR THE STOCK

2 celery stalks, chopped
1 garlic clove, peeled
1 onion, coarsely chopped
1 large carrot, sliced
A sprig of thyme
1 bay leaf
Stems from 1 bunch flat-leaf parsley, leaves reserved
A few black peppercorns
A splash of white wine

FOR THE SOUP

2 garlic cloves
1 large onion
2 celery stalks
2 leeks
1 pound russet potatoes
2 tablespoons canola or olive oil
½ teaspoon fennel seeds, coarsely crushed
4 to 6 ounces cleaned squid, or 4 to 8 scallops (optional)
Leaves from the parsley bunch, finely chopped
Sea salt and freshly ground black pepper
Whole-wheat croutons, to serve

FOR THE ROUILLE (OPTIONAL)

1 hot red chile
Mayonnaise (recipe follows), made with 1 garlic clove

EDITOR'S WINE CHOICE
Citrusy, minerally white
Burgundy: 2010 Patrick Piuze
Terroirs de Courgis Chablis

This is a pleasingly frugal recipe. You buy an inexpensive fresh fish, get the fishmonger to fillet it for you, then use the head, skin, and bones to make a flavorful stock. The broth is enhanced with a few herbs and vegetables, the fish flesh goes in at the end, and you can splash out on a bit of squid or a few scallops, if you like. The finishing touch is a swirl of garlicky, chile-hot rouille, though I have to say, the soup is delicious even without it. And croutons, made from leftover bread, add crunch.

First, make a simple fish stock: Put the fish head, skin, and bones in a saucepan with all the other ingredients for the stock. Add 4 cups cold water and bring to a gentle simmer. Cook very gently for half an hour; do not allow it to boil hard, as this spoils the flavor. Strain the stock, discarding the fishy bits and vegetables.

For the soup, finely chop the garlic, onion, celery, and leeks. Peel the potatoes and cut into ½-inch cubes. Heat the oil over low heat in a large saucepan, add the fennel seeds, garlic, onion, celery, and leeks, then cover and cook for about 10 minutes, until soft. Add the potatoes and the stock and return to a gentle simmer. Cook for 15 minutes, or until the potatoes are tender.

Meanwhile, make the rouille, if you are serving it, by chopping the chile very finely and mixing it with the garlic mayonnaise; set aside.

Now, slice the fish fillets into bite-sized pieces. If using squid, slice the pouches into rings; if using scallops, clean and slice horizontally in half. Add all the fish and any shellfish to the simmering broth. Cook for 2 minutes, until the fish is just done, then remove from the heat. Add the parsley and season to taste.

Serve the soup in warm bowls, topped with a few crisp croutons and a good blob of rouille, if you like.

VARIATION When fennel is in season, in summer and autumn, try using it instead of the leeks.

MAYONNAISE

I'm not a total mayo fascist: like most families, we usually have a jar of commercial mayo in the fridge. However, I make my own if I have time and I hope you will too, as it will be far superior to standard store-bought options. Adding a teaspoonful of ready-made mayo to your raw egg yolk at the start reduces the risk of separating.

Crush the garlic to a paste with a pinch of salt. Transfer it to a bowl, add the mustard, egg yolk, vinegar, mayo if using, plus a little pepper and a tiny pinch of sugar, then whisk together.

Combine the oils in a pitcher. Pour a few drops into the yolk mixture and whisk to emulsify. Repeat this once or twice, then start pouring in the oil in a very thin, steady stream, whisking all the time.

When all the oil has been whisked in and you have a thick, glossy mayonnaise, taste it and add more salt, pepper, sugar, and some lemon juice if it needs it. If it's too thick, thin it with a little warm water. Refrigerate until needed and use within a week.

MAKES ABOUT ¾ CUP

¼ garlic clove
Sea salt, freshly ground black pepper,
    and a little superfine sugar
¼ teaspoon English mustard
1 egg yolk
1 teaspoon wine vinegar
    or cider vinegar
1 generous teaspoon commercial
    mayonnaise (optional)
⅓ cup sunflower oil
⅓ cup canola oil or a mild olive oil
Lemon juice (optional)

BAKED CHICKEN CURRY

SERVES 6

- 2 heaping teaspoons cumin seeds
- 2 heaping teaspoons coriander seeds
- 1 heaping teaspoon fennel seeds
- 2 teaspoons ground turmeric
- 2 teaspoons ground fenugreek
- 1 large onion, coarsely chopped
- 3 large garlic cloves, coarsely chopped
- 1 large green chile, coarsely chopped
- 1 thumb-sized piece of fresh ginger, coarsely chopped
- 3 to 4 tablespoons sunflower or peanut oil
- 1 chicken, cut into 6 pieces, or 6 skin-on, bone-in chicken pieces (about 3 pounds total)

Sea salt and freshly ground black pepper
One 14-ounce can tomatoes
One 14-ounce can coconut milk

EDITOR'S WINE CHOICE
Substantial, concentrated Rhône blend: 2011 Domaine Gramenon Vie on y Est Côtes du Rhône Blanc

This may not be quite as quick as opening a jar of curry sauce, but it tastes far better. If you want to put a little curry "banquet" together, you could serve this dish with flatbreads, lamb and squash curry, and green onion bhajis with radish raita.

If you've got the time, toast the cumin, coriander, and fennel seeds in a dry frying pan for a minute or two, until fragrant. Grind the whole spices (toasted or otherwise) to a coarse powder in a spice grinder or with a mortar and pestle, then mix with the turmeric and fenugreek.

Put the onion, garlic, chile, and ginger in a food processor or blender. Blend to a coarse paste, stopping to scrape down the sides a few times.

Preheat the oven to 350°F.

Heat 2 tablespoons of the oil in a large frying pan over medium-high heat. Add half the chicken pieces, season well, and brown them all over, making sure you get the skin a good color. Transfer them to a large roasting dish, skin side up. Repeat with the remaining chicken pieces.

Reduce the heat under the frying pan, add the spice mix, and fry for a minute or two, then add the onion paste. Fry, stirring frequently, for about 5 minutes, until the paste is soft, fragrant, and reduced in volume. Add a little more oil if it seems to be sticking.

Add the tomatoes and coconut milk to the food processor (no need to wash it out first) and blend to combine. Pour into the frying pan and bring to a simmer, stirring constantly. Add 1 teaspoon of salt and a grinding of pepper, then pour the sauce over the chicken pieces. Make sure they are all coated in the sauce, then push most of the sauce off the top of the chicken—if there's too much sauce sitting on them, the skin won't brown in the oven.

Bake, uncovered, for 1 hour or until the chicken is cooked through and nicely browned on top, turning and basting it a couple of times. Serve with lots of basmati rice to soak up the sauce.

LEEK & GOAT CHEESE SPELTOTTO

SERVES 4

- ½ stick (2 ounces) unsalted butter
- 2 tablespoons extra-virgin olive oil, plus more for drizzling
- 3 medium leeks, white and light green parts only, halved lengthwise and thinly sliced crosswise

Sea salt and freshly ground pepper

- 4 cups vegetable stock or low-sodium broth
- 1 onion, finely chopped
- 1 garlic clove, minced
- 1 teaspoon finely chopped thyme
- 1½ cups pearled spelt (see Editor's Note)
- ½ cup dry white wine
- ½ cup freshly grated aged goat cheese or Parmigiano-Reggiano, plus more for serving

EDITOR'S NOTE
Pearled spelt, which has had the outer husks removed, is a good alternative to rice or wheat. It's available at natural food stores.

EDITOR'S WINE CHOICE
Lively, medium-bodied northern Italian white: 2010 Venica & Venica Jesera Pinot Grigio

For his creamy leek "speltotto"—a playful marriage of spelt and risotto—Fearnley-Whittingstall replaces rice with nutty-tasting spelt.

1. In a large skillet, melt 2 tablespoons of the butter in 1 tablespoon of the olive oil. Add the leeks and cook, stirring occasionally, until translucent and softened, about 10 minutes. Season with salt and pepper.

2. In a medium saucepan, bring the stock to a simmer; keep warm. In a large pot, melt the remaining 2 tablespoons of butter in the remaining 1 tablespoon of oil. Add the onion, garlic and thyme and season with salt and pepper. Cook over moderate heat, stirring occasionally, until softened, about 10 minutes. Add the spelt and cook, stirring, until lightly toasted, about 2 minutes. Add the wine and cook until absorbed, about 5 minutes. Add 1 cup of the hot stock to the spelt and cook, stirring frequently, until nearly absorbed, about 5 minutes. Continue adding the hot stock, 1 cup at a time and stirring frequently, until the spelt is al dente, 20 to 25 minutes. Stir in the leeks and ½ cup of cheese and season with salt and pepper. Drizzle the speltotto with oil and serve, passing additional cheese at the table.

HUGH FEARNLEY-WHITTINGSTALL
ONLINE
rivercottage.net

 River Cottage

@rivercottage

BOBBY FLAY'S BAR AMERICAIN COOKBOOK

bobby flay with stephanie banyas & sally jackson

why we love this book

In his 11th cookbook, the star chef approaches regional American dishes and ingredients with a French-inflected sense of creativity, reflecting the bold-flavored food he serves at his New York City brasserie, Bar Americain. For example, Flay transforms chicken cordon bleu into a panko-crusted chicken cutlet that he tops with a triple-cream cheese, country ham and a peppery arugula salad (page 82).

on regional american cuisine

"When most people look at a map of America, they see cities and towns and states; I see ingredients. The Pacific Northwest is all about wild salmon, Dungeness crab and geoduck clams; the Southwest makes me think of blue corn, red chiles, green chiles. Louisiana, with all of its Cajun and Creole dishes, represents an entire cuisine of its own, and that's just one state. I think American food may be the most diverse in the world—and it's absolutely different from state to state."

the french connection

"Besides My-T-Fine pudding and deviled eggs, my first real dish was shrimp with mustard from Wolfgang Puck's *Modern French Cooking for the American Kitchen*. That was my go-to dish at home when I was 15 or 16. Wolfgang was the first celebrity chef in the country, and the only chef I had ever heard of."

on bar americain

"Great French brasseries might seem slightly chaotic, but they're organized. Everybody has a distinct role. For Bar Americain I wanted to translate that style, and the casual food and plating, and make it American. For instance, we do a take on classic French onion soup, but it's made entirely from American ingredients: Vidalia onions, white Vermont cheddar instead of Gruyère, a Parker House roll for the crouton. The feel of the recipe is French, but the taste is American."

PUBLISHED BY CLARKSON POTTER, $35

SMOKED CHILE COLLARD GREENS

SERVES 4

- 2 tablespoons canola oil
- 1 medium Spanish onion, finely diced
- 4 cloves garlic, finely chopped
- 2 to 3 teaspoons pureed canned chipotle chiles in adobo, to taste
- 2½ pounds collard greens, stems and ribs removed, coarsely chopped
- Kosher salt and freshly ground black pepper
- 3 tablespoons apple cider vinegar

Collard greens are a point of southern pride. Any barbecue or soul food restaurant worth its salt has a place for these mustardy-flavored greens. In the South, collard greens are typically cooked with a ham hock or smoked turkey wings to give a great smoky flavor to the greens and the broth—or pot liquor as it is referred to in local parlance. You can definitely add either to this recipe, but I like to use chipotle chiles to give not only smokiness but also a little heat to this dish. I prefer my collard greens to retain some bite and cook them until tender, not to melting. The greens have a natural sweetness that is both accentuated and balanced by the finishing splash of apple cider vinegar. Sweet, smoky, and slightly vinegary, these collard greens definitely deliver a touch of soul to the table.

1. Heat the oil in a large deep sauté pan over high heat until the oil begins to shimmer. Add the onion and cook until soft, about 4 minutes. Add the garlic and cook for 1 minute.

2. Add 1½ cups water and the chipotle puree and bring to a boil. Add the collards, season with salt and pepper, and turn to coat in the mixture. Reduce the heat to low, cover the pot, and cook, stirring occasionally, until the greens are crisp-tender, 15 to 20 minutes. Transfer to a platter and drizzle with the vinegar.

CHICKEN CUTLET

american triple cream cheese, southern ham, arugula

SERVES 4

CHICKEN

- 1 cup all-purpose flour
- 3 large eggs, lightly beaten
- 2 cups panko bread crumbs

Kosher salt and freshly ground black pepper

Four 6-ounce boneless, skinless chicken breast halves

- 6 tablespoons (¾ stick) unsalted butter
- 2 tablespoons olive oil
- ¼ pound Red Hawk triple cream cheese, Brie, or Camembert, thinly sliced
- 8 thin slices country ham or prosciutto

ARUGULA SALAD

- 2 tablespoons red wine vinegar
- 1 teaspoon Dijon mustard

Kosher salt and freshly ground black pepper

- ¼ cup extra-virgin olive oil
- ¼ pound baby arugula

EDITOR'S WINE CHOICE
Elegant, berry-rich Pinot Noir: 2010
Freeman Russian River Valley

Here is that American favorite, chicken cordon bleu, deconstructed. This gorgeous dish pulls the soggy ham and cheese out of the stuffing, layering them instead over a crisp, juicy chicken cutlet. The rich triple cream cheese begins to melt when it hits the panko-crusted chicken, which then anchors the paper-thin slices of cured ham to them both. Baby arugula is tossed in a bright, acidic vinaigrette of Dijon mustard and red wine vinegar before being placed atop the dish. The peppery arugula and mustardy vinaigrette cut through the richness of the cheese and complement the salty ham. I serve this at lunch, but it would be wonderful at dinner as well.

1. To cook the chicken, put the flour, eggs, and bread crumbs in 3 separate shallow bowls and season each with salt and pepper.

2. Place each chicken breast between 2 pieces of wax paper and pound to ¼-inch thickness.

3. Season the chicken on both sides with salt and pepper and then dredge each breast in the flour and tap off the excess. Dip into the egg wash and let the excess drip off, then dredge on both sides in the bread crumbs. Place on a wire rack set over a baking sheet.

4. Preheat 2 large nonstick sauté pans over high heat. Add 3 tablespoons of the butter and 1 tablespoon of the oil to each pan and heat until the butter is melted and sizzling. Place 2 breasts in each pan and cook until golden brown, about 4 minutes. Flip the breasts over and continue cooking until golden brown and the chicken is cooked through, about 3 minutes.

5. To make the arugula salad, whisk together the vinegar and mustard in a large bowl. Season with salt and pepper. Slowly whisk in the oil until emulsified. Add the arugula and toss to coat the leaves with the vinaigrette.

6. Transfer each breast to a large plate and immediately top with a few slices of cheese, then a few slices of ham, and some of the arugula salad.

This extra-crispy riff on chicken cordon bleu is layered, not rolled.

DEEP-DISH CHOCOLATE CREAM PIE

SERVES 8

CHOCOLATE PUDDING

⅔	cup sugar
¼	cup unsweetened Dutch-processed cocoa powder
2	tablespoons cornstarch
½	teaspoon fine salt
3½	cups whole milk
3½	cups heavy cream
1	vanilla bean, split and seeds scraped, or 1½ teaspoons vanilla extract
1¼	pounds bittersweet chocolate (60 percent cacao), coarsely chopped
2	tablespoons unsalted butter

GRAHAM CRACKER DISKS

½	pound (2 sticks) unsalted butter
½	vanilla bean, split and seeds scraped
2½	cups graham cracker crumbs (about 20 crackers)
1	cup sugar

RUM WHIPPED CREAM

2	cups heavy cream, very cold
2	tablespoons confectioners' sugar
1	tablespoon dark rum (optional)

Seeds scraped from ½ vanilla bean or ½ teaspoon vanilla extract

Chocolate cream pie has a place of honor in roadside diner pie cases across the country. This deconstructed version inverts the classic format because the gorgeous, silky, deeply chocolaty pudding is worth digging for. Break though a crunchy, buttery graham cracker crust and a smooth layer of whipped cream before making your way to the rich chocolate depths of this decadent "pie." Chocolate lovers, rejoice.

1. To make the pudding, whisk together the sugar, cocoa, cornstarch, and salt in a medium heavy pan. Slowly whisk in the milk and cream and add the vanilla bean and seeds (if using).

2. Slowly bring the mixture to a boil over medium heat, whisking constantly. Once the mixture comes to a boil, let it boil for 1 minute. Remove the pan from the heat and whisk in the chocolate and butter, along with the vanilla extract, if using, until smooth. Strain the pudding through a fine-mesh sieve into a bowl and press a piece of plastic wrap directly onto the surface. Let cool at room temperature for 30 minutes; then transfer to the refrigerator and let chill completely, at least 4 hours and up to 24 hours.

3. To make the graham cracker disks, preheat the oven to 350°F.

4. Combine the butter and vanilla bean and seeds in a small saucepan and melt over low heat. Remove from the heat and keep warm. Discard the vanilla bean before using.

5. Combine the graham cracker crumbs and sugar in a medium bowl, add the melted butter, and stir until combined. Pat the mixture evenly and firmly into an 18-by-12-inch rimmed baking sheet. Bake until light golden brown and set, about 10 minutes. Let cool completely on a wire rack.

6. Using a 3-inch cookie cutter or a very sharp paring knife, carefully cut out 8 disks.

7. To make the whipped cream, combine the cream, sugar, rum, if using, and vanilla seeds in a large bowl and whip, using a handheld mixer or a balloon whisk, until soft peaks form.

8. Divide the pudding among 8 shallow bowls and spread some of the whipped cream evenly over the pudding. Top each with a graham cracker disk.

SMOKED TOMATOES

with ancho bread crumbs & creamy cilantro vinaigrette

SERVES 6

¼ cup unseasoned rice wine vinegar
1½ tablespoons Dijon mustard
2 teaspoons honey
¾ cup lightly packed cilantro
⅓ cup canola oil
Kosher salt and freshly ground pepper
6 medium tomatoes, cored
½ cup fresh bread crumbs
1 teaspoon ancho chile powder
1 teaspoon granulated garlic
½ teaspoon granulated onion
Extra-virgin olive oil, for brushing
and drizzling

Flay gives ripe, juicy tomatoes a double dose of smokiness. First he smokes them on the grill, then he tops them with smoky, ancho chile–spiced bread crumbs.

1. In a blender, combine the vinegar, mustard, honey, cilantro and 3 tablespoons of water; puree until smooth. With the blender running, slowly drizzle in the canola oil until emulsified. Season the vinaigrette with salt and pepper.

2. Light a very small charcoal or wood fire on one side of a charcoal grill. Lay ½ cup of soaked hardwood chips over the fire and replace the grate. When the chips begin to smoke, set the tomatoes on the grate opposite the fire. Close the grill and smoke for 15 minutes.

3. Meanwhile, preheat the oven to 325°F. In a small bowl, toss the bread crumbs with the chile powder, garlic and onion and season with salt and pepper. Spread the bread crumbs in a pie plate and bake for about 10 minutes, stirring once, until golden brown. Remove the ancho bread crumbs from the oven and increase the oven temperature to 375°F.

4. Transfer the smoked tomatoes to a baking sheet, brush with olive oil and season with salt and pepper. Roast for 15 to 20 minutes, until the tomatoes just start to soften. Let cool slightly.

5. Cut the tomatoes in half crosswise and arrange cut side up on the baking sheet. Sprinkle the ancho bread crumbs over the tomatoes and drizzle with olive oil. Roast for 5 minutes, until just heated through. Transfer the tomatoes to a platter and serve, passing the vinaigrette at the table.

BOBBY FLAY ONLINE

bobbyflay.com

f Bobby Flay

t @bflay

Hominy salad, page 89

A SOUTHERLY COURSE

martha hall foose

why we love this book

Southern classics and dishes from immigrants who've helped define the New South come together in this homespun book. Martha Hall Foose collects recipes from throughout the Mississippi Delta to create "an immersion in Southern culinary eccentricity, ingenuity and creativity." Yet her food is always comforting, as in her sausage bake that puffs up like a popover (page 90).

her welcome-home dinner

"It's always grilled catfish. It's nice that catfish is finally getting some props. People have worked for a long time to improve its reputation; the best farms culture the fish in beautiful, alluvial, filtered water. Now, if they'd take those hillbilly fishing shows off TV . . ."

the original locavores

"I think the Southern approach to cooking what's local and in season is catching on around the country. They call it locavore. We call it sensible."

defining southern food

"I kind of seize up when people say 'the South.' That's like saying 'Eastern Europe.' The South is huge, and its food differs from region to region. Compare South Carolina low-country and Louisiana cooking: Both use grits and rice, but the results are so different."

the international south

"The South isn't just about fried chicken and biscuits. I have a close friend who grew up in India; my cousin Daniel married a Korean woman; there's a market in Yazoo City [Mississippi] that sells *kibbeh* [a Lebanese meatball]. My aunt and uncle used to own a farm in Mexico, so they would make ceviche all the way back in the sixties. You can see these international influences in my food. My Hominy Salad (page 89), for instance, has Mexican seasonings like cumin, cilantro and chili powder. It's a fun alternative to regular potato salad."

PUBLISHED BY CLARKSON POTTER, $32.50

DEVILED TOMATOES

SERVES 6

- 6 slices bacon, cut in ½-inch pieces
- 1 cup chopped green bell pepper
- 1 cup chopped red onion
- 2 jalapeño peppers, seeded and diced
- 2 garlic cloves, minced
- 3 large tomatoes, peeled and halved
- 1 tablespoon chopped fresh oregano

Salt and freshly ground black pepper
- 6 slices sourdough bread, toasted
- ¼ pound pepper Jack cheese, shredded (½ cup)

My friend Cindy Nix Sturdivant lives on the Countiss Place near Swan Lake, Mississippi. She has a nice plot of tomatoes, herbs, and peppers out the back door of her kitchen. This hot and spicy dish is inspired by her. She is so much fun because she can always get folks fired up for a party, like her epic dove hunt party, which grows every year, on Labor Day weekend. She needs to plant a bigger plot.

In a large skillet set over medium heat, cook the bacon until crisp, about 6 minutes. Transfer the bacon to paper towels and reserve the bacon drippings in the pan. Add the bell pepper, onion, jalapeños, and garlic to the pan. Cook, stirring occasionally, for 5 minutes.

Meanwhile, scoop the flesh out of the center of the tomatoes and chop, reserving the shells. Add the chopped flesh to the pan. Stir in the oregano, season with salt and pepper, and cook for 2 minutes.

Place an oven rack in the center of the oven and heat the broiler.

Put the bread slices in a 9-by-13-inch baking dish. Top each slice of bread with a tomato half. Divide the vegetable mixture evenly among the tomato halves. Top each with the bacon and cheese. Broil for 3 minutes or until the cheese is melted.

AUTHOR'S NOTE Nix [no relation to Cindy] vs. Hedden was the case that brought the question of whether a tomato is a fruit or a vegetable before the U.S. Supreme Court in 1893. Although the tomato is a fruit, the court unanimously ruled that the tomato would be thought of as a vegetable in regards to the Tariff Act of 1883, setting a precedent that still holds today.

HOMINY SALAD

SERVES 8

One 14½-ounce can golden hominy,
    rinsed and drained
One 14½-ounce can white hominy,
    rinsed and drained
  2 cups chopped fresh tomatoes
  ¼ pound sharp Cheddar cheese,
     shredded (1 cup)
  ½ cup mayonnaise
  ¼ cup chopped green bell pepper
  ¼ cup chopped red bell pepper
  4 green onions, white
     and green parts, chopped
  2 tablespoons chopped
     fresh cilantro
  1 teaspoon chili powder
  1 teaspoon cumin seeds
  1 teaspoon salt

Hominy and tomatoes with a South Texas chili spice are a great change from boring potato salad. It is sort of like changing the radio dial from a typical oldies station to a feisty, fun Mexican one.

Put the golden hominy, white hominy, tomatoes, cheese, mayonnaise, green bell pepper, red bell pepper, green onions, cilantro, chili powder, cumin seeds, and salt in a large bowl. Toss well to combine. Chill for at least 1 hour before serving.

AUTHOR'S NOTE The band Wall of Voodoo came out with a song called "Mexican Radio" when I was in high school. It was spicy and infectious and like nothing else on the radio at that time.

EDNA FERBER, FROM *GIANT,* A STORY SET IN TEXAS
"This was due partly to habit and partly to affection born of a mixture of superiority and inferiority. . . . It was part of the Texas ritual. We're rich as son-of-a-bitch stew but look how homely we are, just as plain-folksy as Grandpappy back in 1836. We know about champagne and caviar but we talk hog and hominy."

SAUSAGE DINNER

SERVES 3

- ⅓ cup whole milk
- ⅔ cup unbleached all-purpose flour
- 1 large egg

Six 3-ounce sweet Italian sausages

- 1 yellow onion, thinly sliced
- 1 tablespoon vegetable oil

Salt and freshly ground black pepper

This simple batter puffs up in the oven like a popover and envelops the sweet sausage nestled down in it like a snuggly down comforter. This is a family favorite on cold winter Sunday nights.

In a measuring cup with a spout, combine the milk with ¼ cup water.

Sift the flour into a small bowl and make a well in the center. Add the egg and, using a whisk, begin to incorporate it into the flour. Slowly add the milk mixture, whisking until the batter is smooth. Set aside to rest.

Heat the oven to 450°F.

Prick the sausages several times with a sharp knife and put them in an ovenproof skillet with the onion, oil, and ½ cup water. Bake for 18 minutes, turning occasionally, until the onions are browned, the sausages have begun to brown, and the water has reduced to just a thin coating in the bottom of the skillet.

Remove the skillet from the oven and pour the batter around the sausages. Season with salt and pepper. Return to the oven and bake for 30 minutes or until the batter is puffed and deep golden brown.

GULF COAST–STYLE CRAB ROLLS

SERVES *6*

ROLLS

- 2¼ teaspoons active dry yeast (1 envelope)
- ½ cup warm water
- 2 cups bread flour, plus more for dusting
- 2 large eggs, 1 beaten with 1 tablespoon of water and a pinch of salt
- 1 large egg yolk
- 3 tablespoons raw sugar
- 2 tablespoons vegetable oil, plus more for greasing

Sea salt

Poppy seeds, for sprinkling

CRAB SALAD

- ¼ cup seeded and finely diced English cucumber
- ¼ cup finely diced celery
- 3 tablespoons mayonnaise
- ¼ teaspoon cayenne pepper
- 1 pound lump crabmeat, picked over

Sea salt

Finely shredded cabbage, for serving

EDITOR'S WINE CHOICE
Green apple–inflected, stainless steel Chardonnay: 2010 Foxglove

Inspired by road trips along the Gulf Coast, Foose's soft, golden rolls are filled with sweet Southern crab salad made with cucumber and a hint of cayenne.

1. MAKE THE ROLLS In a large bowl, combine the yeast with the warm water and let stand until foamy, about 5 minutes. Add the 2 cups of flour, the whole egg, egg yolk, sugar, the 2 tablespoons of oil and 1 teaspoon of salt. Using a wooden spoon, stir the mixture until the dough comes together and starts to pull away from the side of the bowl, about 5 minutes. Scrape the dough onto a lightly floured work surface. Knead the dough until it becomes smooth and silky, 10 to 15 minutes. Transfer the dough to a lightly oiled bowl, cover with a damp kitchen towel and let rise in a warm place until doubled in bulk, about 1 hour.

2. Line a baking sheet with parchment paper. Punch down the dough and cut it into 6 pieces. Roll each piece into the shape of a hot dog, about 5 inches long. Arrange the rolls 2 inches apart on the prepared baking sheet and let rise in a warm place until nearly doubled in bulk, about 1 hour.

3. Preheat the oven to 350°F. Brush the rolls with some of the egg wash and let stand for 5 minutes. Brush the rolls with more egg wash and sprinkle with poppy seeds. Bake for about 30 minutes, until deeply golden and slightly puffed. Transfer the rolls to a rack to cool.

4. MEANWHILE, MAKE THE CRAB SALAD In a large bowl, combine the cucumber, celery, mayonnaise and cayenne pepper. Gently fold in the crabmeat and season with salt. Split the top of each roll halfway through. Fill the rolls with the crab salad, top with cabbage and serve immediately.

MAKE AHEAD The baked rolls can be frozen in an airtight container for up to 1 month.

MARTHA HALL FOOSE ONLINE

marthafoose.com

 Martha Foose

Bolognese balls, page 98

THE MEATBALL SHOP COOKBOOK

daniel holzman & michael chernow
with lauren deen

why we love this book

The Meatball Shop is a New York City phenomenon, serving meatballs both traditional (Bolognese Balls, page 98) and ingenious (Chicken Cordon Bleu Meatballs, page 99) from three neo-retro locations. This cookbook celebrates the humble dish with a surprisingly wide range of recipes—including sides, salads and sweets—from the restaurant's owners, chef Daniel Holzman and manager Michael Chernow.

best cooking technique

Holzman: "There's really no wrong way to do a meatball, so I'm a big fan of cooking them the easiest way: roasting them in the oven. You do get a nice golden crust when you fry meatballs, and they become more tender when they're braised, but roasting is the fastest, simplest and most consistent cooking method, especially when you're making a lot of meatballs. And they're actually super-delicious. Also, cleaning up all the splatter from frying is a nightmare."

weirdest meatball recipe

Holzman: "Our Reuben Sandwich Ball is the most bizarre meatball we've ever created. I was 100 percent sure that it wouldn't succeed, but the chef at our West Village location made it work. They were so good and out of control. Almost as out-there are the Mini Buffalo Chicken Balls (page 94), which just slap you in the face with Buffalo wing flavor."

on new york city

Chernow: "We opened our first Meatball Shop on the Lower East Side, knowing that our cheap, hearty food would appeal to a young, hungry, late-night crowd. But we've been amazed at who comes in: Our first week, we had a table of 75-year-old guys celebrating a birthday. Weekends are packed with families and kids. Lunch is lots of Wall Street guys. It's like all of New York City condensed into a 39-seat restaurant."

PUBLISHED BY BALLANTINE BOOKS, $28

MINI BUFFALO CHICKEN BALLS

MAKES ABOUT FORTY ¾-INCH MEATBALLS

- 2 tablespoons vegetable oil
- 4 tablespoons (½ stick) unsalted butter
- ⅓ cup Frank's RedHot sauce or any other favorite hot sauce
- 1 pound ground chicken, preferably thigh meat
- 1 large egg
- ½ celery stalk, minced
- ¾ cup bread crumbs
- 1 teaspoon salt

EDITOR'S WINE CHOICE
Peppery, raspberry-scented
Zinfandel: 2010 Bogle Old Vine

These balls will definitely get any party started. Buffalo's finest bar food minus the bones makes it the perfect food to serve up for the big game, a surprising appetizer, or even passed as a fancy hors d'oeuvre. It's the best part of hot and spicy wings with none of the mess. If you like your balls extra spicy, you can always add an extra tablespoon or two of hot sauce to the recipe. Make one batch and you'll know why these are a staff fave and top seller at the Shop. Serve with blue cheese dressing.

Preheat the oven to 450°F. Drizzle the vegetable oil into a 9-by-13-inch baking dish and use your hand to evenly coat the entire surface. Set aside.

Combine the butter and hot sauce in a small saucepan, and cook over low heat, whisking until the butter is melted and fully incorporated. Remove from the heat and allow the mixture to cool for 10 minutes.

Combine the hot sauce mixture, ground chicken, egg, celery, bread crumbs, and salt in a large mixing bowl and mix by hand until thoroughly incorporated.

Roll the mixture into round, ¾-inch balls, making sure to pack the meat firmly. Place the balls in the prepared baking dish, being careful to line them up snugly and in even rows vertically and horizontally to form a grid. The meatballs should be touching one another.

Roast for 15 to 20 minutes, or until the meatballs are firm and cooked through. A meat thermometer inserted into the center of a meatball should read 165°F.

Allow the meatballs to cool for 5 minutes in the baking dish before serving.

Thigh meat
makes these
meatballs
especially juicy.

SMASHED TURNIPS
with fresh horseradish

SERVES 4 TO 6

- 8 large turnips (about 2 pounds), peeled and quartered
- ½ cup sour cream
- 6 scallions, thinly sliced
- 2 tablespoons freshly grated horseradish or more to taste
- 2 teaspoons salt

We love turnips and don't want you to pass them by the next time you're at the market. When cooked right, their earthy flavor is seriously irresistible. At the Shop people go crazy for them. The kick from the horseradish brings out the natural sweetness, and the sour cream adds a tangy, rich element.

Place the turnips in a large pot with enough water to cover by 2 inches. Bring to a boil over high heat, then reduce the heat to low and simmer until fork-tender, about 25 minutes. Drain thoroughly, until completely dry.

Place the turnips in a bowl and, while they are still hot, add the sour cream, scallions, horseradish, and salt. Mash with a wire whisk or potato masher until well combined but still chunky. Serve immediately.

Try serving these instead of potato salad or mashed potatoes.

BOLOGNESE BALLS

MAKES ABOUT 2 DOZEN
1½-INCH MEATBALLS

- 2 tablespoons olive oil
- 1¾ pounds 80 percent lean ground beef
- ½ pound mortadella, cut into ¼-inch cubes
- 2 large eggs
- 1 carrot, finely diced
- 1 celery stalk, finely diced
- 1 onion, finely diced
- ¼ cup chopped fresh parsley
- ¼ cup heavy cream
- ¼ cup crushed canned tomatoes
- 1 cup bread crumbs
- 1 tablespoon chopped fresh oregano or 1 teaspoon dried
- 2 teaspoons salt
- 1 teaspoon freshly ground black pepper

EDITOR'S WINE CHOICE
Medium-bodied, spicy Sangiovese:
2010 Casamatta Toscana Rosso

Both classic and inventive, these balls were one of the first meatball "specials" we served at the Shop, and they remain incredibly popular. While traditional Bologna-style meatballs call for braising in tomatoes and heavy cream, our version uses ground beef, with the tomatoes and cream added to the actual meatball. This makes for one mean spaghetti and meatballs.

Preheat the oven to 450°F. Drizzle the olive oil into a 9-by-13-inch baking dish and use your hand to evenly coat the entire surface. Set aside.

Combine the ground beef, mortadella, eggs, carrots, celery, onions, parsley, cream, tomatoes, bread crumbs, oregano, salt, and pepper in a large mixing bowl and mix by hand until thoroughly incorporated.

Roll the mixture into round, golf ball–size meatballs (about 1½ inches), making sure to pack the meat firmly. Place the balls in the prepared baking dish, being careful to line them up snugly and in even rows vertically and horizontally to form a grid. The meatballs should be touching one another.

Roast for 20 minutes, or until the meatballs are firm and cooked through. A meat thermometer inserted into the center of a meatball should read 165°F.

Allow the meatballs to cool for 5 minutes in the baking dish before serving.

QUICK TIP People have lots of tricks for rolling meatballs, but we've found that one of the best shortcuts to help cut down on time is to use a ¼-cup (2-ounce) ice-cream scooper. Simply pull a rounded scoop from the bowl of thoroughly mixed meatball mixture and drop it into the prepared baking dish, lining 'em up, one by one, as directed.

CHICKEN CORDON BLEU MEATBALLS

MAKES ABOUT FORTY
1½-INCH MEATBALLS

Olive oil, for greasing
1½   pounds ground chicken thighs
½   pound Emmental cheese,
      cut into ⅛-inch dice
½   pound baked ham, cut into
      ⅛-inch dice
½   cup fresh bread crumbs
¼   cup dry white wine
2   large eggs
2   teaspoons kosher salt

EDITOR'S WINE CHOICE
Juicy, fruit-forward dry rosé:
2011 Montes Cherub

Holzman's little chicken meatballs have a distinct ham and Swiss cheese flavor; serve them with mustard and toothpicks.

1. Preheat the oven to 450°F and grease a 9-by-13-inch baking dish with olive oil. In a large bowl, combine the ground chicken with the cheese, ham, bread crumbs, wine, eggs and salt. Mix well with your hands and form into 1½-inch meatballs.

2. Arrange the meatballs snugly in the prepared baking dish. Roast for 15 to 20 minutes, until an instant-read thermometer inserted in the center of a meatball registers 165°F. Let the meatballs stand for 5 minutes, then serve.

MAKE AHEAD The cooked meatballs can be refrigerated overnight. Reheat gently before serving.

DANIEL HOLZMAN
& MICHAEL CHERNOW ONLINE

themeatballshop.com

 The Meatball Shop

@MEATBALLERS

DESSERTS FROM THE FAMOUS LOVELESS CAFE

alisa huntsman

why we love this book

There are about a million Southern baking books, but Alisa Huntsman, pastry chef at the 60-year-old Loveless Cafe in Nashville, brings a new perspective to classics like chocolate cake—hers includes mashed potatoes (page 108). Huntsman's down-home desserts are simple but never "unsophisticated or dull," as in her Southern Belle Raspberry Pie (page 102), made fragrant with orange zest and rose water.

the southern sweet tooth

"I came to the cafe from San Francisco, and when I first started making desserts, people said, 'That's not sweet enough.' I had to correct myself pretty quickly, notching up the sweetness without going overboard."

baking with honey

"I always look for ways to use honey—I add freshly harvested wildflower honey to my chess pie. The more fragrant and flowery it is, the better the pie tastes."

on banana pudding

"I never had banana pudding before I started at the Loveless Cafe, but on the first day I was told I had to make it. I said, 'Well, then everything will be from scratch—no Nilla Wafers.' They just looked at me. In the end, the pudding looks like grandma put it together, but I've used classic French technique. I don't advertise all the work that goes into the dish, so the customers don't know what they're getting."

her top sellers

"We sell around 100 desserts a day, and usually half of those are pie. It's just what people in the South want for dessert, so I have six to eight different pies on the menu every day. The most popular is the Coconut Cream Pie, though I always have the Chocolate Cookie–Peanut Butter Pie (page 105) on the menu; Southerners just seem to love peanut butter."

PUBLISHED BY ARTISAN, $25

SOUTHERN BELLE RASPBERRY PIE

MAKES A 9-INCH PIE; SERVES 8

9-inch prepared pie shell, unbaked
- ¾ cup sugar
- ¼ cup cornstarch
- 2 teaspoons grated orange zest
- 2 teaspoons rose water
- ½ vanilla bean, split lengthwise in half
- 1½ pounds fresh raspberries (5 to 6 cups)

Lattice Dough (recipe follows)

Nothing is as intense as raspberry pie. Or as jewel-like in color or, it turns out, as easy to make. This version adds a citrusy floral undertone with orange zest and rose water, the kind Southern belles used to dab at their temples in the heat.

Since this country pie uses a generous amount of berries, don't apologize if you resort to frozen. Just choose unsweetened, individually quick-frozen raspberries. Measure the fruit while frozen and thaw thoroughly before using. Serve plain or with a small scoop of chocolate or orange sorbet.

1. Preheat the oven to 350°F. Line a sturdy baking sheet with parchment paper and lightly grease the paper. Place the pie shell on the baking sheet and set aside.

2. In a mixing bowl, combine the sugar, cornstarch, orange zest, and rose water. With the tip of a small knife, scrape the seeds from the vanilla bean into the bowl. Rub the ingredients together with your fingertips to combine them. Add the raspberries and toss to coat. Turn them into the pie shell.

3. For the top crust, make the Lattice Dough. Roll out, cut into 1-inch-wide strips, and arrange in a lattice on top.

4. Bake for 1 hour and 15 minutes, or until the juices are bubbling in the center and the lattice top is golden brown. Let cool and set for at least 4 to 6 hours, or the filling will be runny when the pie is cut. Serve at room temperature.

continued on page 104

RASPBERRY PIE *continued*

MAKES ENOUGH DOUGH
FOR 1 LATTICE TOP

- 1 cup unbleached all-purpose flour
- 6 tablespoons confectioners' sugar
- 6 tablespoons cold unsalted butter, cut into small cubes
- 1 egg yolk

LATTICE DOUGH

This dough is very forgiving; it can be rolled out several times without becoming stiff and dry. Because it's so flexible, it's ideal for making lattice strips.

Place the flour and confectioners' sugar in a food processor and whirl briefly to blend. Scatter the butter evenly over the top of the dry ingredients. Pulse to cut in the butter, processing until no lumps are visible and the mixture is the texture of cornmeal.

Add the egg yolk and pulse to blend, mixing only until the dough comes together; do not overprocess.

CHOCOLATE COOKIE–PEANUT BUTTER PIE

MAKES A 9-INCH PIE; SERVES 8

No-Bake Cookie Crust (recipe follows),
    made with chocolate wafer cookies
  ½ cup packed light brown sugar
  ¾ cup light corn syrup
  ½ cup half-and-half
  ½ cup smooth peanut butter,
    at room temperature
  1 teaspoon vanilla extract
  3 eggs
Whipped cream and chopped peanuts,
    for topping

This is one pie that is always on the menu. Peanut butter is hugely popular in the South, and pairing it with chocolate creates a dessert that appeals to everyone. Of course, ours is special, served in a crunchy homemade chocolate cookie crust.

1. Preheat the oven to 350°F. Place the prepared crust on a sturdy baking sheet and set aside.

2. In a large mixing bowl, use your fingertips to break up any lumps in the brown sugar. Add the corn syrup, half-and-half, peanut butter, and vanilla. Using a whisk, mix the ingredients until smooth and completely combined. Whisk in the eggs and scrape the filling into the pie crust.

3. Bake for 40 to 45 minutes, until the edges are puffed and set but the center of the pie appears soft and shimmies slightly. Let the pie cool completely before topping with whipped cream and a sprinkling of chopped peanuts.

BAKING TIP Use a commercial homogenized peanut butter for this recipe. "Natural" or freshly ground peanut butter will not work well here.

continued on page 106

CHOCOLATE COOKIE–PEANUT BUTTER PIE *continued*

MAKES A 9-INCH PIE SHELL

- 1 cup cookie crumbs
- 2 tablespoons sugar
- 1 tablespoon very finely chopped nuts (optional)
- 3 tablespoons unsalted butter, melted

NO-BAKE COOKIE CRUST

The best cookies to use for this crust are those with a lower fat content. Depending on the flavor you want, some suggestions include biscotti (but not those that have been dipped in chocolate), gingersnaps, graham crackers, and chocolate wafers. Higher-fat butter cookies will produce a looser, oilier crust without the pleasing crisp texture you want.

Place the cookie crumbs, sugar, and nuts, if using, in a bowl and stir to mix. Add the melted butter and toss with a fork until evenly moistened. Pour into a 9-inch pie pan. Using your fingertips, pat the mixture evenly across the bottom and up the sides of the pan, pressing gently to pack it.

BAKING TIPS Work quickly while the butter is still warm and liquid; the crumbs will be much easier to manipulate. Once the butter chills and sets, it's almost impossible to shape a smooth, even crust.

This easy pie shell can be stored in the refrigerator for up to a week or wrapped well and frozen for up to 2 months.

This pie (left)
is especially
tasty when
served chilled.

CHOCOLATE MASHED POTATO CAKE

MAKES A 9-BY-12-INCH SHEET
CAKE; SERVES 12 TO 16

- 2 cups sugar
- 1¾ cups cake flour
- 1½ teaspoons baking soda
- ¾ cup warm (not hot), unseasoned mashed potatoes
- 4 ounces unsweetened chocolate, melted and slightly cooled
- 1 stick (4 ounces) unsalted butter, softened
- 2 eggs
- ¾ cup buttermilk
- 1 teaspoon vanilla extract
Light Chocolate Frosting (recipe follows)

We often have leftover mashed potatoes at the cafe, which we're happy to put to good use. They add moisture and structure to many breads and cakes, such as this one. Because you cannot taste the potato in the finished product, no one will know it's there. This is a stiff batter that is best prepared in a stand mixer or with a very strong hand mixer.

1. Preheat the oven to 350°F. Grease a 9-by-12-inch rectangular baking dish.

2. Place the sugar, cake flour, and baking soda in a mixing bowl and beat on low speed to combine, about 1 minute. Add the mashed potatoes, melted chocolate, and butter; mix until blended. Raise the speed to medium and beat until fluffy, about 2 minutes.

3. In another bowl, whisk the eggs, buttermilk, and vanilla together until blended. Pour into the chocolate mixture in two additions, scraping the bowl well between additions. Turn the batter into the greased baking dish.

4. Bake for 45 to 50 minutes, or until a toothpick or cake tester inserted in the center comes out clean. Let the cake cool completely in the dish before frosting the top with Light Chocolate Frosting. Cut into squares to serve.

LIGHT CHOCOLATE FROSTING

MAKES ABOUT 1½ CUPS

- 6 tablespoons unsalted butter, softened
- 1½ cups confectioners' sugar, sifted
- 1½ ounces unsweetened chocolate, melted and slightly cooled
- 2 tablespoons half-and-half

1. Place the butter in a mixing bowl. Add the confectioners' sugar and blend on low speed to combine. Raise the speed to medium and beat until fluffy, about 2 minutes.

2. Add the chocolate and mix well, scraping the bowl to incorporate completely. Add the half-and-half and beat until blended. Use immediately.

This cake is so good you can skip the frosting and just top with confectioners' sugar.

ONE-BOWL BROWNIE DROPS

MAKES ABOUT 2½ DOZEN COOKIES

- ¾ cup chopped walnuts
- 4 ounces unsweetened chocolate, chopped
- 5 tablespoons unsalted butter
- 1⅓ cups sugar
- 2 eggs
- 1 teaspoon vanilla extract
- ⅓ cup unbleached all-purpose flour
- ½ teaspoon baking powder
- ¾ cup semisweet chocolate chips

These fudgy cookies will stay soft for up to three days in an airtight tin.

1. Preheat the oven to 350°F. Line 2 sturdy cookie sheets with parchment paper or silicone liners.

2. Toast the walnuts in a baking dish for 5 to 7 minutes, until lightly browned and fragrant. Transfer to a plate and let cool.

3. Place the chocolate and butter in a heatproof bowl set over (not in) a pan of barely simmering water. Heat, stirring often, until the chocolate melts, 3 to 5 minutes. Remove from the heat.

4. Add the sugar, eggs, and vanilla to the melted chocolate and butter. With an electric mixer on medium speed, beat until well blended. Sift the flour and baking powder over the batter and fold in by hand. Add the walnuts and chocolate chips, stirring just enough to combine. Drop the dough by tablespoons at least 2 inches apart onto the lined cookie sheets.

5. Bake for exactly 12 minutes. Remove from the oven and let stand for 2 minutes before carefully transferring the cookies to a wire rack to finish cooling.

RED VELVET CHEESECAKE BARS

MAKES 24 BARS

TOPPING

- 8 ounces cream cheese, at room temperature
- ¾ cup sugar
- ½ teaspoon pure vanilla extract
- 1 large egg

CAKE

- 1½ sticks (6 ounces) unsalted butter, plus more for greasing
- 4 ounces bittersweet chocolate, chopped
- 1⅔ cups all-purpose flour
- 3 tablespoons unsweetened cocoa powder
- 1½ teaspoons baking powder
- ½ teaspoon salt
- 4 large eggs
- 2 cups sugar
- 2 tablespoons red food coloring
- 1 teaspoon pure vanilla extract

A cross between a brownie and cheesecake, Huntsman's chewy bars have a chocolate cakey bottom swirled with a cheesecake topping.

1. MAKE THE TOPPING In the bowl of a food processor, combine the cream cheese with the sugar and vanilla and puree until smooth. Scrape down the side of the bowl. Add the egg and puree until incorporated. Transfer the topping to a small bowl.

2. MAKE THE CAKE Preheat the oven to 350°F. Grease a 9-by-13-inch baking pan and line it with parchment paper; grease the paper. In a microwavable bowl, melt the 1½ sticks of butter with the chocolate at low power in 20-second intervals, stirring, until most of the chocolate is melted. Stir until completely melted, then set aside to cool slightly.

3. In a medium bowl, whisk the flour with the cocoa, baking powder and salt. In a large bowl, whisk the eggs with the sugar until pale. Whisk in the food coloring, vanilla and the melted chocolate. Sift the dry ingredients over the batter and, using a rubber spatula, fold in the dry ingredients until no streaks remain. Scrape the batter into the prepared baking pan.

4. Dollop the topping over the cake batter. Using a knife, decoratively swirl the topping into the batter, creating a marbled pattern. Bake for 35 to 45 minutes, until the cake is set and the cheesecake swirls are just starting to brown. Transfer the baking pan to a rack and let the cake cool completely. Cover the pan tightly with plastic wrap and refrigerate until chilled, about 2 hours. Cut into bars and serve.

ALISA HUNTSMAN ONLINE

lovelesscafe.com

f Loveless Cafe

t @LovelessCafe

Pappardelle with chicken liver ragù, page 116

BOCCA COOKBOOK

jacob kenedy

why we love this book

Named after his London restaurant, Bocca di Lupo, Jacob Kenedy's cookbook might not be the most exhaustive guide to Italian cooking, but it's one of the liveliest and funniest. Kenedy traveled the length of Italy for a year researching the book. Along the way he gathered recipes that capture the character of each region—his Pappardelle with Chicken Liver Ragù (page 116) reflects the spare aesthetic of Tuscany, for instance—to create dishes that are as "direct and pleasurable as possible."

on removing ingredients

"You always want to remove what's unnecessary from a recipe, so you don't cloud the soul of what you're cooking. It will make the dish better. For example, I don't use chicken stock in my Gorgonzola, Asparagus and Hazelnut Risotto (page 117) because I don't want it to taste like chicken. I make it with water, and you can taste the ingredients more cleanly as a result."

italy's best desserts

"Sicily and Naples are the dessert capitals of Italy. Both regions benefited from culinary expertise and traditions passed on to them by foreign powers. In Sicily, it's the strong Arabic influence—a love of almonds, citrus, spice and sugar. The French rule of Naples left behind the techniques of the *pâtisserie,* so bakers there can create a hundred different textures and tastes out of flour, egg, butter and sugar."

his top ingredients

"My three favorite ingredients are *guanciale,* which is like pancetta but made from pork cheek; Pecorino Romano, a really hard, salty, sheepy grating cheese that I use in my Calabrian-style orecchiette (page 114); and capers, which I hated when I was a kid but love now. The first year my restaurant was open, I used more capers than rice."

PUBLISHED BY BLOOMSBURY, $45

CALABRIA

ORECCHIETTE WITH 'NDUJA

SERVES 4 BRAVES AS A STARTER,
2 AS A MAIN

- 9 ounces fresh *orecchiette* (see Editor's Note), or 7 ounces dried (but only if you must)
- 1 red onion, halved and sliced with the grain
- ¼ pound cherry tomatoes, quartered
- 3 tablespoons extra-virgin olive oil
- ¼ pound *'nduja* (see Author's Note and Editor's Note)
- ¼ cup white wine
- ⅓ cup heavy cream
- 1½ cups arugula, very roughly chopped

Freshly grated Pecorino Romano, to serve

EDITOR'S NOTE
Kenedy makes his own *orecchiette* and *'nduja* for this dish, and includes those recipes in *Bocca Cookbook.*

EDITOR'S WINE CHOICE
Ripe, full-bodied Sicilian white: 2010 Ajello Majus Grillo-Catarratto

Even a small amount of 'nduja is enough to make for an extremely spicy pasta, but the heat is tempered slightly by the cream. Nonetheless it is imperative to serve a crisp yet aromatic white (Grillo or Fiano or Falanghina, say), or an ice-cold beer, to help you through.

Just before you put the *orecchiette* on to boil (or just after if they are dried), fry the onion and tomatoes in the oil over a high heat for 3 minutes, until softened and slightly browned. Crumble in the *'nduja* and fry for 30 seconds, then add the wine and a small ladleful of water. Let it bubble for a few moments, then add the cream.

Allow the sauce to cook until the cream has reddened, and thickened if it looked watery, then add the drained pasta (still a little wet) and the arugula. Cook until the arugula is wilted and the pasta coated in the sauce. Serve with grated Pecorino on top.

AUTHOR'S NOTE *'Nduja* (extremely spicy *salame*) can be replaced with ¼ pound crumbled Italian sausage and as much chili—dried, fresh or both—as the cook can bear.

TUSCANY

PAPPARDELLE WITH CHICKEN LIVER RAGÙ

**SERVES 4 AS A STARTER,
2 AS A MAIN**

- 7 ounces dried *pappardelle*, or 9 ounces fresh

Freshly grated Parmesan, to serve

CHICKEN LIVER RAGÙ

- ½ pound chicken livers
- ⅓ cup extra-virgin olive oil
- ½ small onion, chopped
- 1 celery stalk, chopped
- 1 garlic clove, chopped
- ⅔ cup dry Marsala
- ½ cup white wine
- 1 scant tablespoon chopped rosemary
- 3 tablespoons chopped flat-leaf parsley
- 3 tablespoons butter

EDITOR'S WINE CHOICE
Substantial, cherry-rich Italian
rosé: 2011 Cataldi Madonna

I ate this dish somewhere in Tuscany, at an old convent where they served a few plates of food. I cannot remember exactly where, but it was idyllic—we sat outside, under an old oak tree which shaded a hill from the summer sun. I think I was twelve, perhaps a year or two older; it is a happy memory.

Heat a wide frying pan over a high heat until smoking profusely. Toss the chicken livers in a bowl with 1 tablespoon of the olive oil and some salt and pepper, then pour into the hot pan, spreading them out as much as you can. Let them fry without moving them for 2 minutes, until well browned on one side. Turn them over, and fry the second side in the same way, then transfer to a plate to cool. When safe to handle, chop them finely with a knife, reserving any juices that oozed on to the plate as they sat.

Fry the onion, celery and garlic in the remaining oil with salt and pepper in a small saucepan over a medium-low heat. After 10 minutes, or when very soft, add the chopped chicken liver and its juices and fry for a couple of minutes until hot through. Add the Marsala and wine and cook at the gentlest of simmers until the sauce is very thick (almost like a pâté) with a little oil risen to the surface, at least an hour. For such a small quantity, you may need to add ½ cup or so of water during the cooking—don't let it fry. Stir in the rosemary and take off the heat: this sauce can be refrigerated for a few days, or used straightaway.

When ready to eat, put the pasta on to boil in lots of salted boiling water, and heat the sauce in a wide frying pan. Add a splash of the pasta water to thin the sauce slightly (the liquid part should be creamy). When the pasta is *al dente*, drain it and add to the sauce with the parsley and butter. Cook together for a few moments, until the butter has melted and the pasta is well coated in the sauce, then serve with a light sprinkling of Parmesan.

LOMBARDY

GORGONZOLA, ASPARAGUS & HAZELNUT RISOTTO

SERVES 3 TO 4 AS A STARTER,
2 AS A MAIN

- ½ medium onion, chopped
- 5 tablespoons butter
- ¾ cup *carnaroli* rice
- ½ cup white wine
- 1 large bunch (¾ pound) thin asparagus, cut into ½- to ¾-inch sections with the hard parts of the stem discarded
- ¼ pound Gorgonzola *dolce*
- ½ cup shelled hazelnuts, toasted and coarsely chopped

EDITOR'S WINE CHOICE
Crisp, slightly nutty Italian white:
2011 Gini Soave Classico

I learned a valuable lesson from Sam and Sam at Moro; don't use stock unless you want to add flavour. This risotto is a case in point—asparagus, Gorgonzola and hazelnuts are a wonderful trinity, and need only the plainest of backdrops to really sing.

Fry the onion in 3 tablespoons of the butter over a moderate heat with a pinch of salt for 10 minutes until tender. Add the rice, fry for 2 minutes more, then pour in the wine and simmer until absorbed. You'll need about 1½ cups water for this recipe, which should be added a little at a time, waiting for it to be mostly absorbed between additions. Taste for seasoning all the time and, about 5 minutes before the end (about 10 minutes after you started adding water), add the asparagus.

When the rice is still a touch too *al dente* for you, the liquor just on the wet side, add three-quarters of the Gorgonzola (crumble it in; you can use or lose the rind as you like) and the remaining butter. Continue to stir until you are satisfied, and serve with hazelnuts and the remaining Gorgonzola scattered on top.

LAZIO
BURNED RICOTTA PIE

SERVES 8 TO 12

- 1 quantity Sweet Pastry (recipe follows)
- Generous 2 pounds fresh ricotta, sheep's milk if possible
- 1 small egg, or ½ large one
- ⅓ cup superfine sugar
- ⅔ cup sour cherry jam, or 3½ ounces bittersweet chocolate, finely chopped (not both)
- 1 large egg yolk
- Generous ¼ cup confectioners' sugar

There is a tiny Jewish bakery in the Ghetto in Rome, on the corner of Via del Portico and Via della Reginella. It is called Antico Forno del Ghetto, but that's no help as there's no name outside. They burn everything—croissants come out completely black, as do the ricotta cakes (either chocolate or cherry flavoured) for which they are famous. This signature char is delicious—only skin-deep, but it adds that slight bitter edge that makes Roman pizza so exquisite, and grounds this rich but refreshing ricotta cake in the earth.

Divide the pastry into two unequal balls, one of them one-and-a-half times the weight of the other. Roll the smaller into a 7-inch disc, and the larger one 9¾ inches. The dough is fragile, and it is easiest to roll it between two sheets of parchment paper, flouring the sheet below and the top of the dough to prevent sticking. Peel off the top sheet of paper, and leave the rolled pastry on the lower one. Put the smaller disc of pastry, still on its sheet of parchment paper, on to a baking sheet. If using jam, spread it on this disc, leaving about a ¾-inch border.

Mix together the ricotta, egg and superfine sugar with a wooden spoon, as well as the chocolate, if using. Pile this filling in a tall, domed heap in the centre of the smaller round of pastry, leaving about a ¾-inch border. Carefully pick up the larger circle of pastry (to prevent it breaking, it is best to wrap it, with its under-paper, around a rolling pin) and lay it over the filling. Peel off the top sheet of paper, and crimp the edges all the way around.

Mix together the egg yolk and confectioners' sugar, add a drop of water if needed to make a thick glaze, and paint it over the top of the pie to help it burn. Bake the pie in an oven preheated to its very maximum— best with the fan off for that perfect *brûlée*. The pie will spread a little, crack in a couple of places, and ebonise. As soon as the whole surface of the pie is blackened, or very dark chocolate brown, turn the oven down to 350°F and continue to bake, until the cake has cooked for a total of 45 minutes. Turn off the oven, and leave the cake inside for 20 minutes to rest. Take it out, let cool and serve at room temperature. As with many Italian desserts, it is just as good for breakfast as for dessert.

continued on page 120

There's a surprise layer of jam or chocolate filling under the crust.

BURNED RICOTTA PIE *continued*

MAKES ENOUGH FOR
1 BURNED RICOTTA PIE

Scant 4 cups all-purpose flour
1⅔ cups confectioners' sugar
A pinch of salt
1 tablespoon baking powder
¾ cup unsalted butter, cold, diced
2 large eggs
1 large egg yolk
1 tablespoon vanilla extract
Finely grated zest of 1 small lemon

SWEET PASTRY

Sift together the flour, sugar, salt and baking powder. Add the butter, and quickly work it in with your fingers, trying not to warm it up too much. Add the whole eggs, the yolk, the vanilla and the lemon zest. Bring the dough together, but do not overwork as it would become tough if really kneaded, then wrap it in plastic wrap in a flattened patty and rest in the refrigerator until firm—half an hour or more.

YOUNG SWISS CHARD, FENNEL & PARMESAN SALAD

SERVES 4 TO 6 AS A FIRST COURSE

One 1-pound fennel bulb—halved lengthwise, cored and very thinly sliced (preferably on a mandoline)

¾ pound young Swiss chard, stems removed and leaves sliced ¼ inch thick

3 tablespoons extra-virgin olive oil

2 tablespoons fresh lemon juice

Salt and freshly ground pepper

2 ounces Parmigiano-Reggiano cheese, shaved (about 1 cup)

The trick to Kenedy's sublime and simple salad is soaking the fennel slices in ice water, which makes them extra-crisp.

1. In a medium bowl, soak the fennel in ice water until crisp, about 10 minutes. Drain well and dry thoroughly with paper towels.

2. In a large bowl, toss the Swiss chard with the fennel, olive oil and lemon juice and season with salt and pepper. Add the cheese and toss to combine. Transfer the salad to plates and serve right away.

JACOB KENEDY ONLINE

jacobkenedy.com

 @boccadilupo

Salt-roasted potatoes, page 126

MOURAD: NEW MOROCCAN

mourad lahlou with susie heller, steve siegelman & amy vogler

why we love this book

In his first cookbook, San Francisco chef Mourad Lahlou offers innovative Moroccan recipes that are, as he says, "not the same 20 or 30 dishes found in every other Moroccan book." It's his interpretation of his native cuisine—inspired by nostalgia but cooked with a modern Northern Californian sensibility—that earned his restaurant Aziza a Michelin star. His Roast Chicken with Preserved Lemons and Root Vegetables (page 128), for example, is a reimagined tagine in which he forgoes traditional braising in broth to give the bird a crispy, golden skin.

essential ingredient

"Preserved lemon. It's cured in salt and lemon juice and you can use it in different forms—in a puree, vinaigrette, stew or marinade. It just gives your food so much complexity and brightness. It doesn't taste like lemon anymore; it's a completely different animal. It's like the kimchi of Morocco."

morocco's iconic dish

"*Basteeya.* I don't know of any other culture that mixes poultry with almonds, then bakes it in phyllo dough with sugar and cinnamon. This harmony of sweet and savory together captures the essence of Moroccan food."

unique moroccan seasoning

"In Morocco, instead of salt and pepper on the table, we season with salt and cumin. Moroccan cumin is unique. It's so fragrant and powerful."

DIY harissa

"Commercial harissa is usually disappointing. A quick homemade alternative is a mix of Chinese chile-garlic paste and preserved lemon rind. Or you can simply make the harissa powder for my Spiced Almonds (page 124). I add it to popcorn, deviled eggs, even to whipped cream as a garnish for chocolate cake."

PUBLISHED BY ARTISAN, $40

SPICED ALMONDS

MAKES 6 CUPS (660 GRAMS)

- ¼ cup plus 3 tablespoons (87 grams) granulated sugar
- 2 teaspoons (6 grams) kosher salt
- 2 teaspoons (4.5 grams) cayenne
- 1½ teaspoons (3.8 grams) ground cumin
- 1 teaspoon (2.7 grams) ground cinnamon
- 1 teaspoon (2.4 grams) Harissa Powder (recipe follows)
- ½ teaspoon (1 gram) ground allspice
- ¼ teaspoon (0.6 gram) ground cloves
- ¼ teaspoon (0.4 gram) grated nutmeg
- 2 large egg whites, at room temperature
- 4 cups (688 grams) skin-on whole almonds

The idea hit me when I was eating a pointy almond meringue called a rocher at Tartine, a favorite urban-cool bakery in San Francisco's Mission District. I realized I was liking the meringue, but I was really loving the big chunks of toasted almonds in every bite. So, I thought, why not reverse the proportions and make almonds coated with just a bit of meringue? I worked out a nice balance of spicy, salty, and sweet, and this is where I ended up.

We've served these as a little predinner nibble and bar snack for years. I use Mission almonds, which have an extra-nutty flavor that can stand up to all the spice. Their small size, round shape, and wrinkled skin make them just right for this kind of coating and seasoning. That said, you can also use regular almonds, as well as pecans or walnuts.

I love the crunch of both the coating and the nuts when they're cold, so I usually refrigerate them, then serve right from the fridge. You can sprinkle them (chopped if you use larger nuts) on salads as a garnish, adding them at the last second after you've tossed and plated the greens so they don't get wet. Packed into a jar, they make a very cool gift to take to someone's house—a nice reversal of the whole Moroccan welcoming thing.

Preheat the oven to 325°F. Line a baking sheet with a Silpat.

Combine the sugar, salt, and spices. Put the egg whites in a large bowl and whisk to soft peaks. Whisk in the spice mix, then fold in the almonds. Spread the almonds in a single layer on the Silpat and bake for 10 minutes.

Use a spatula to turn the almonds, breaking up any that have stuck together; return to the oven and continue to bake for 20 to 30 minutes, turning the nuts every 10 minutes. Break a nut open; the inside should be a rich golden brown. Spread the nuts on another baking sheet to cool completely.

Store the nuts in an airtight container at cool room temperature (so the meringue doesn't melt) for up to 3 days, or store in the refrigerator for up to 2 weeks.

MAKES ABOUT 1 CUP
(110 GRAMS)

- ½ cup plus 1 tablespoon (64.8 grams) Aleppo pepper
- 1½ tablespoons (15.4 grams) granulated garlic
- 1½ teaspoons (7 grams) citric acid
- 2¼ teaspoons (5.9 grams) pimentón (Spanish paprika)
- 2¼ teaspoons (5.7 grams) ground cumin
- 1½ teaspoons (4.8 grams) roasted garlic powder
- 1½ teaspoons (4.5 grams) kosher salt
- 1½ teaspoons (4 grams) sweet paprika
- 1½ teaspoons (2.7 grams) ground caraway
- ⅛ teaspoon (0.3 gram) cayenne

HARISSA POWDER

I came up with this dry spice blend to use whenever I want the flavor of harissa *without its moisture. Fried chickpeas are a perfect example—* harissa *would make them gloppy, but* harissa *powder and a squeeze of lemon juice coats them perfectly.*

Harissa *powder has the added advantage that you can store it for up to 6 months, while* harissa *lasts only about half as long. And it's as simple as stirring together a bunch of dry ingredients in a bowl. The citric acid is a stand-in for lemon juice and/or vinegar, and it's important in the overall flavor balance. Look for it in specialty grocery and natural foods stores, or order it online.*

Combine all the ingredients in a bowl. Transfer to a tightly sealed glass jar and store at room temperature for up to 6 months.

SALT-ROASTED POTATOES

SERVES 6

- 12 ounces (340 grams) 1-inch marble potatoes or 2-inch fingerlings (about 2 cups)
- 3½ cups (1 pound/453 grams) kosher salt
- ¼ cup (21.7 grams) fennel seeds
- ¼ cup (15.2 grams) coriander seeds
- 2 (2.2 grams) star anise
- 10 (1.6 grams) green cardamom pods, shelled and seeds reserved
- ½ orange, preferably a blood orange
- ¼ large grapefruit
- ½ lemon
- 3 large egg whites

Grapeseed or canola oil (if sautéing the potatoes)

Rosemary leaves

Extra-virgin olive oil for finishing (optional)

Crunchy sea salt (optional)

Salt-roasting cooks potatoes evenly, so they're moist and creamy inside, and the spices and seasonings in the salt crust add just a hint of subtle flavor and mystery. Smashed and browned in oil, as described below, they make a nice passed appetizer, topped with crème fraîche and caviar. Once roasted, the potatoes can be stored in olive oil in the fridge for up to 3 days. The salt-roasting technique can also be used for carrots, parsnips, turnips, and beets.

Wash and dry the potatoes. Put the salt in a large bowl. Put a piece of parchment paper on the work surface.

Combine the fennel, coriander, star anise, and cardamom seeds in a medium heavy frying pan, set it over medium heat, and swirl the pan, flipping or stirring the spices occasionally so they toast evenly, until fragrant, 2 to 3 minutes. Pour onto the parchment paper and let cool.

Lift the edges of the parchment and pour half the spices into a spice grinder. Coarsely grind them and add to the bowl of salt. Repeat with the remaining spices and mix to combine all the ingredients.

Using a Microplane, grate the zest from the orange, grapefruit, and lemon. You should have about 1 generous tablespoon (12.5 grams) total. Mix it into the salt mixture.

Preheat the oven to 400°F.

Beat the egg whites until they are just beginning to hold a shape, and stir them into the salt mixture.

Line a 9-inch square baking dish with parchment paper. Form a 1-inch-thick bed of salt in the baking dish and arrange the potatoes on it in a single layer. Cover with the remaining salt, to completely encase the potatoes.

Roast for 30 minutes for 1-inch potatoes, or 35 minutes for 2-inch potatoes, or until they are tender. Remove from the oven and let rest for 10 minutes.

You can break away the salt crust with your hand or hit it with a wooden spoon to crack it. Remove the potatoes and brush off any excess salt clinging to them.

There are two ways to serve the potatoes: **FOR THIN, CHIP-LIKE POTATOES,** put the potatoes between pieces of parchment paper lightly brushed with oil and press a meat pounder against them to flatten. Heat a generous film of oil in a nonstick skillet over medium-high heat and sauté the potatoes on both sides to brown, about 2½ minutes per side. Drain on paper towels. Add some rosemary leaves to the oil and fry and crisp them for about 30 seconds. Arrange the potatoes on a plate and sprinkle with crunchy sea salt and the rosemary. **OR SERVE THE POTATOES WHOLE,** in a bowl, tossed with fresh rosemary leaves and drizzled with olive oil.

ROAST CHICKEN
with preserved lemons & root vegetables

SERVES 6 TO 8

BRINE

4	quarts (3.7 kilograms) cold water
¾	cup (150 grams) granulated sugar
1½	cups (216 grams) kosher salt
2	lemons, cut into quarters
1	cup (220 grams) cracked green olives, with their brine
12	(42 grams) flat-leaf parsley sprigs
3	tablespoons (24 grams) sliced garlic
1	tablespoon (9 grams) Tellicherry peppercorns
8	thyme sprigs
10	(1.7 grams) bay leaves
4	quarts (1.96 kilograms) ice cubes

CHICKEN

3	(450 grams) preserved lemons
2	air-chilled chickens (3½ pounds/1.58 kilograms each), excess fat removed
8	(8 grams) thyme sprigs
	Kosher salt
8	tablespoons (4 ounces/ 113 grams) unsalted butter, at room temperature

VEGETABLES

12	medium turnips
3	small rutabagas
4	small parsnips
12	medium carrots
8	cipollini onions, about 1½ inches in diameter, left unpeeled
2	tablespoons (27 grams) extra-virgin olive oil
2	teaspoons (2 grams) coarsely chopped thyme
18	garlic cloves
	Kosher salt

continued on page 130

continued on page 130

If chicken legs braised in a tagine with preserved lemons and olives is my faithful adaptation of a Moroccan institution, this recipe takes that dish one step further. I'm extremely fond of the not-at-all-Moroccan idea of roast chicken—that and some buttered couscous would be my pick for a last meal—and I love how when you buy a great air-chilled bird and roast it, the flavor that really comes through is unmistakably chicken. In Morocco, between the slow braising and the assertive seasonings that generally go into any chicken dish, that comforting, brothy poultry flavor is sacrificed, along with the thrill of crispy skin, for the greater good of the dish.

But sometimes I want both—chicken that tastes like peak-experience, crisp-skinned chicken and sauce with Moroccan richness, depth, and intensity—and that's when I make this recipe. I brine whole chickens just like they do in Morocco with plenty of salt, lemon, and olives. But then, instead of braising them, I roast them whole over a bed of vegetables, with preserved lemons and thyme tucked under the skin.

I promise you, it's worth the effort. Also, not that you would, but don't compromise on the vegetables. The nicest ones you can find at the farmers' market will make a great difference as they caramelize and their sweetness comes out. If you have very small vegetables, you can leave them whole; larger ones should be cut and trimmed to even shapes with a paring knife. Use burgundy carrots if you can find them; they're great here. Peel them lightly so you don't remove too much of their color. And if you've got time to make the spiced prunes, go for it. They add a lot.

FOR THE BRINE Put the water in a 10- to 12-quart stockpot and bring to a simmer. Add the brine ingredients (except the ice) and stir to dissolve the sugar and salt. Turn off the heat and let sit at room temperature for 20 minutes to infuse the flavors.

Add the ice to chill the brine. If the brine isn't completely cold, refrigerate it until it is. Add the chickens to the cold brine and weight them with a plate or smaller pot lid to keep them submerged. Refrigerate for 8 to 12 hours.

continued on page 130

The vegetables
absorb all
the delicious
chicken juices.

ROAST CHICKEN *continued*

12 Spiced Prunes
    (recipe follows; optional)
 1 tablespoon (16 grams) preserved
    lemon liquid
 2 tablespoons (1 ounce/
    28 grams) cold unsalted butter,
    cut into pieces
 2 teaspoons (3 grams) coarsely
    chopped flat-leaf parsley

FOR THE CHICKENS Cut the preserved lemons into quarters. Cut the flesh away from the rinds and reserve both the rinds and flesh. Remove the chickens from the brine (discard the brine), rinse them, and dry well with paper towels. Place 1 chicken on a work surface with the legs facing you. Starting at the cavity, work the handle of a wooden spoon between the skin and one breast to create a pocket, working slowly and gently to avoid tearing the skin. Repeat on the other side. Holding the chicken in place with one hand, slide the index and middle fingers of your other hand into each pocket to enlarge it, then slide your fingers down to create a pocket over the thigh. Repeat with the second chicken.

Insert the pieces of preserved lemon rind, white pith side down, and thyme sprigs into the pockets over the thighs and breasts. Sprinkle the cavities with salt, and rub the chickens with the reserved flesh from the preserved lemons.

I like to truss poultry without using kitchen twine, which saves tying and untying them and makes for a more natural presentation. Position 1 chicken breast side up, with the legs facing you. Cut a vertical slit in one side, about 1 inch back from the cavity, alongside the thigh. Cross the end of the opposite drumstick over the drumstick on this side and poke the end of the top drumstick through the slit. (Depending on the condition of the chicken's skin, it may rip as you try to poke the drumstick through it, so have some kitchen twine on hand just in case, and tie the legs together if necessary.) Repeat with the other chicken. Sprinkle the chickens with salt.

Preheat the oven to 500°F.

FOR THE VEGETABLES Peel the turnips and rutabagas with a paring knife. (Because they have thick skins, a vegetable peeler won't cut deeply enough to remove all the tough peel.) Cut them into pieces of about the same size—I usually cut small turnips in half from the top to bottom and quarter small rutabagas lengthwise.

Peel the parsnips and carrots with a vegetable peeler. If the carrots are small, leave them whole. Cut large carrots and parsnips into 1½-inch pieces. If you'd like the vegetables to have a less rustic appearance, they can be trimmed (turned) into oval shapes, cutting away the sharp edges. Peel the onions and trim the root ends.

EDITOR'S WINE CHOICE
Fragrant, apple-scented white
blend: 2010 Chateau Musar Musar
Jeune Blanc

TO FINISH THE DISH Put all the vegetables in a large bowl and toss them with the olive oil, thyme, garlic cloves, and 3 pinches of salt. Spread them in a large roasting pan. Put a roasting rack in the pan and set the chickens breast side up on it, leaving a space between the chickens. They should rest just above the vegetables, not touching them.

Roast for 15 minutes. Spread the room-temperature butter over the breasts. Roast for another 30 minutes. Add the prunes, if you are using them, to the pan and roast the chickens for another 15 to 20 minutes, or until the skin is richly browned and the temperature in the meatiest sections registers 160°F. Remove from the oven and put the chickens on a carving board to rest for 20 minutes.

Meanwhile, remove the rack, set the roasting pan on the stove so that it spans two burners, and bring the cooking liquid to a simmer. Whisk in the preserved lemon liquid and simmer for 2 minutes. Stir in the butter bit by bit to emulsify the sauce and glaze the vegetables. Stir in the parsley.

Present the chickens whole or carved, arranged over the vegetables in the roasting pan or on a large platter.

SPICED PRUNES

I use Moyer prunes here for their flavor, texture, and deep, rich color. Unlike French prunes, which are often pitted, Moyers are usually sold with the pits, and it's important to use prunes with pits here, so that the brine doesn't get inside the prune and make it mushy. The pits also add an almondy sweetness.

MAKES 4 CUPS (1.7 KILOGRAMS)

- 4 cups (630 grams) unpitted Moyer or other prunes
- 1 cup (234 grams) water
- ¾ cup (175 grams) champagne vinegar
- ¾ cup (150 grams) granulated sugar
- 2 tablespoons (27 grams) brandy

One 3-inch (3.3 grams) cinnamon stick
- ¾ teaspoon (2.3 grams) Tellicherry peppercorns
- 3 (0.4 gram) allspice berries
- 1 (0.2 gram) bay leaf

Put the prunes in a medium bowl.

Combine all the remaining ingredients in a saucepan and bring to a boil over medium-high heat, stirring to dissolve the sugar. Pour over the prunes and let cool to room temperature.

Let stand in an airtight container at room temperature for at least a week before using. The prunes can be stored at room temperature for up to 6 months.

CHICKEN SKEWERS

SERVES 6

MARINADE
- 3 tablespoons (24 grams) sweet paprika
- 1 tablespoon (7.7 grams) ground cumin
- ¾ teaspoon (1.5 grams) ground ginger
- 1 tablespoon (12 grams) finely chopped garlic
- 3 tablespoons (8 grams) coarsely chopped thyme
- 1½ tablespoons (7 grams) coarsely chopped flat-leaf parsley
- 1 tablespoon (4 grams) coarsely chopped cilantro
- 1½ cups (318 grams) extra-virgin olive oil
- 6 boneless, skinless chicken breasts (6 ounces/170 grams each)

Kosher salt and freshly ground black pepper

VINAIGRETTE
- ¼ cup (48 grams) finely diced preserved lemon rind
- ¼ cup plus 3 tablespoons (93 grams) extra-virgin olive oil
- 2½ tablespoons (11 grams) finely chopped flat-leaf parsley
- 1 tablespoon (15 grams) fresh lime juice

EDITOR'S NOTE
Charmoula is a tangy sauce of olive oil, garlic, herbs and spices.

EDITOR'S WINE CHOICE
Full-bodied, tropical-scented Chardonnay: 2010 Errazuriz Casablanca Valley

If you're browsing for a totally simple recipe in this book to start with, here you go: quick, tasty chicken skewers with a marinade and finishing vinaigrette that work together to give you an easy approximation of the pleasures of red charmoula [see Editor's Note]. If you're having people over, you can prepare the skewers in advance so you'll have only a few minutes of grilling to do when it's time to eat. For a barbecue picnic at the beach or in a park, pack the skewers, uncooked, in the marinade so you can grill them on the spot. They work well as a starter, or as a main course over couscous with some grilled asparagus, drizzled with the vinaigrette.

FOR THE MARINADE Mix all the ingredients in a large bowl.

Trim the chicken breasts of excess fat. Remove the tenders and reserve for another use. Cut the meat into 1½-inch pieces. Add the chicken to the marinade and refrigerate for at least 6 hours, or as long as overnight.

FOR THE VINAIGRETTE Whisk all the ingredients together. Set aside.

FOR THE CHICKEN Soak 6 long wooden skewers in cold water for 30 minutes.

Lift several pieces of the chicken at a time from the marinade and squeeze them over the bowl to drain the extra marinade. Skewer the chicken, leaving ¼ inch between the pieces to allow all sides of the chicken to cook evenly. Season the chicken lightly with salt and pepper.

Preheat a grill to medium-high heat.

Place the skewers on the grill and cook for 2 to 3 minutes without moving them, to mark the chicken. Turn the skewers 90 degrees to mark with a crosshatch pattern and grill for another 1 minute. The marks should be well browned but not burnt. Turn the skewers over and cook for about 2 minutes to finish cooking the chicken.

Carefully remove the chicken from the skewers and place in a bowl. Toss with a light coating of the vinaigrette, and serve the extra vinaigrette on the side.

PIQUILLO PEPPER JAM

MAKES ABOUT 1¼ CUPS

- 2 tablespoons sugar
- 2 teaspoons powdered pectin
- 1 tablespoon grapeseed oil
- 1 large shallot, thinly sliced
- 1 large garlic clove, thinly sliced

Kosher salt

- ½ cup Riesling

Two 9-ounce jars piquillo peppers,
    drained and chopped

- 2 jalapeños, seeded
    and coarsely chopped
- 2 tablespoons honey
- 1 tablespoon fresh lemon juice

Toasted baguette slices and Manchego
    cheese, for serving

Lahlou's sticky-sweet jam is ideal on toast with a salty cheese like Manchego, but it's also great with duck or pork.

1. In a small bowl, combine the sugar and pectin. In a large, deep skillet, heat the grapeseed oil until shimmering. Add the shallot and garlic and a generous pinch of salt. Cook over moderately low heat until softened, about 3 minutes. Add the Riesling and simmer until the wine is reduced to about 1 tablespoon, about 5 minutes. Add the piquillos, jalapeños and honey and cook over moderate heat until most of the liquid is evaporated, about 5 minutes. Add 1 cup of water and bring to a simmer. Stir in the pectin mixture and simmer over moderately low heat, stirring occasionally, until a jamlike consistency forms, 35 to 45 minutes.

2. Scrape the jam into a bowl. Stir in the lemon juice and season with salt. Serve the jam barely warm, with baguette slices and Manchego cheese.

MAKE AHEAD The jam can be refrigerated for up to 1 month. Reheat gently and serve warm.

MOURAD LAHLOU ONLINE

aziza-sf.com

f Mourad Lahlou

t @mouradlahlou

CREATING COMMUNITY THROUGH FOOD

TASTINGS

MARCH 31ST.
NUMA SNACKS

APRIL 2ND
ECCO COFFEE

LOCAL OR
FULL BELLY
RANUNCU
$10.9

BUY FRESH
BUY LOCAL

Organically Grown
Vegetable & Herb
Starts
6 pk → $2.99/ea
3.5 in pot → $2.99/ea
Greenhouse Grown Richmond, CA

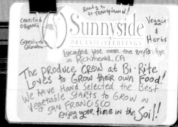
Ready to be transplanted!
Certified
Organic
Greenhouse
Grown

Sunnyside
ORGANIC SEEDLINGS

Veggies
& Herbs

Located just over the Bay Bridge
in Richmond, CA

The PRODUCE CREW at Bi-Rite
Loves to GROW their own Food!
We HAVE Hand Selected the Best
Vegetable STARTS to Grow in
SAN FRANCISCO
Enjoy your time in the Soil!

BI-RITE MARKET'S EAT GOOD FOOD

sam mogannam & dabney gough

why we love this book

Sam Mogannam's first cookbook is a complete guide to ethical grocery shopping—from navigating the fish counter to deciphering olive oil labels. *Bi-Rite Market's Eat Good Food* also includes great informal dishes like Romesco Chicken Salad (page 138). The owner of San Francisco's beloved Bi-Rite Market and a former chef, Mogannam shares Cal-Italian recipes that are both deeply practical (there's ketchup in his Sicilian Meatballs with Fresh Basil Marinara, page 140) and incredibly delicious.

a new kind of caesar salad

"The first time I had a kale Caesar salad (page 142) was at Il Buco in Manhattan. I was blown away by its simplicity. Caesar dressing is typically served with tender sweet romaine hearts, but its boldness is a better match for something sturdy like kale. I use young dinosaur kale, which is peppery and pleasantly bitter. It marries perfectly with the dressing."

growing up in a grocery store

"My dad and uncle owned Bi-Rite in the sixties, so I spent my childhood stocking shelves, serving as cheap labor. I would be there from after school until the store closed at nine. I'd be working when my friends were out playing; I was always late to the high school dances."

cooking from the pantry

"Ketchup is a great way to add umami and acidity while also complementing other flavors. In my Sicilian meatballs, its sweetness helps balance out heat and salt in a way that other ingredients just can't."

favorite quick fix

"I love *broccoli di cicco*—an Italian sprouting broccoli that is sweet and tender, with just enough bitterness. I love it sautéed with garlic, anchovy, chile flakes, lots of good olive oil and a squeeze of lemon."

PUBLISHED BY TEN SPEED PRESS, $32.50

SEARED SAFFRON ALBACORE TUNA
with fennel-olive tapenade

SERVES 4 TO 6

TAPENADE

1	large clove garlic

Kosher salt

1	tablespoon capers, coarsely chopped
1	tablespoon champagne vinegar
1	tablespoon freshly squeezed lemon juice
1	medium shallot, minced
1	anchovy fillet, minced
¼	teaspoon lightly packed saffron threads
¼	cup extra-virgin olive oil
½	teaspoon chopped fresh thyme
2	teaspoons roughly chopped fennel fronds or dill
⅓	cup pitted oil-cured olives, coarsely chopped

TUNA

¼	cup dry bread crumbs
¼	teaspoon lightly packed saffron threads

Kosher salt

1¾-pound piece Pacific albacore or tombo tuna, about 4 inches on each side

1	tablespoon extra-virgin olive oil
2	tablespoons unsalted butter

EDITOR'S WINE CHOICE
Zesty, lemony Sauvignon Blanc:
2011 Ferrari-Carano Fumé Blanc

This entrée can easily be turned into a one-dish meal by serving it atop a bed of young escarole, sliced carrots, and shaved fennel—or any other hearty salad veggies—dressed with a little lemon juice and extra-virgin olive oil. This recipe will work well with other firm fish like swordfish.

TO MAKE THE TAPENADE Coarsely chop the garlic, sprinkle with a generous pinch of salt, and use the side of the blade to smash and crush the garlic into a paste. Put in a medium bowl along with the capers, vinegar, lemon juice, shallot, anchovy, and saffron. Whisking constantly, drizzle in the olive oil.

Add the thyme, fennel fronds, and olives and whisk again. Set aside and let the saffron infuse while you prepare the tuna.

TO COOK THE TUNA Combine the bread crumbs, saffron, and ¼ teaspoon salt in a food processor and pulse to blend and chop the saffron a bit (7 or 8 pulses). Pour onto a plate and set aside.

Cut the tuna lengthwise along the grain to make 2 long logs. Trim any connective tissue and season all over with ½ teaspoon salt. Roll the logs in the bread crumbs to coat each broad side lightly.

Heat a large, heavy skillet (ideally cast iron) over medium heat. When hot, add the oil and 1 tablespoon of the butter and let the butter melt. Cut the remaining 1 tablespoon butter into 4 pieces and set aside.

Gently place the tuna logs in the pan and let cook undisturbed for 3 minutes. Use a thin spatula to gently lift the log and check the progress of the browning. Once the first side is golden brown (about 4 minutes), turn to a new side and add a chunk of the butter next to each of the logs. Gently nudge the logs into the newly added butter as it melts. Cook this side until golden and repeat on the remaining sides, adding the 2 remaining chunks of butter after flipping, for a total of 12 to 14 minutes cooking time.

Transfer the tuna to a cutting board and let rest for 5 to 10 minutes. Cut the tuna into ½-inch-thick slices (a sharp knife with a thin blade works best).

Arrange on a serving platter or individual plates and drizzle the tapenade over the slices.

Searing in butter helps the tuna brown without overcooking.

ROMESCO CHICKEN SALAD

MAKES ABOUT 2½ CUPS, ENOUGH
FOR ABOUT 4 SANDWICHES

- 5 tablespoons Romesco Sauce (recipe follows)
- 2 tablespoons mayonnaise
- 2 teaspoons freshly squeezed lemon juice, more as needed

Pinch of cayenne pepper (optional), more as desired

- 2 cups shredded or diced cooked chicken (about 8 ounces)
- ¼ cup finely diced small celery
- 2 tablespoons finely diced red onion
- 1 tablespoon chopped fresh parsley

Kosher salt

This unique chicken salad is bound together with romesco sauce, the Spanish puree of red peppers, almonds, and olive oil. It takes the classic chicken salad sandwich to another level, but piled on crostini, sliced baguette, or even mini tart shells, you can also turn it into a fabulous hors d'oeuvre.

In a medium bowl, combine the romesco, mayonnaise, lemon juice, and cayenne and stir to blend. Add the chicken, celery, red onion, and parsley and stir to combine. Taste and add more salt or lemon juice as needed.

ROMESCO SAUCE

This incredible sauce is particularly versatile and serves as the backbone for the Romesco Chicken Salad. It's important to avoid over-processing the sauce; not only does heat cause the mixture to become gelatinous, but the sauce simply tastes better when left a little chunky.

If you can't find piquillo peppers, roasted red bell peppers would work, too. Roasting and peeling them yourself is the ideal, because it gives you more of that nice smoky flavor.

MAKES ABOUT 1¾ CUPS

1 medium Roma tomato
3 tablespoons extra-virgin olive oil, plus more for the tomato
⅓ cup toasted blanched almonds, preferably Marconas
One 10-ounce jar roasted piquillo peppers, drained, seeds picked out (about 1¼ cups)
1 medium clove garlic, smashed and peeled
1 tablespoon sherry vinegar, more as needed
1 teaspoon smoked Spanish paprika
Kosher salt

Rub the tomato with a few drops of olive oil to very lightly coat. Using tongs, hold the tomato over a gas flame until charred all over (3 to 4 minutes). If you don't have a gas range, you can put the tomato under the broiler, turning it frequently and watching carefully so that it doesn't go up in flames! Let the tomato cool enough to handle, then remove and discard the skin and seeds. Set aside.

Put the almonds in a food processor and pulse until they're just coarsely chopped, about 10 pulses. It's okay if they're uneven; you just want to start the chopping process. Transfer to a bowl and set aside.

Put the tomato, peppers, garlic, vinegar, paprika, and 1 teaspoon salt in the food processor (you don't need to wash it after chopping the almonds). Blend until it forms a coarse paste, 10 to 15 seconds. Add the almonds and olive oil and pulse just until coarsely chopped; it should still have distinct pieces of almonds. Taste and stir in more vinegar or salt as needed.

SICILIAN MEATBALLS
with fresh basil marinara

MAKES 6 LARGE MEATBALLS

½	cup fresh bread crumbs
¼	cup whole milk
1	large egg
¾	cup grated Parmigiano-Reggiano, more for sprinkling
¼	cup ketchup
2	tablespoons chopped parsley
1	teaspoon finely chopped fresh oregano
1	teaspoon finely chopped fresh thyme
1	small onion, finely chopped
4	large cloves garlic, minced

Kosher salt and freshly ground black pepper

1½	pounds ground beef
3	tablespoons extra-virgin olive oil

One 28-ounce can crushed tomatoes
Sugar, as needed

2	tablespoons chopped fresh basil

AUTHOR'S NOTE
This marinara sauce is as versatile as it is simple. Add some capers, anchovies, and olives for a puttanesca sauce or a pinch of chile flakes for arrabbiata.

EDITOR'S WINE CHOICE
Smoky, black cherry–scented Italian red: 2009 Sabbie Morellino di Scansano

These baseball-size meatballs are a mainstay of the market's deli case. They're flavorful and tender and stay good for several days after they're made. If you have leftovers, they make an incredible meatball sandwich; just slice them up, reheat in the sauce, and put them in the middle of a good crusty roll. Then top with mozzarella or provolone if you have it.

Put a rack in the center of the oven and heat to 375°F. Line a large rimmed baking pan with parchment or a nonstick liner and set aside.

Put the bread crumbs and milk in a large mixing bowl, stir to blend, and set aside for 5 minutes. With your hands, squeeze and mash the bread crumbs so that they make a smooth paste. Add the egg and whisk, then add the Parmigiano, ketchup, parsley, oregano, thyme, half the onion, half the garlic, 2 teaspoons salt, and ½ teaspoon pepper. Stir to blend.

With your hands, break the beef into small chunks and add to the bowl. Mix gently but thoroughly; overmixing will make the meatballs tough and dry. When all the ingredients are evenly combined, shape the mixture into 6 balls and arrange on the baking sheet.

Bake until an instant-read thermometer reads 165°F at the center of a meatball, 40 to 45 minutes.

While the meatballs are baking, make the sauce. Heat the olive oil in a medium saucepan over medium heat. Add the remaining half onion and 1 teaspoon salt and increase the heat to medium-high. Cook, stirring frequently, until translucent, about 3 minutes. Add the remaining half garlic and cook until aromatic, about 1 minute. Add the tomatoes, bring to a boil, and lower the heat to maintain a vigorous simmer. Cook, stirring occasionally, until reduced to a thick sauce, 10 to 15 minutes. Taste the sauce and add a pinch or two of sugar if it seems too tangy, and season with more salt if necessary. Stir in the basil and keep warm until the meatballs come out of the oven.

Spoon the sauce generously over the meatballs and bake for another 5 to 10 minutes to blend the flavors. Garnish with a sprinkling of Parmigiano.

These giant meatballs brown in the oven, not in a skillet.

LEMONY KALE CAESAR SALAD

SERVES 4 TO 6

- 1 medium bunch dino or lacinato kale (about 10 ounces) (see Author's Note)
- 2 medium cloves garlic

Kosher salt

- 2 anchovy fillets, minced (about 1 teaspoon)
- 1 large egg yolk
- 2 tablespoons freshly squeezed lemon juice, more to taste
- ½ teaspoon Dijon mustard
- ¼ cup extra-virgin olive oil
- ⅓ cup grated Parmigiano-Reggiano cheese, more for garnish

Freshly ground black pepper

AUTHOR'S NOTE
We've used regular kale, red leaf kale, and others to make this salad, and they're all delicious. Whatever the variety, the younger and smaller the leaves, the more tender they are and the better for eating raw. You can also use tender inner young escarole leaves, radicchio, or a mix of chicories.

EDITOR'S WINE CHOICE
Vibrant, unoaked Chardonnay: 2010 Lioco Sonoma County

This salad is inspired by the incredible version I had at New York City's Il Buco restaurant. One bite will convince you that compared to romaine, kale is a better match for assertive Caesar dressing. You can omit the egg yolk if you want to play it safe, but don't try this without anchovy; it makes the dish. This version is crouton-less; if you add them, make a bit more dressing.

Strip off and discard any thick stalks from the kale. If the leaves are very tender, you can tear them into bite-size pieces. Otherwise, cut them by stacking 6 or 8 of the leaves, rolling into a tight cigar, and slicing crosswise into ¼-inch strips. Repeat with the remaining kale; pile any particularly wide strips on the cutting board and cut across the pile once or twice. Put in a large bowl and set aside.

Coarsely chop the garlic and sprinkle with a generous pinch of salt. Use the flat side of a chef's knife to smash and press the garlic into a paste (you should have about ¾ teaspoon). Transfer to a small bowl and add the anchovy, egg yolk, lemon juice, and Dijon. Whisking constantly, slowly drizzle in the oil until completely incorporated. Dip a leaf of kale into the dressing and taste. Add more lemon juice or salt as needed.

Put the kale into a large bowl and drizzle about 1½ tablespoons of the dressing over the kale. With your hands, gently toss until the leaves are evenly coated, adding just enough dressing to coat the leaves lightly. Sprinkle the cheese over and toss again to blend. Taste and add more dressing or salt as needed.

Garnish with an extra sprinkling of cheese and a grind or two of pepper. You can serve the salad right away, but you can also let it sit for a few minutes before serving (in this time, the acid in the dressing will tenderize the leaves a bit).

CRISPY FRESH SALMON CAKES

SERVES 6 AS A FIRST COURSE

- 1 tablespoon extra-virgin olive oil
- 1 cup finely diced celery
- 1 large leek, white and light green parts only, finely diced (about 1 cup)

Kosher salt and freshly ground black pepper

- 1 pound skinless salmon fillet, cut into 1-inch cubes
- 1 large egg
- 1½ tablespoons fresh lemon juice
- ¼ teaspoon cayenne pepper
- ¼ cup mayonnaise
- 3 tablespoons capers—drained, rinsed and coarsely chopped
- 2 tablespoons chopped dill
- 1 cup panko (Japanese bread crumbs)

Grapeseed or vegetable oil, for frying

Tartar sauce, for serving

EDITOR'S WINE CHOICE
Earthy, minerally rosé: 2011 Unti

Mogannam's nicely crispy salmon cakes are a fantastic way to make a pound of fish serve six people; you can also make mini cakes and serve them as an hors d'oeuvre.

1. In a medium skillet, heat the olive oil. Add the celery and leek, season with salt and black pepper and cook over moderately low heat, stirring occasionally, until softened, about 10 minutes. Let cool completely.

2. In a food processor, combine the salmon, egg, lemon juice and cayenne with 1 teaspoon of salt and ¼ teaspoon of black pepper. Pulse until the salmon is finely chopped and the ingredients are incorporated. Scrape the mixture into a bowl. Stir in the leek and celery along with the mayonnaise, capers, dill and ¼ cup of the panko.

3. In a shallow bowl, spread the remaining ¾ cup of panko. Form the salmon mixture into six 3½-inch patties. Dredge the patties in the panko and transfer to a parchment paper–lined baking sheet.

4. In a large nonstick skillet, heat ¼ inch of grapeseed oil until shimmering. Add the salmon patties and fry over moderately high heat until browned on the bottom, about 2 minutes. Turn and fry until golden brown and cooked through, about 3 minutes longer. Transfer to a paper towel–lined plate to drain. Serve the salmon cakes with tartar sauce.

SERVE WITH A green salad.

SAM MOGANNAM ONLINE
biritemarket.com

 Bi-Rite Market

@sammogannam

THE ART OF LIVING ACCORDING TO JOE BEEF

frédéric morin, david mcmillan & meredith erickson

why we love this book

Frédéric Morin and David McMillan, the chefs and owners of the wildly popular Joe Beef in Montreal, have a more-is-more take on French market cuisine that has made them a darling among food cognoscenti like chefs David Chang and Anthony Bourdain. Morin and McMillan's first book reveals their irreverent sense of humor and eccentric tastes.

the concept of joe beef

Morin: "The vibe is like hanging out all day with friends. When there's too much discipline, it's not fun. There has to be that blissful chaos. At Joe Beef, you can slouch and eat things like Chicken Skin Tacos (page 152)."

quebec as inspiration

McMillan: "We created Joe Beef with nostalgia in mind—the sense that the original paint is likely better than what's covering it. We're inspired by the traditions of Quebec and the ingredients in our own backyard."

culinary hero

Morin: "There should be a statue of Daniel Boulud in New York. That guy still cooks. When I saw him at his restaurant Daniel, he knew exactly how many grams of sausage and brioche went into the saucisson dish that I had at one of his other restaurants."

favorite seafood

McMillan: "On a fishing trip to Prince Edward Island, we learned that mussels are amazingly sustainable and should be eaten as much as possible. For our version of Mouclade (page 150), we serve mussels in a creamy wine sauce with simmered vegetables and tarragon."

on choosing recipes

Morin: "We change our menu like we change underwear. This book is our Joe Beef menu, but with Ritalin. It's the things we remembered and were able to focus on."

PUBLISHED BY TEN SPEED PRESS, $40

BAKED MUSHROOMS
with new (or old!) garlic

SERVES 4

- 16 large white mushrooms, stem ends trimmed
- ¼ cup (55 grams) salted or unsalted butter
- 1 tablespoon olive oil

Salt and pepper

- ¼ teaspoon smoked paprika (pimentón de la Vera)
- 2 garlic flowers or garlic cloves
- 6 sprigs thyme

Here is a simple way to enjoy big Paris mushrooms. I like chanterelles, morels, and even matsutakes, but these common white mushrooms— the kind you see in supermarkets—remind me of culinary school; they smell like la bonne cuisine française. *We use banker watch–size mushrooms—as big as you can find. If you're looking for an upscale alternative, porcini will also work.*

This dish is best prepared in a cast-iron frying pan, served family style at the table. Bring it out hot and bubbling.

1. Preheat the oven to 450°F (230°C). Score each mushroom cap with shallow cuts about ⅛ inch (3 millimeters) deep. Spread the butter and oil in the bottom of a heavy ovenproof pan. Season the bottom of the pan with salt, pepper, and the paprika. Place the mushrooms, cap down and side by side, in the pan. Tuck the garlic flowers and thyme among them.

2. Bake the mushrooms for 18 to 20 minutes, or until the pan juices are bubbling and the mushrooms have shrunk and roasted. Serve bubbly.

The young garlic scapes here have a milder flavor than mature cloves.

PETITS FARCIS

SERVES 4

- 4 small new onions, with tops attached
- 4 small pattypan squashes
- 4 small tomatoes
- 4 small eggplants
- 4 bell peppers
- 4 small zucchini

STUFFING

- 1 small onion, finely chopped
- 1 tablespoon neutral oil
- 8 ounces (225 grams) ground veal
- 8 ounces (225 grams) ground pork
- 1 egg, lightly beaten
- 1 slice white bread, crust removed, crumbled and soaked in 2 tablespoons milk
- ¼ cup (30 grams) grated Parmesan cheese
- 1 teaspoon finely chopped fresh thyme leaves
- ½ teaspoon fennel seeds
- ¼ teaspoon finely chopped garlic
- ¼ teaspoon dried chile flakes

Salt and pepper

Olive oil for drizzling

EDITOR'S WINE CHOICE
Crisp, dry Provençal rosé: 2011
Commanderie de la Bargemone

We remember falling in love with a photograph of petits farcis *in an old issue of* Cuisine et Vins de France. *We're sure that most chefs our age who had dreamed of cooking professionally since childhood feel the same when they open a vintage copy of* Cuisine et Vins de France, *or of Georges Blanc's* De la Vigne à l'Assiette. *There is no greater food era than when Michel Guérard, Bernard Loiseau, Paul Bocuse, Alain Chapel, Georges Blanc, and Roger Vergé were at the top.*

Petits farcis *are vegetables stuffed with sausage mix, then baked and eaten lukewarm. We make them in the summer when the growers show up with pattypan squashes. What else are you supposed to do with those little squashes other than admire them? The stuffed vegetables are awesome with a mâche salad and partner perfectly with a nice rosé or pastis. Get the smallest vegetables you can find, about the size of a golf ball.*

1. Cut the top one-third off the onions, squashes, tomatoes, eggplants, and peppers, and set aside to use as caps. Cut the zucchini in half lengthwise. With a melon baller or an espresso spoon, scoop out the inside of each vegetable the best you can. Leave the walls about ¼ inch (6 millimeters) thick. Set the vegetables aside.

2. Preheat the oven to 400°F (200°C). To make the stuffing, in a small frying pan, sweat the onion in the oil over medium heat for 4 to 5 minutes, or until translucent. Remove from the heat.

3. In a bowl, combine the veal, pork, cooked onion, egg, bread, Parmesan, thyme, fennel seeds, garlic, chile flakes, and a pinch each of salt and pepper. Mix together using your hands; it should have the texture of a raw meatball.

4. Divide the meat mixture among the vegetables, stuffing it carefully and deeply inside each one. Stand the vegetables, without their caps, in an oiled gratin dish or cake pan. Bake for 20 minutes, or until the meat is cooked but not colored. Remove from the oven, top each vegetable with its cap, and return to the oven for another 10 minutes, or until the tops are getting crispy and the meat is sizzling.

5. Remove from the oven and drizzle olive oil on top. Serve lukewarm.

The sausage stuffing here is tasty in baby or full-size vegetables.

MOUCLADE

SERVES 4

1 carrot, peeled and finely diced
1 celery stalk, finely diced
1 small onion, finely diced
1 small PEI or Yukon Gold potato, finely diced
3 tablespoons unsalted butter
2 pounds (900 grams) PEI mussels, washed and picked through (see Editor's Note)
½ cup (125 milliliters) dry white wine
¾ cup (180 milliliters) whipping cream (35 percent butterfat)
1 egg yolk
1 tablespoon chopped fresh tarragon

EDITOR'S NOTE
Morin and McMillan prefer shellfish from Prince Edward Island (PEI) for this dish of steamed mussels in a creamy sauce.

EDITOR'S WINE CHOICE
Floral, strawberry-scented rosé: 2011 Mas Carlot

We do not have a story for this recipe. Sorry.

1. In a sauté pan over medium heat, sweat the carrot, celery, onion, and potato in 2 tablespoons of the butter for 3 to 4 minutes, or until the onion is translucent. Set aside.

2. In a pot with a lid, combine the mussels and wine, cover, place over high heat, and steam for 4 or 5 minutes, or until the mussels open. Discard any mussels that failed to open. Then, take the mussels one by one and remove the top shell, allowing the mussel liquor to fall back into the pan. Set the mussels in their bottom shells, meat side up, in a shallow bowl.

3. Simmer the mussel juice over medium heat until reduced by half. Add the remaining 1 tablespoon butter and the cream, bring to a boil, and remove from the heat.

4. Buzz the sauce with a hand blender and add the egg yolk and tarragon. Add the sweated vegetables and return the pan to low heat. Do not allow the sauce to boil or the egg will curdle.

5. When the sauce is nice and warm, pour it on top of the mussels and serve immediately.

This is also delicious tossed with pasta.

CHICKEN SKIN TACOS

MAKES 8 TACOS

About 1½ pounds (680 grams)
  chicken skins
2 tablespoons canola oil
Salt and pepper

RUB
2 teaspoons salt
2 teaspoons sugar
1 teaspoon pepper
1 teaspoon red chile powder
1 teaspoon ground cumin
1 teaspoon ground coriander
1 teaspoon achiote powder
  (optional)

POTATO DE GALLO
1 cup (140 grams) minutely
  diced peeled potato
¼ cup (60 milliliters) canola oil
⅓ red onion, very finely diced
1 jalapeño chile, seeded
  and diced superfine
1 tablespoon Mayonnaise
  (recipe follows)
¼ cup (10 grams) chopped
  fresh cilantro
3 tablespoons fresh lime juice
Salt
8 small corn tortillas, warmed
8 hard-boiled quail egg yolks
  (optional)
8 sprigs cilantro

EDITOR'S BEER CHOICE
Citrusy, spiced wheat beer: Dieu
du Ciel Blanche du Paradis

We made this dish because we like the "potato" de gallo idea. (In fact, you can make only the rub and eat it on almost anything, especially eggs.) Make certain that the potatoes are tiny and crisp, so you get that salt-and-vinegar potato chip taste.

1. Preheat the oven to 425°F (220°C). Cut the skins into 4 or 5 pieces, each roughly 1 inch (2.5 centimeters) square. With your hands, combine the skin pieces and canola oil in a roasting pan and season with a pinch each of salt and pepper.

2. Roast the skins for 1 hour, stirring and tossing them every 15 minutes with your trusty tongs.

3. While the skins are roasting, make the rub. In a small bowl, stir together the salt, sugar, pepper, chile powder, cumin, coriander, and achiote powder.

4. When the skins are ready, they should be crispy, golden, and delicious looking. Remove from the oven, drain, and pat dry with paper towels. Chop finely while still lukewarm, and season to taste with the rub. Keep warm. (The remaining rub will keep well in a tightly capped jar in a cool, dry cupboard.)

5. Just before the skins are ready, make the potato de gallo. In a nonstick frying pan, fry the potato in the oil for about 6 minutes, or until they have a French-fry color and are crispy. Transfer to paper towels and pat dry. Just before you are going to serve the tacos, combine the potato, onion, chile, mayonnaise, chopped cilantro, and lime juice and season with salt. Don't mix the ingredients any sooner; it is important that the "salsa" tastes fresh.

6. Now, build each taco: warm tortilla, some skin, some spud, a yolk (as dressing), and a cilantro sprig.

MAKES ABOUT 1 CUP
(250 MILLILITERS)

  1 egg yolk
  1 tablespoon Dijon mustard
  1 cup (250 milliliters) canola oil
Salt and pepper
Juice from ½ lemon
Purée de Fines Herbes (recipe follows),
    optional

MAKES 2 CUPS
(500 MILLILITERS)

  1 bunch chervil
  1 bunch chives
  1 bunch flat-leaf parsley
  1 bunch tarragon
  1 bunch watercress, blanched
     and chilled in an ice bath
Squeeze of fresh lemon juice
  2 teaspoons neutral oil
  ½ cup (125 milliliters) water
Pinch of salt

MAYONNAISE

A classic mayo.

1. In a large bowl, whisk together the egg yolk and mustard. Pour in the oil in a steady, fine, slow stream and whisk, whisk, whisk. Always have a glass of water nearby in case the mayonnaise starts splitting and you need to thicken and mend. Season with salt, pepper, and lemon juice to taste. Mix in some of the puréed herbs if you want to add a bit of flavor.

2. Use right away, or cover and refrigerate for up to 2 days.

PURÉE DE FINES HERBES

This is part of our mise en place *at the restaurant. We mix it with mayonnaise, serve it straight up with potatoes or fish, or use it to punch up sauces, soups, stews, or anything raw like tartare. Do not use woodsy herbs like rosemary, thyme, or sage in this purée, and be sure to wash all of your herbs well.*

1. In a food processor, combine the herbs, watercress, lemon juice, oil, and water and process until smooth. Season with the salt.

2. Store in a tightly sealed container for up to a week.

SCHNITZEL OF PORK

SERVES 4

3 cups (385 grams) all-purpose flour
Salt and pepper
4 eggs
1 cup (250 milliliters) sour cream
¼ teaspoon freshly grated nutmeg
4 cups (170 grams) *panko*
(Japanese bread crumbs), pulsed
for a few seconds in a food
processor until the texture of
regular bread crumbs
1 cup (115 grams) grated sbrinz
or grana padano cheese
4 large pork schnitzels
(loin cutlets), pounded
by the butcher to ¼ inch
(6 millimeters) thick
¼ cup (60 milliliters) canola oil
or more if needed

EDITOR'S WINE CHOICE
Focused, cherry-rich red Burgundy:
2009 Philippe Pacalet Pommard

Not long ago, restaurants were just fun places to eat out—not the foodist temples of today. And they were often an ode to the owner's homeland, hobby, or previous livelihood: a ski or fishing lodge, a Bahamian beach hut, a Chinese pagoda. At the top of our list is the stube, the Austrian ski shack with crossed skis hung over the mantel, beer steins, pretzel buns as bread, schnapps, and kabinnet. The menus here would invariably feature sides of mustard in glass jars, parsleyed potatoes, krauts and wursts of all kinds, and, ultimately, the schnitzel— crisp and hot and overlapping the plate like Dom DeLuise on a bar stool.

We include schnitzel on the Joe Beef menu twice a year: in the spring with peas, cream, and morels, and in the fall with chanterelles, eggs, and anchovies (of course). Ask your butcher for 4 large, pounded schnitzels. Sizewise, default to your biggest pan. You can top the schnitzel with a fried egg with a lemon wedge alongside.

1. Prepare 3 flat containers, each big enough to contain 1 schnitzel at a time. Put the flour and a good pinch each of salt and pepper in the first container. In the second container, whisk together the eggs, sour cream, nutmeg, and another good pinch each of salt and pepper. In the third container, mix together the processed *panko* and the cheese.

2. Dip a schnitzel in the flour and shake off the excess; drop it in the egg mixture and drain off the excess; and lay it in the third container with the *panko* mixture and coat it well. Shake off the excess crumbs and put it on a platter. Repeat with the remaining schnitzels, then put the platter, uncovered, in the fridge, and leave it to dry a little.

3. Heat the oil in a big frying pan over medium-high heat. Do not wait until the oil smokes, but it should be hot enough so that a pinch of crumbs sizzles on contact. Place 1 schnitzel in the pan. Remember to lay it down away from you, so you don't splash yourself. Cook, turning once, for 3 minutes on each side, or until golden brown. You want to maintain a steady sizzle the whole time the schnitzel cooks, but you don't want it to overcolor. Transfer to paper towels to absorb the excess oil, and season with salt and pepper. Repeat with the remaining schnitzels, adding more oil to the pan if needed.

4. Serve the schnitzels one at a time as they are ready, or leave them on the paper towels and place in a low oven until serving.

YUKON GOLD SOUP

with smoked fish & pumpernickel croutons

SERVES 6 TO 8

- 2 pounds Yukon Gold potatoes, peeled and cut into 1-inch pieces (about 5 potatoes)
- 3 cups chicken stock or low-sodium broth
- 2 cups milk
- 1 cup heavy cream
- 1 garlic clove, thinly sliced
- ½ stick (2 ounces) unsalted butter, softened

Kosher salt and freshly ground pepper
- ¾ pound smoked trout fillets, skin removed, flesh flaked

Pumpernickel croutons and freshly snipped chives, for garnish

EDITOR'S WINE CHOICE
Flinty, green apple–inflected Chardonnay: 2010 Gilbert Picq et ses Fils Chablis

Morin and McMillan like to think of this ultrasmooth potato soup as a "big white page on which to do anything you want." Here they top the soup with smoked trout and croutons, but feel free to experiment with other ingredients.

1. In a large pot of boiling salted water, cook the potatoes over moderate heat until tender, about 15 minutes. Drain well. Transfer the potatoes to a bowl and cover with plastic wrap.

2. Wipe out the pot. Add the chicken stock, milk, cream and garlic and bring to a simmer. Cook over moderately low heat until the garlic is very tender, about 8 minutes. Add half of the potatoes to the pot. Using an immersion blender, puree the potatoes until smooth. Add the remaining potatoes and the butter and puree until smooth and slightly thickened. Season with salt and pepper. Ladle the soup into bowls and top with some of the trout, croutons and chives; serve right away.

MAKE AHEAD The soup can be refrigerated overnight. Reheat gently before serving.

FRÉDÉRIC MORIN
& DAVID MCMILLAN ONLINE

joebeef.ca

f Joe Beef - Liverpool House

t @joebeef

Silken tofu and pork soup, page 161

MY VIETNAM

luke nguyen

why we love this book

Part autobiography, part cookbook, *My Vietnam* is a journey into traditional Vietnamese cuisine from Australia-based chef and TV host Luke Nguyen. He traveled to his ancestral homeland, gathering recipes from his extended family in Saigon, old women in markets and little restaurants throughout the country. Many of his recipes will require a trip to an Asian grocer for ingredients like preserved cabbage and shrimp paste, but the dishes come together quickly. The reward: uniquely bright, spicy, fresh flavors.

his favorite ingredient

"Before you call tofu bland, experiment with it a bit. In its natural state it's so delicate, but then you can flash-fry tofu and it becomes crisp, or you can pan-fry it and it firms up. Tofu is also an amazing flavor carrier—if you cook it with the right ingredients. I have a lot of simple tofu recipes that'll blow you away, like my Silken Tofu and Pork Soup (page 161). It's perfect comfort food."

adventurous eating

"At my restaurant Red Lantern in Sydney, I serve goat on the bone and whole fish with the head on. But traveling through Vietnam was a real eye-opener in terms of trying new foods like rat and dog. Before freaking out, you have to realize that it's a wild rat that eats off coconut trees in the jungle, and the dog is bred to be cooked; it's very lean and flavorful. I want to push people to be a bit more adventurous with my book. For instance, my Sautéed Jumbo Shrimp (page 158) calls for tomalley, which you squeeze out of the shrimp heads. It has the most intense shrimp flavor, and it makes the sauce incredible."

on minimalist cooking

"I'm trying to demystify cooking. In Vietnam, cooks have a burner, a pan, a charcoal grill and a chopping block and cleaver. That's all you really need."

PUBLISHED BY LYONS PRESS, $40

SAUTÉED JUMBO SHRIMP

tôm kho tàu

SERVES 4 TO 6 AS PART
OF A SHARED MEAL

- 8 raw jumbo shrimp or scampi
- 2 tablespoons fish sauce
- 1 tablespoon sugar
- A pinch of salt
- 1 teaspoon freshly ground black pepper
- 3 tablespoons finely chopped red Asian shallots
- 3 tablespoons finely chopped garlic
- 1 tablespoon lemon juice
- 3 tablespoons vegetable oil
- 1 long red chili, julienned
- 8 spring onions (scallions), white part only, cut into 5-centimeter (2-inch) lengths

EDITOR'S BEER CHOICE
Light, refreshing lager: 333

With jumbo shrimp comes shrimp "butter," also known as tomalley. Shrimp butter is a delicacy in Vietnam and is found in the shrimp's head. I use shrimp butter in this recipe; when cooked it has a powerful concentrated shrimp flavor. To obtain the shrimp butter, squeeze the shrimp head until all the innards have been excreted, then scoop out the orange-colored butter.

It is common to find shrimp cooked and served in Vietnam with the heads still intact—suck out the juice in the shrimp's head before making your way to its body. In this recipe, you'll need to peel the shrimp to remove the shrimp butter from the heads, but try leaving a few shrimp with their heads on, and eat them the Vietnamese way.

Peel and devein the shrimp, leaving the tails intact. Scoop out the shrimp butter from the shrimp heads, and reserve the butter. If desired, leave a few of the shrimp with their heads and tails intact, and peel only their bodies.

In a bowl, combine the fish sauce, sugar, a pinch of salt, 1 teaspoon freshly ground black pepper, 1 tablespoon of the shallots and 1 tablespoon of the garlic. Add the shrimp, toss to coat in the marinade, then cover and place in the fridge to marinate for 20 minutes. Drain, reserving the marinade.

To make the sauce, mix the shrimp butter with the lemon juice and 1 tablespoon of the oil. Set aside.

Place a large frying pan over medium-high heat, add the remaining oil, then sauté the shrimp for 1 minute on each side to seal. Remove the shrimp and set aside.

Wipe the pan clean and turn the heat to low, then add the sauce along with the reserved marinade from the shrimp, and simmer for 2 minutes. Now add the shrimp, the remaining shallots and garlic, the chili and spring onions, and stir-fry for 2 minutes. Serve with jasmine rice.

A little bit of sugar makes this dish sweet and savory.

WOK-TOSSED BEEF WITH KOHLRABI
bò xào su hào

SERVES 4 TO 6 AS PART
OF A SHARED MEAL

1 kohlrabi, peeled and sliced into 3-centimeter (1¼-inch) long pieces, about 3 millimeters (⅛ inch) thick
2 tablespoons vegetable oil
1 tablespoon finely chopped garlic
1 small onion, thinly sliced
300 grams (10½ ounces) beef sirloin, trimmed and sliced into 3-millimeter (⅛-inch) thick strips
1 tablespoon fish sauce
2 teaspoons light soy sauce
2 teaspoons oyster sauce
2 teaspoons sugar
1 teaspoon freshly ground black pepper

EDITOR'S WINE CHOICE
Smoky, fruit-forward Malbec:
2010 Mapema

Kohlrabi means "cabbage turnip"; it is in the same family as the cabbage and broccoli, its texture as crisp as its cousins. There are two types of kohlrabi—purple and light green—but go for the green ones, as they don't seem to be as tough in texture. When buying it at the market, look for a vegetable that resembles a round Sputnik satellite.

Bring 1 liter (35 fluid ounces/4 cups) of water to a boil in a large saucepan. Add the kohlrabi and blanch for 2 minutes. Drain, then submerge in ice-cold water for 2 minutes, then drain again.

Heat 1 tablespoon of the oil in a wok over high heat and fry half the garlic and half the onion for 1 minute until fragrant. Add the beef and stir-fry for 1 minute, then remove the beef and onion and set aside.

Add the remaining oil to the wok over high heat and stir-fry the kohlrabi with the remaining garlic and onion for 2 minutes. Return the beef to the wok, add the fish sauce, soy sauce, oyster sauce, sugar and 1 teaspoon freshly ground black pepper, and stir-fry for a further 2 minutes. Transfer to a serving bowl and serve with jasmine rice.

SILKEN TOFU & PORK SOUP
canh đậu hũ hẹ heo xay

SERVES 4 TO 6 AS PART
OF A SHARED MEAL

- 200 grams (7 ounces) minced pork
- 2 teaspoons salt
- 1 teaspoon sugar
- 1 tablespoon fish sauce
- 250 grams (9 ounces) silken tofu, cut into bite-sized pieces
- 1 tablespoon preserved cabbage
- 1 bunch garlic chives, cut into 4-centimeter (1½-inch) pieces
- 4 spring onions (scallions), green part only, thinly sliced lengthways
- 1 handful cilantro leaves, roughly chopped
- A pinch of freshly ground black pepper
- 1 bird's eye chili, thinly sliced
- Fish sauce, for dipping

Tofu is a dietary staple throughout Vietnam. It acts as a sponge and carries the flavors it is cooked with. I use mainly silken tofu in my cooking as I enjoy its soft creamy texture. I cook this recipe when I'm feeling unwell—it's comfort food—even preparing it makes me feel better. Leftover tofu should be kept in cold water and refrigerated. Change the water daily and use it within three days.

Pour 1.5 liters (52 fluid ounces/6 cups) of water into a saucepan and bring to a boil. Add the pork and stir for 3 minutes to break up the mince, skimming any impurities off the surface. Now add 2 teaspoons salt, the sugar, fish sauce and tofu. When the tofu rises to the surface, add the preserved cabbage and garlic chives. Remove the saucepan from the heat.

Transfer the soup to large serving bowls and garnish each bowl of soup with some spring onions, cilantro and a pinch of freshly ground black pepper. Serve with jasmine rice, and a small bowl of sliced chili and fish sauce for dipping.

HANOI CHICKEN & VERMICELLI NOODLE SOUP

bún thang hà nội

SERVES 4 TO 6

- 2 liters (70 fluid ounces/8 cups) Chicken Stock (recipe follows)
- 2 teaspoons sugar
- 3 tablespoons fish sauce
- 2 teaspoons Garlic Oil (recipe follows)
- 2 teaspoons salt
- 100 grams (3½ ounces) boneless, skinless chicken breast
- 100 grams (3½ ounces) pork fillet, trimmed
- 250 grams (9 ounces) dried rice vermicelli noodles
- 2 eggs, lightly beaten
- 2 tablespoons vegetable oil
- 100 grams (3½ ounces) Pork Terrine (recipe follows), sliced into thin strips (optional)
- 2 tablespoons sliced spring onion (scallion)
- 1 large handful cilantro leaves
- A pinch of freshly ground black pepper
- 1 large handful mint leaves
- 1 large handful Vietnamese mint leaves
- 90 grams (3¼ ounces/1 cup) bean sprouts
- Shrimp paste, to taste (optional)
- 1 bird's eye chili, thinly sliced
- Fish sauce, for dipping

This vermicelli soup is as popular as pho *in the streets of Hanoi and, like* pho, *it can be eaten for breakfast, lunch or dinner. I have never found this dish anywhere else in Vietnam, so be sure to try a bowl of the local specialty if you ever find yourself in Hanoi. If you decide to make it at home, please add the shrimp paste. I know that shrimp paste can be too intense for some people's palates (and noses), but I assure you that when dissolved into the broth, you won't be able to smell it, and it will truly add another dimension to your soup.*

In a large saucepan, combine the chicken stock, sugar, fish sauce, garlic oil and 2 teaspoons salt. Bring to the boil, then add the chicken and pork. Reduce the heat to low and cook for 20 minutes. Remove the chicken and pork, cool, then cut into 1-centimeter (½-inch) slices. Reserve the chicken stock.

Put the rice vermicelli in a saucepan of boiling water and bring back to a boil. Cook for 5 minutes, then turn off the heat and leave in the water for 5 minutes. Drain the noodles, rinse under cold water, and set aside.

Place a non-stick frying pan over medium-low heat and add a little oil. Combine the eggs and ½ teaspoon of the oil in a bowl, then pour about a quarter of the beaten egg into the pan to form a thin layer over the base. Cook for 1 minute, or until the egg sheet will slide off the pan, then turn it over and cook for a further 30 seconds. Remove and place on a chopping board. Repeat this process until all the egg mixture is cooked; you should end up with three or four egg sheets. Stack the egg sheets on top of each other as they are cooked, then roll them together into a tight roll and slice thinly.

Divide the vermicelli among serving bowls. On top of the vermicelli, arrange even amounts of pork terrine (if using), followed by egg strips, then the chicken and pork. Pour enough hot stock into each bowl to cover the noodles. Garnish with the spring onions and cilantro, adding a pinch of freshly ground black pepper to each bowl.

Serve with a platter of mint, Vietnamese mint and bean sprouts, to add to the soup as desired. For a more intense flavor, add about ¼ teaspoon of shrimp paste to each bowl, stirring to dissolve the paste. Serve with a small bowl of sliced chili and fish sauce for dipping.

continued on page 164

For a dinner party, let guests add their own garnishes.

VERMICELLI NOODLE SOUP *continued*

MAKES ABOUT 5 LITERS
(175 FLUID OUNCES/20 CUPS)

- 6   garlic cloves
- 8   spring onions (scallions),
      white part only
- 1   whole chicken (1.6 kilograms/
      3 pounds 8 ounces)
- One 4-centimeter (1½-inch) piece
      of ginger, sliced

MAKES 2 TABLESPOONS
FRIED GARLIC; 250 MILLILITERS
(9 FLUID OUNCES/1 CUP)
GARLIC OIL

- 250   milliliters (9 fluid ounces/1 cup)
        vegetable oil
- 6   garlic cloves, finely chopped

MAKES 1 KILOGRAM
(2 POUNDS 4 OUNCES)

- 1   tablespoon sea salt
- 1   kilogram (2 pounds 4 ounces)
       pork leg, minced (ask your
       butcher to mince the pork finely)
- 2½   tablespoons fish sauce
- 1   large banana leaf

CHICKEN STOCK *nước lèo gà*

Crush the garlic and spring onions into a paste using a mortar and pestle. Wash the chicken thoroughly under cold running water, making sure to remove all traces of blood, guts and fat from the cavity.

Put the chicken in a large saucepan or stockpot with 6 liters (210 fluid ounces/24 cups) of water and bring to the boil. Reduce the heat to a slow simmer and skim the surface for 10 minutes until you have removed most of the fat, then add the ginger and the garlic and spring onion paste. Cook for a further 2 hours, then strain and allow the stock to cool. Refrigerate for up to 3 days, or freeze until required.

FRIED GARLIC & GARLIC OIL *tỏi phi và mỡ tỏi*

Pour the oil into a wok and heat to 180°C (350°F), or until a cube of bread dropped into the oil browns in 15 seconds. Add the garlic to the oil and fry for 45 to 60 seconds, or until the garlic is golden, then strain through a metal sieve and place on paper towel to dry. Be careful not to overcook the garlic in the oil, as it continues to cook once it is removed from the wok. Reserve the garlic oil. Store the fried garlic in an airtight container for up to 4 days. The garlic oil will keep for up to 1 week in the fridge.

PORK TERRINE *chả lụa*

Dry-roast the sea salt in a dry wok for a few minutes over medium heat until aromatic. Place the pork, salt and fish sauce in a food processor and pulse until it forms a very fine paste.

Soak the banana leaf in hot water for 5 minutes, dry and lay it flat on the work surface. Cut the leaf in half and cross one piece over the other. Place the pork paste in the center and draw up all sides to form a tight parcel. Secure with string and cook in a large saucepan of simmering salted water for 1 hour. Remove from the pan, allow to cool, then remove the banana leaf and slice the pork when needed. Refrigerate up to 1 week.

AUTHOR'S NOTE You can freeze leftover pork terrine in small portions to use for next time, or use as a filling for Vietnamese baguettes.

GRILLED EGGPLANT SALAD
with prawns

SERVES 4

- 8 Japanese eggplants (about 2¼ pounds)
- 2 tablespoons canola oil, plus more for brushing
- 1 large shallot, halved lengthwise and thinly sliced crosswise
- 2 garlic cloves, thinly sliced
- ½ cup chopped cilantro
- 2 tablespoons low-sodium soy sauce
- 2 tablespoons fresh lime juice
- 2 tablespoons finely chopped roasted peanuts
- 2 teaspoons toasted sesame seeds

Salt and freshly ground pepper

- 8 prawns or jumbo shrimp, shelled and deveined (1 pound)

Lime wedges, for serving

Inspired by Nguyen's travels through Yangon, Myanmar, this smoky, tangy eggplant salad is excellent with sweet charred prawns.

1. Light a grill or preheat a grill pan. Using a toothpick or a fork, pierce the eggplants all over. Grill the eggplants over high heat, turning occasionally, until the skin is blackened and the eggplants are tender, about 10 minutes. Transfer to a plate and let cool completely. Peel the eggplants and roughly chop the flesh.

2. In a small skillet, heat the 2 tablespoons of oil until shimmering. Add the shallot and garlic and cook over moderately low heat, stirring, until golden and crisp, about 3 minutes. Using a slotted spoon, transfer the garlic and shallot to a paper towel–lined plate to drain. Reserve the oil.

3. In a large bowl, combine the chopped eggplant with the cilantro, soy sauce, lime juice, peanuts, sesame seeds and the reserved garlic-shallot oil. Season with salt and pepper, then stir in the crispy garlic and shallot.

4. Brush the prawns with oil and season with salt and pepper. Grill the prawns over high heat, turning once, until lightly charred and cooked through, about 4 minutes. Spoon the eggplant salad onto plates, top with the prawns and serve with lime wedges.

MAKE AHEAD The recipe can be prepared through Step 3 except for adding the garlic and shallot; refrigerate for up to 3 hours. Bring to room temperature and stir in the garlic and shallot before serving.

LUKE NGUYEN ONLINE

redlantern.com.au

 Red Lantern

@luke_nguyen

Pork chops with yuzu-miso marinade, page 172

THE JAPANESE GRILL

tadashi ono & harris salat

why we love this book

Tokyo-born, Manhattan-based chef Tadashi Ono ingeniously combines Japanese flavors with standards of the American backyard grill. Staples like turkey burgers, which Ono flavors with miso, sake, sesame oil and scallion (page 169), feel original and fresh.

grilling in japan

"In Japan grilling is not home cooking, like it is in America. People don't have grills or even backyards to put them in. Instead, grilling is something that professionals do at yakitori spots."

grill prep

"Before grilling, preheat the grate for at least five minutes. Then clean it with a wire brush, every single time. Finally, using long, sturdy tongs, wipe the grate with a rag or paper towel soaked in vegetable oil. The oil on the grate will flare up, then burn off in a few seconds. If you follow all three steps, your food won't stick."

the perfect setup

"Keep the grate five to ten inches from the fire. If you're using charcoal, you want the food far from the flames, beyond the reach of any flare-ups."

fast marinating

"Take a nice cut of meat—porterhouse, rib eye and lamb chops are my favorites—and marinate it in soy sauce, garlic, olive oil and black pepper. Or use bone-in chicken breasts; my recipe for chicken breasts in soy sauce (page 168) requires only 15 minutes of marinating."

his go-to sides

"I love to cook whole vegetables—onion, garlic or eggplant—in foil. Let the packet cook on the side of the grill for 15 or 20 minutes. To see if a vegetable is done, you just press it with your tongs. If it gives easily, it's ready. Drizzle soy sauce on top and dig in."

PUBLISHED BY TEN SPEED PRESS, $25

BONE-IN CHICKEN BREAST
with soy sauce

SERVES 4

- 1 tablespoon rice vinegar
- 1 tablespoon mirin
- 1 tablespoon sake
- 2 teaspoons *shichimi togarashi* (see Editor's Note)
- 2 teaspoons *sansho* (see Editor's Note)
- 1 tablespoon grated fresh ginger
- 1 tablespoon sesame oil
- ½ cup soy sauce
- 4 bone-in chicken breast halves (3 to 4 pounds)

EDITOR'S NOTE

Shichimi togarashi is a Japanese seasoning blend that includes chiles, sesame seeds and orange peel. Lemony-flavored *sansho* is ground Sichuan peppercorns.

EDITOR'S WINE CHOICE

Rich, spicy Gewürztraminer: 2010 Navarro Vineyards

One of Tadashi's culinary mantras is, "I love to cook birds with bones." Why bones? The chicken's skeleton acts as a conduit for heat, so it helps cook the inside of the bird while you grill it. And as it cooks, the bones release their own juices and flavors, so the meat turns out incredibly tasty and moist. Case in point, this dish. You'll be amazed how tender this breast turns out, and so appealing, too, lavished with soy sauce and other traditional Japanese flavors.

Mix together the rice vinegar, mirin, sake, *shichimi togarashi, sansho,* ginger, sesame oil, and soy sauce in a bowl to make the marinade. Pour three-fourths of the marinade into a baking dish or rimmed sheet pan; reserve the rest for brushing on the chicken as it grills. Lay the chicken breasts in the marinade and flip them 4 times to generously coat all sides. Once they're coated, marinate the chicken for 15 minutes.

Preheat a grill to medium heat. Remove the chicken from the marinade. Grill the chicken, covered, for a total of about 20 minutes this way: Start by grilling the chicken skin side down for about 9 minutes. Flip the chicken, brush on the reserved marinade, and grill for another 9 minutes. Grill the chicken for 2 minutes more, flipping twice, and brushing on more marinade after each turn. The breasts are ready when they are browned and glossy. Let the chicken rest for 3 minutes. Slice and serve.

TURKEY BURGER
with quick barbecue sauce

SERVES 4

BARBECUE SAUCE

- 1 tablespoon miso
- ¼ cup ketchup
- 1 tablespoon mirin
- 1 tablespoon sake
- 2 teaspoons sesame oil

TURKEY BURGER

- 1 pound ground turkey
- 1 tablespoon red miso
- 2 tablespoons sesame oil
- 2 teaspoons sake
- ½ teaspoon *sansho* (see Editor's Note on previous page)
- ¼ cup chopped scallions (white and green parts)

EDITOR'S WINE CHOICE
Medium-bodied, red cherry–rich
Pinot Noir: 2009 Wairau River Estate

Here's Tadashi's take on a turkey burger, Japanese style, accompanied by a quick and easy barbecue sauce. In Japan, hamburger is usually served as "hamburger-steak," that is, a patty served on a plate covered in sauce. You can enjoy your turkey burger this way, too, or—sacrilege—stick it in a bun.

To prepare the sauce, mix together the miso, ketchup, mirin, sake, and 2 teaspoons sesame oil in a bowl. Divide the marinade equally between 2 separate bowls (you'll use half the barbecue sauce for grilling and half for dabbing on the finished burgers). Set aside.

To prepare the burgers, mix together the ground turkey, miso, 1 tablespoon of the sesame oil, sake, *sansho,* and scallions in a large mixing bowl. Knead the meat until it becomes sticky and binds together; divide the mixture into 4 equal parts. For each patty, use your palms (coated with the remaining 1 tablespoon sesame oil to prevent sticking) to roll 1 part into a ball, then flatten the ball by shifting it from hand to hand, until you form a ½-inch-thick patty (patting like this compresses the meat and removes air pockets, which will prevent even heat distribution). Press down in the center of each patty to make an indentation, which prevents the burger from puffing up into a ball as it grills. Place each patty on a piece of aluminum foil to make it easier to transfer to the grill. (Remove the aluminum foil before grilling.)

Preheat a grill to medium. Grill the burgers for about 8 minutes, flipping once, until they're nicely browned. Brush on the barbecue sauce and grill for 1 more minute, flipping once, and brushing on more barbecue sauce after turning. Let the burgers rest for 2 minutes. Spoon the reserved barbecue sauce on top and serve.

SALMON WITH SHISO PESTO

SERVES 4

2 pounds salmon fillet,
   cut into 4 pieces
Salt
2 bunches shiso leaves
   (about 20 leaves), thinly sliced
½ cup olive oil
1 tablespoon soy sauce

EDITOR'S WINE CHOICE
Vibrant, minerally Italian white:
2010 Colle dei Bardellini Vigna
U Munte Vermentino

Lightly season the salmon fillets with salt on all sides. Let them rest at room temperature for 30 minutes. Wipe off moisture that accumulates on the surface of the fish with paper towels.

Add the shiso leaves, olive oil, soy sauce, and salt to the jar of a blender, cover, and pulse until the pesto is smooth, about 1 minute. Reserve 2 tablespoons of the pesto and set aside. Pour the remaining marinade into a baking dish or rimmed sheet pan. Lay the salmon fillets in the pesto and gently turn them 4 times to generously coat all over.

Preheat a grill to medium-hot. Brush the cooking grate clean and oil it well. Grill the salmon for about 6 minutes for medium-rare (8 minutes for well done), turning once. If the salmon is more than 1 inch thick, grill it for about 2 minutes top and bottom and about 1 minute on each side. Right before you pull the fillets off the grill, dab the reserved marinade on top. Serve immediately.

The Japanese herb shiso gives salmon a slightly minty flavor.

PORK CHOPS WITH YUZU-MISO MARINADE

SERVES 4

- ¼ cup red miso
- 1 tablespoon sake
- 1 tablespoon mirin
- 2 teaspoons red *yuzu kosho* (see Editor's Note)
- ¼ cup finely chopped scallions (white and green parts)
- 1 tablespoon plus 1 teaspoon sesame oil
- 4 bone-in pork chops (about 1½ pounds)

EDITOR'S NOTE
Yuzu kosho is a hot, spicy and aromatic Japanese condiment made from hot chiles and ultra-citrusy yuzu zest.

EDITOR'S WINE CHOICE
Bold, juicy rosé: 2011 Artazuri

With these pork chops, you marinate the meat in miso overnight for two reasons: First, it takes time for the pork to absorb the miso flavor. Second, it gives the active bacteria cultures in miso time to tenderize the meat. The result is tender, lip-smacking chops with a pleasing touch of heat from the yuzu kosho.

Mix together the miso, sake, mirin, *yuzu kosho,* scallions, and sesame oil in a bowl to make the marinade. Pour three-fourths of the marinade into a baking dish or rimmed sheet pan and reserve the rest for brushing on the pork as it grills. Lay the pork chops in the marinade and flip them 4 times to generously coat all over. Marinate the pork chops for 12 hours, or overnight, in the refrigerator.

Preheat a grill to a two-zone fire (medium and hot). Grill the pork chops for about 10 minutes this way: Start on hot heat for about 1 minute, then shift the chops to medium heat. After about 4 minutes, flip the chops, brush on the reserved marinade, and repeat the two-zone grilling on the other side. When the pork is ready, it'll be glossy and juicy on the outside. Let the pork chops rest for about 2 minutes and serve.

YUAN YAKI–STYLE GRILLED SPANISH MACKEREL

SERVES 4

- ½ cup soy sauce
- ½ cup mirin
- ½ cup sake
- 2 ounces fresh ginger, peeled and thinly sliced (about ¼ cup)
- 1 lemon, thinly sliced crosswise
- 4 Spanish mackerel fillets with skin (1½ to 2 pounds total)

Canola oil, for brushing

EDITOR'S WINE CHOICE
Concentrated, citrusy Riesling:
2010 Hugel Tradition

Yuan yaki *is a Japanese cooking method that involves marinating ingredients in a deliciously sweet-and-sour mix of soy sauce, mirin, sake and citrus. Ono uses Spanish mackerel here but also suggests other firm-fleshed fish, such as grouper, striped bass or tilefish.*

1. In a large glass baking dish, combine the soy sauce with the mirin, sake, ginger and lemon. Spoon about 2 tablespoons of the marinade into a small bowl and reserve. Add the fish to the baking dish, turn to coat and refrigerate, turning once, for about 30 minutes.

2. Light a grill or preheat a grill pan. Remove the fish from the marinade and brush with oil. Grill over moderately high heat, turning once, until lightly charred and cooked through, about 6 minutes. Transfer the fish to a platter and brush with the reserved marinade. Serve right away.

TADASHI ONO ONLINE
thejapanesegrill.com

PLENTY

yotam ottolenghi

why we love this book

This vegetarian collection from London chef and *Guardian* food columnist Yotam Ottolenghi includes beautiful, often rich vegetable dishes boldly flavored with intriguing spices—his Green Bean Salad, for instance, calls for mustard, coriander and nigella seeds (page 178). Some recipes are clearly Mediterranean, like the Marinated Pepper Salad (page 176); others are definitely Middle Eastern. Either way, as he says, "they are as substantial and basic as any cut of meat."

overlooked vegetables

"People don't cook many roots and tubers, like turnips, rutabagas and parsnips. They seem old-fashioned and not as sexy as tomatoes or courgettes [zucchini], but I think there is a lot of potential in them. For example, even in winter I would make a root vegetable slaw with some dried cherries, sour cream, scallions, chives, oil and a good vinegar—then you've taken something humble and given it a lot of sparkle."

on vegetarian food

"Meat has always been very central to the British diet, but I think that people have begun to realize that it makes a lot of sense—for both environmental and health reasons—to eat more vegetables. So it seems that Londoners were ready for my food, which presents vegetables and pastas and grains in a very exciting way. I'm not a vegetarian—I probably have meat every other day. But I do think that you can have less meat and fish and still feel completely satisfied."

his perfect meal

"It would have to include many elements, because I am always disappointed with one main dish. I prefer the Middle Eastern–Mediterranean style of dining, with meze or tapas. For me, a meal should be a whole experience made up of many little things. Just a little bit of everything would satisfy me. I'm very modest."

PUBLISHED BY CHRONICLE BOOKS, $35

MARINATED PEPPER SALAD WITH PECORINO

SERVES 2 AS A STARTER

- 1 red bell pepper, quartered
- 1 yellow bell pepper, quartered
- 4 tablespoons olive oil

Salt

- 1 tablespoon balsamic vinegar
- 1 tablespoon water
- ½ teaspoon muscovado sugar
- 2 thyme sprigs
- 1 garlic clove, thinly sliced

Black pepper

- 2 tablespoons flat-leaf parsley, leaves picked
- ⅔ cup basil leaves
- 1 cup watercress
- 2 ounces mature pecorino, shaved
- 1 tablespoon drained capers

Crusty bread is essential to soak up the sweet dressing left after finishing this salad.

Preheat the oven to 375°F. Toss the peppers with 1 tablespoon of the oil and a little salt. Scatter in a roasting pan and roast for 35 minutes, or until they soften and take on some color. Remove to a bowl and cover it with plastic wrap. Once cooled to room temperature, peel the peppers and cut into thick strips.

Whisk together 2 tablespoons of the oil, the balsamic vinegar, water, sugar, thyme, garlic, and some salt and pepper. Pour this over the peppers and leave aside for at least an hour, or overnight in the fridge.

To assemble the salad toss together the herbs, watercress, drained pepper strips, pecorino and capers. Add the remaining 1 tablespoon olive oil and 1 tablespoon (or more if you like) of the marinade. Taste and adjust the seasoning as needed.

Tuck this salad inside a baguette for a vegetarian sandwich.

GREEN BEAN SALAD
with mustard seeds & tarragon

SERVES 4

1¼ cups green beans, trimmed
2¼ cups snow peas, trimmed
1¾ cups green peas (fresh or frozen)
2 teaspoons coriander seeds, roughly crushed with a mortar and pestle
1 teaspoon mustard seeds
3 tablespoons olive oil
1 teaspoon nigella seeds
½ small red onion, finely chopped
1 mild fresh red chile, seeded and finely diced
1 garlic clove, crushed
Grated zest of 1 lemon
2 tablespoons chopped tarragon
Coarse sea salt
1 cup baby chard leaves (optional)

This salad—offering a good balance of clean freshness from the beans with the punchy complexity of the herbs and spices—works in plenty of contexts. Try it as a side dish with grilled lamb chops.

Fill a medium saucepan with cold water and bring to the boil. Blanch the green beans for 4 minutes, then immediately lift them out of the pan and into iced water to refresh. Drain and dry.

Bring a fresh pan of water to the boil and blanch the snow peas for 1 minute only. Refresh, drain and dry. Use the same boiling water to blanch the peas for 20 seconds. Refresh, drain and dry. Combine the beans, snow peas and peas in a large mixing bowl.

Put the coriander seeds, mustard seeds and oil in a small saucepan and heat up. When the seeds begin to pop, pour the contents of the pan over the beans and peas. Toss together, then add the nigella seeds, red onion, chile, garlic, lemon zest and tarragon. Mix well and season with salt to taste.

Just before serving, gently fold the chard leaves, if using, in with the beans and peas, and spoon the salad onto plates or into bowls.

Nigella seeds give this salad a slight oniony taste.

CRUSTED PUMPKIN WEDGES
with sour cream

SERVES 4

- 1½ pounds pumpkin (skin on)
- ½ cup grated Parmesan
- 3 tablespoons dried white breadcrumbs
- 6 tablespoons finely chopped parsley
- 2½ teaspoons finely chopped thyme
- Grated zest of 2 large lemons
- 2 garlic cloves, crushed
- Salt and white pepper
- ¼ cup olive oil
- ½ cup sour cream
- 1 tablespoon chopped dill

You can use most varieties of pumpkin for these satisfying wedges. Serve with green gazpacho to make a light and healthy-feeling supper. They will also make a perfect veggie main course for Christmas as the crust is a bit like stuffing.

Preheat the oven to 375°F. Cut the pumpkin into ⅜-inch-thick slices and lay them flat, cut-side down, on a baking sheet that has been lined with parchment paper.

Mix together in a small bowl the Parmesan, breadcrumbs, parsley, thyme, half the lemon zest, the garlic, a tiny amount of salt (remember, the Parmesan is salty) and some pepper.

Brush the pumpkin generously with olive oil and sprinkle with the crust mix, making sure the slices are covered with a nice, thick coating. Gently pat the mix down a little.

Place the pan in the oven and roast for about 30 minutes, or until the pumpkin is tender: stick a little knife in one wedge to make sure it has softened and is cooked through. If the topping starts to darken too much during cooking, cover loosely with foil.

Mix the sour cream with the dill and some salt and pepper. Serve the wedges warm, sprinkled with the remaining lemon zest, with the sour cream on the side.

YOTAM OTTOLENGHI ONLINE

ottolenghi.co.uk

🅑 @ottolenghi

ESSENTIAL PÉPIN

jacques pépin

why we love this book

One of the world's most famous TV chefs and food educators distills six decades of cooking into this 750-recipe, 685-page book. The dishes here are a "diary of my life," says F&W contributing editor Jacques Pépin, who includes recipes that reflect his childhood growing up as the son of restaurateurs near Lyon (like his mother's chicken ragout, page 187) as well as dishes he discovered in America, like grits. Though Pépin trained in some of France's most legendary restaurants, the food here is humble, simple and frugal.

on his eclectic cooking style

"For many people, I may be the quintessential French chef, but I'm also influenced by my wife, who was born in New York City to a Cuban father and a Puerto Rican mother, so I don't really feel like a 'French' chef anymore. I make things like ceviche, fried chicken, black bean soup, chicken in a lemon-ginger sauce (page 186)—these are not French recipes."

updating pépin for 2012

"Many things have changed since some of these recipes were originally written: the amount of fat people use, the cooking times for vegetables and fish. The updated recipes retain the spirit and flavor of the originals, but they're more usable, friendly and current."

cooking improv

"The greatest food comes from *cuisine d'opportunité,* just by using leftovers. You take some demiglace and tomato sauce, then sauté a kidney, deglaze with wine and so on. You build the flavors without thinking."

the importance of technique

"Food trends change, but basic techniques do not, whether it's boning a chicken or making an omelet. To become a great cook you have to become a technician. The only way to do that is through endless repetition."

PUBLISHED BY HOUGHTON MIFFLIN HARCOURT, $40

BROCCOLI VELVET PUREE

SERVES 4

- 1½ pounds broccoli
- 1½ cups water
- ¾ teaspoon salt
- 1 garlic clove
- 1 teaspoon coarsely chopped jalapeño pepper
- 2 tablespoons unsalted butter
- 1 tablespoon extra-virgin olive oil

This is a delicious way to serve broccoli. First I cook it with some garlic and jalapeño pepper until it is tender. Then I emulsify the mixture with a little butter and olive oil in a blender to create a smooth, creamy puree.

Cut the broccoli heads from the stalks and separate the florets. Peel the stalks and cut them into 2-inch-long pieces.

Bring the water to a boil in a medium saucepan. Add the broccoli, salt, garlic, and jalapeño pepper and bring back to a boil over high heat. Cover the pan and cook for 10 minutes, or until the broccoli is very tender.

Transfer the broccoli and ⅔ cup of the cooking liquid to a blender. Add the butter and oil and blend for about 1 minute, until the mixture is very smooth. Serve.

HALIBUT STEAKS GRENOBLE-STYLE

SERVES 4

- ¼ cup olive oil
- 2 slices firm white bread, crusts trimmed and cut into ¾-inch cubes (about 1 cup)
- 1 large lemon
- 1 teaspoon salt
- ½ teaspoon freshly ground black pepper
- 4 halibut steaks (about 6 ounces each and ¾ to 1 inch thick)
- ¼ cup all-purpose flour
- 8 tablespoons (1 stick) unsalted butter
- 3 tablespoons drained capers
- 2 tablespoons chopped fresh parsley

EDITOR'S WINE CHOICE
Vibrant, citrusy Sauvignon Blanc: 2010 Domaine Bailly-Reverdy La Mercy-Dieu Sancerre

Sautéed halibut sprinkled with a garnish of croutons, lemon, and capers and some brown butter is simple and tasty. The garnish is also excellent with other fish, from trout and sole to cod and catfish.

Heat 2 tablespoons of the oil in a large skillet until hot. Add the bread cubes and cook, turning them with a spoon, until uniformly browned on all sides. Drain in a sieve and set aside.

Using a sharp knife, remove the rind and white pith from the lemon. Cut the flesh into ½-inch cubes, removing the seeds as you go. (You should have about ⅓ cup.)

Sprinkle the salt and pepper on both sides of the fish and dip the steaks in the flour to coat on all sides; shake off any excess flour.

Heat 3 tablespoons of the butter and the remaining 2 tablespoons oil in a large heavy skillet. When the mixture is foaming, add the fish and cook over medium heat for about 3 minutes. With a wide spatula, turn the fish and cook for another 3 minutes, or until browned and crusty on both sides.

Arrange the fish on a serving platter with the nicest side showing. Sprinkle the croutons, lemon, and capers on top and set in a warm place (such as a 150°F oven).

Melt the remaining 5 tablespoons butter in a skillet and cook until it takes on a hazelnut color. Pour the hot butter on top of the fish, sprinkle with the parsley, and serve.

SPICY GINGER & LEMON CHICKEN

SERVES 1

- 1 teaspoon olive oil
- 1 whole chicken leg (10 to 12 ounces), skin removed, tip of drumstick cut off

Pinch of salt

- ⅛ teaspoon chili powder
- ⅛ teaspoon ground cumin

Pinch of dried thyme

Pinch of cayenne pepper

- ½ teaspoon all-purpose flour
- ½ teaspoon finely grated lemon rind
- ½ teaspoon finely grated orange rind
- 1 teaspoon chopped ginger
- 1 small garlic clove, crushed and chopped
- ¼ cup apple cider
- ¼ cup water

EDITOR'S WINE CHOICE
Juicy, spicy Gewürztraminer:
2011 Gundlach-Bundschu

Intended for people who dine alone, this dish is made with a single chicken leg that is skinned and then cooked with a sweet-and-spicy mixture that is especially complementary to the meat. It can be prepared ahead and reheated at serving time.

Heat the oil in a large stainless steel saucepan until it is hot but not smoking. Add the chicken leg and brown it over medium-high heat, turning occasionally, for 10 to 12 minutes.

Add the salt, chili powder, cumin, thyme, cayenne, flour, citrus rinds, ginger, garlic, cider, and water and bring to a boil. Reduce the heat to low, cover, and cook gently for 15 minutes.

Serve the chicken with the sauce.

MY MOTHER'S CHICKEN RAGOUT

SERVES 4

- 1 tablespoon canola or safflower oil
- 4 whole chicken legs (about 2½ pounds), skin removed
- 4 ounces salt pork, as lean as possible, or pancetta, cut into ½-inch pieces
- 6 scallions, trimmed (leaving some green) and cut into ½-inch pieces (⅔ cup)
- 1 large onion, coarsely chopped (1¼ cups)
- 2 teaspoons all-purpose flour
- 1¼ cups water
- ½ cup fruity dry white wine (such as Sémillon or Sauvignon Blanc)
- 2 large garlic cloves, crushed and coarsely chopped (1 teaspoon)
- ½ teaspoon dried thyme
- 2 bay leaves
- ½ teaspoon salt
- 1 pound small Red Bliss potatoes (8 to 10), peeled
- ¼ teaspoon Tabasco sauce (optional)
- 2 tablespoons coarsely chopped fresh parsley

EDITOR'S WINE CHOICE
Fresh, strawberry-scented Beaujolais: 2010 Château Thivin Brouilly

JACQUES PÉPIN ONLINE
kqed.org/food/jacquespepin

@jacques_pepin

The taste of certain dishes you had as a child stays in your memory forever. This is one of those dishes for me.

In France, salt pork is called lard—*hence the name* lardons, *for the small pieces that we add to stews and other dishes. Look for a salt pork slab with as much meat on it as possible, or use pancetta. The stew tastes even better when made ahead and reheated at serving time.*

Heat the oil in a large heavy stainless steel saucepan until hot. Add the chicken legs and sauté over medium heat for 6 to 8 minutes, turning occasionally, until lightly browned on all sides.

Meanwhile, place the salt pork or pancetta in a saucepan with 2 cups water, bring to a boil, and boil for 1 minute. Drain in a sieve and rinse under cold water.

When the chicken is browned, transfer it to a plate. Add the salt pork or pancetta to the drippings in the pan and sauté, partially covered (to prevent splattering), over medium heat for 5 minutes, or until browned. Add the scallions and onion, mix well, and cook for 1 minute, stirring occasionally. Add the flour, mix well, and brown the mixture for about 1 minute, stirring.

Add the water and wine and mix well. Stir in the garlic, thyme, bay leaves, and salt and bring to a boil, stirring occasionally. Add the potatoes and chicken legs, bring back to a boil, and boil very gently, covered, over low heat for 30 minutes.

Add the Tabasco, if desired, stir, sprinkle with the parsley, and serve.

Buttermilk panna cottas, page 190

MIETTE

meg ray with leslie jonath

why we love this book

Inspired by the *pâtisseries* of Paris, San Francisco's Miette bakery and candy shop is a pastel-hued, fondant-filled place of impeccable triple-layer cakes, artisanal marshmallows and dainty bags of tea cookies. For owner Meg Ray, "presentation is as important as the pastry itself," but her flavors are just as memorable, from her airy Banana Bread with Nutty Streusel (page 197) to her signature Fleur de Sel Caramels (page 191), cooked to exactly 246 degrees to achieve their wonderful chewy-yet-soft texture.

small-scale sweets

"Miette's cakes are small partly because I'm fond of small things. But I also think that a six-inch cake is an elegant sufficiency. I carry this sense of proportion through everything we do at the bakery, from bite-size cookies to individual custards. We adopted the principle of less is more, also taking a page from the Japanese: Small is better; balance is everything."

on organic baking

"My goal isn't to make the most delicate cake—which is usually flavorless. My goal is to make the most delicious cake using organic, unrefined ingredients. I use real, full-fat organic butter; I use organic cane sugars and flours from local mills. I want to challenge the stereotype of earthy 'hippy' organic baking with light, tender and elegant cakes and pastries."

baking essentials

"I cannot do anything in a kitchen until I tie my apron strings tightly around my waist. I also must have an offset spatula, a thermometer, bowls for *mise en place*, parchment paper and disposable pastry bags."

beyond her comfort zone

"Red velvet cake. I'm certain I wouldn't be able to dump that much food coloring in anything I was going to eat."

PUBLISHED BY CHRONICLE BOOKS, $27.50

BUTTERMILK PANNA COTTA

MAKES TWELVE TO FOURTEEN
2-OUNCE PANNA COTTAS

- 2 cups heavy cream
- 1 teaspoon unflavored gelatin powder (about ½ packet)
- ⅓ cup (2⅓ ounces) sugar
- ⅓ vanilla bean
- 1 cup plus 2 tablespoons buttermilk

Fresh berries, finely diced, for garnish

The tangy buttermilk and vanilla bean make this panna cotta a luscious base for any summer fruit, including strawberries, raspberries, and blueberries.

In this recipe, we use powdered gelatin. Be sure to measure the gelatin since the amounts that come in the packages will vary. Also be sure to follow the directions on the package to fully dissolve the gelatin so the dessert is smooth and properly set.

1. In a medium bowl, pour in ⅓ cup of the cream and scatter the gelatin evenly over the surface. Leave the gelatin to soften for at least 10 minutes. Arrange 14 clean small jars in a baking pan and clear space in your refrigerator for the pan.

2. Meanwhile, combine the remaining 1⅔ cups cream and the sugar in a medium saucepan. Split the vanilla bean lengthwise and scrape the seeds into the cream. Bring to a boil and add the dissolved gelatin mixture into the hot cream. Add the buttermilk to the cream mixture and whisk to combine. Strain the mixture through a medium-mesh strainer into a container with a spout, such as a glass measuring cup.

3. Pour the mixture into the jars just to the base of the neck. Cover the pan with plastic wrap and refrigerate overnight to set the panna cottas. Garnish with the fresh berries. These will keep in the refrigerator, covered with plastic wrap, for up to 3 days; garnish just before serving.

FLEUR DE SEL CARAMELS

MAKES SIXTY-FOUR
1-INCH SQUARE CARAMELS

1½	cups heavy cream
1¼	cups whole milk
2	cups (14 ounces) granulated sugar
1¼	cups (8 ounces) light brown sugar
1	teaspoon kosher salt
2	tablespoons unsalted butter
½	cup light corn syrup
3	tablespoons water

Fleur de sel for sprinkling

Although many people feel they have to choose between a hard and soft caramel, Miette's are right in the middle. The trick to controlling the texture is in the temperature, so you must use a calibrated candy thermometer and watch it very carefully. If you let the temperature rise above 246°F, the result will be a hard, chewy candy. If it doesn't reach that temperature, the caramel will be gooey and pale. We make our caramels dark and buttery with flakes of fleur de sel to finish. We also make Lemon Verbena and Chocolate variations, which are included.

Be sure to cook the caramel in a medium saucepan (at least 6 quarts), as the bubbling mixture will double in volume.

1. Butter the bottom and sides of an 8-inch square baking dish or casserole. Line the bottom with a piece of parchment paper long enough to extend over two opposite sides by about 3 inches, to use later as handles, if needed.

2. In a medium saucepan, combine the cream, milk, granulated and brown sugars, salt, butter, corn syrup, and water. Clip a candy thermometer to the side of the pan. Place over medium-low heat and cook, whisking constantly, until the mixture reaches 246°F, 30 to 40 minutes.

3. When the caramel reaches the correct temperature, remove it from the heat and pour into the buttered pan, scraping out any caramel clinging to the sides of the pan. Be careful because the caramel is very hot. Let the caramel cool for 15 minutes and sprinkle with fleur de sel, then let cool completely to room temperature. Wrap the baking dish in plastic wrap and refrigerate the whole pan for at least 30 minutes and up to 1½ hours to help it set up and make cutting the caramels easier.

continued on page 192

FLEUR DE SEL CARAMELS *continued*

4. To remove the caramel from the pan, loosen the sides by running the tip of a knife around the edges. Lift the caramel out using the parchment paper "handles." If it resists, warm the bottom of the pan briefly with a kitchen torch or over a stove burner. Turn the caramel out onto waxed paper on a cutting board. Measure 1-inch intervals along the sides, and then cut the caramel into 1-inch squares. Peel the caramel squares from the parchment paper.

5. Wrap each caramel in a square of waxed paper or candy cellophane and twist both ends. Store in an airtight container for up to 10 days.

LEMON VERBENA OR BERGAMOT CARAMELS
Stir ¼ teaspoon verbena or bergamot essential oil into the caramel right after you remove it from the heat. Proceed as directed, omitting the fleur de sel.

CHOCOLATE CARAMELS
Add 8 ounces finely chopped 62 percent cacao chocolate to the ingredients and cook, whisking constantly, until the mixture reaches 230°F. Proceed as directed, including the fleur de sel.

ENGLISH TOFFEE

MAKES ABOUT 3½ POUNDS

- 2 cups (9½ ounces) whole almonds (more if coating both sides)
- 1 cup (8 ounces) unsalted butter
- 1 cup (7 ounces) sugar
- 1 tablespoon vanilla extract
- 1½ teaspoons salt
- ⅓ cup water
- 1½ pounds 70 percent cacao chocolate (more if coating both sides)

Miette's version of this classic candy is crisp, crunchy, and especially thin. Our English Toffee is coated in dark chocolate, then tossed in roasted almonds. Our American version [pictured at right] uses milk chocolate and roasted peanuts. Both versions need to be stored in airtight containers.

Make sure you have a pan big enough to spread your toffee thin. A Silpat baking mat is essential to this recipe as it allows you to remove the toffee easily from the pan.

Miette's toffee is coated on both sides with chocolate and nuts. You have the option of stopping at one, but we've provided instructions for coating the second side.

1. Preheat the oven to 350°. Line a baking sheet with sides (a jelly-roll pan) with a silicone baking mat.

2. Toast the almonds on a second baking sheet in the oven until lightly browned, 8 to 10 minutes. Let cool and chop finely.

3. In a medium saucepan, combine the butter, sugar, vanilla, salt, and water over low to medium-low heat. Clip a candy thermometer to the side of the pan. Cook, whisking, until the butter has melted and the mixture has emulsified. Increase the heat to medium-high and cook, whisking constantly at a consistent speed, until the mixture reaches 300°F, 15 to 20 minutes.

4. Pour the hot toffee onto the prepared baking sheet. Be careful as the toffee is very hot. Using an offset spatula, spread into a thin, even layer over the entire baking sheet and let cool for at least 45 minutes before adding the chocolate.

5. Meanwhile, place the chocolate in a heatproof bowl on top of a pot of simmering water and gently stir with a rubber spatula until it has melted completely, looks smooth, and is no more than 110°F. Wipe off any excess oil on top of the toffee with a paper towel. Spread the top of the cooled toffee with the warm chocolate and sprinkle with the nuts. Let set at room temperature until hard, 20 to 30 minutes.

continued on page 196

This toffee
(see next page)
is coated
on both sides
with milk
chocolate and
salted peanuts.

ENGLISH TOFFEE *continued*

6. If desired, once the first side has set, invert the toffee onto a second sheet pan. Remove the Silpat and cover the second side with additional chocolate and nuts.

7. Break the cooled toffee into pieces. Store in an airtight container at room temperature for up to 3 days.

AMERICAN TOFFEE
Substitute milk chocolate and lightly salted peanuts for the dark chocolate and toasted almonds. Proceed as directed.

BANANA BREAD WITH NUTTY STREUSEL

**MAKES FOUR SMALL 5-INCH
LOAVES OR TWO STANDARD
8-INCH LOAVES**

NUTTY STREUSEL

- ½ cup (2 ounces) pecan pieces
- ¼ cup (2 ounces) firmly packed light brown sugar
- ⅓ cup (1½ ounces) all-purpose flour
- 2 tablespoons cold unsalted butter
- ¾ teaspoon ground cinnamon
- ¼ teaspoon vanilla extract
- ⅛ teaspoon kosher salt

BANANA BREAD

- 2¼ cups (11 ounces) all-purpose flour
- 1 teaspoon baking soda
- ¾ teaspoon baking powder
- 1 teaspoon kosher salt
- 1½ cups (10½ ounces) sugar
- 2 large eggs
- 1 teaspoon vanilla extract
- ½ cup vegetable oil
- 4 medium soft, but not black, bananas (about 1 pound total), peeled and roughly mashed
- ½ cup (2 ounces) pecan pieces

Full of pecans, butter, and brown sugar, the nutty streusel in this recipe was the obsession that led to Miette's beloved version of banana tea cake—a bit like getting dressed from the socks up. I asked my staff to come up with different ideas for using streusel and we had a bake-off. The banana bread was a clear winner, with the added benefit of helping us use up a continual stash of overripe bananas.

Delicate in texture, it is more of a cake than a bread and full of banana flavor. Once, one of our sly bakers put chocolate chips in the batter when I wasn't looking, and I have to admit, they are a great addition. But there are times when you want something without chocolate, so here is the pure version.

1. Liberally butter four 5-by-3-inch or two 8-by-4-inch loaf pans and dust with sifted flour. Tap out the excess flour.

2. Preheat the oven to 350°F.

3. To make the streusel: In a food processor, add the pecans, sugar, flour, butter, cinnamon, vanilla, and salt and pulse until coarsely combined. Transfer to a small bowl, cover, and refrigerate until ready to use, up to 5 days.

4. To make the banana bread: Sift together the flour, baking soda, baking powder, and salt into a bowl and set aside.

5. In the bowl of a stand mixer fitted with the whisk attachment, whisk the sugar, eggs, and vanilla on medium speed until well combined and lightened in color, 4 to 5 minutes. Reduce the speed to low and drizzle in the oil, whisking just until combined. Add the banana mash and whisk just until combined. Add the dry ingredients and pecans to the batter in three additions, whisking just to combine after each addition. Do not overmix.

continued on page 198

BANANA BREAD *continued*

6. Divide the batter between the prepared pans. Sprinkle the tops with the streusel, dividing it evenly. (You may not need all of the streusel if making the smaller loaves.) Bake until the breads have risen nicely and a tester inserted in the center comes out clean, 40 to 45 minutes for the small loaves and 45 to 50 minutes for the larger loaves. Transfer to wire racks and let cool in the pans for 20 minutes. Run an offset spatula around the edges of the pans, then invert the cakes onto the racks and let cool for about 20 minutes longer. Serve right away, or wrap tightly in plastic wrap and refrigerate until you are ready to serve, up to 3 days. To freeze, wrap tightly in a second layer of plastic and store in the freezer for up to 2 months. Serve at room temperature.

LEMON CLOUD CAKE

6 TO 8 SERVINGS

- 4 large eggs, separated
- ¾ cup plus 2 tablespoons granulated sugar
- 1 tablespoon finely grated lemon zest
- 2 teaspoons fresh lemon juice
- ½ teaspoon lemon extract
- ⅔ cup all-purpose flour
- ¼ teaspoon salt
- ¼ teaspoon cream of tartar

Confectioners' sugar, for dusting

Ray's lemony cake is light and a little spongy. It's great with sweet, juicy berries and freshly whipped cream.

1. Preheat the oven to 325°F. Grease and flour the bottom (but not the side) of an 8-inch tube pan. In a standing mixer fitted with the whisk, beat the egg yolks on medium speed until pale and thick, about 5 minutes.

2. In a medium saucepan, combine ½ cup plus 2 tablespoons of the granulated sugar with ¼ cup of water and bring to a boil. Insert a candy thermometer and boil the syrup until it reaches 230°F, about 3 to 5 minutes.

3. With the standing mixer at medium speed, slowly drizzle the hot syrup into the yolks, avoiding the whisk. Beat the mixture until cool, about 10 minutes. Add the lemon zest, lemon juice and lemon extract. Reduce the speed to low and beat in the flour and salt until just combined. Scrape the batter into a large bowl.

4. In another large bowl, using a handheld electric mixer, beat the egg whites with the cream of tartar at medium-high speed until frothy, about 1 minute. With the mixer on, slowly beat in the remaining ¼ cup of granulated sugar until stiff peaks form, about 2 minutes.

5. Fold one-third of the beaten egg whites into the batter until incorporated. Gently fold in the remaining egg whites until no streaks remain. Scrape the batter into the prepared pan and bake for 35 to 40 minutes, until the cake is golden and springy and a toothpick inserted in the center comes out clean.

6. Transfer the pan to a rack, invert it and let the cake cool completely. Invert the pan again, run a thin metal spatula around the side of the pan and tube, then invert the pan once more and carefully unmold the cake onto a plate. Dust with confectioners' sugar, cut into wedges and serve.

MEG RAY ONLINE

miette.com

 Miette

 @miettecakes

MADE IN ITALY

david rocco

why we love this book

On his TV show *Dolce Vita,* David Rocco translates authentic dishes from all over Italy into simple recipes. He isn't a chef but he's an excellent cook, and his book has an easygoing feel that's appealing to beginners—recipes call for a handful of this, a splash of that.

an italian-canadian childhood

"My parents were born in Italy; growing up in a Waspy neighborhood in Toronto was tough for me. We felt like the poor immigrants—my friend had a bunny as a pet; we had bunny on the dinner table. My dad cut my first hockey stick in half and used it to prop up tomato vines. I was embarrassed about being Italian, but I came around. I realized we were pretty progressive as a family about food; we had olive oil and buffalo mozzarella in the seventies, and no one had that back then! After seeing the plasticky cheese my friends would call mozzarella in their fridge, I began to think, 'Wow, maybe we're not the poor immigrants after all.'"

letting ingredients do the work

"I joke that 'I'm not a chef. I'm Italian.' But it's true: I don't have formal training. My training is tied to my upbringing and travels in Italy. There's a basic technique in my recipes, then a lot of assembling and letting the ingredients do all the work. For my Penne alla Trapanese (page 204), you could just throw the ingredients in a food processor to make the sauce. People try my food and say, 'Oh my God!' But seriously, my four-year-old could do this. That's the beauty of Italian cooking!"

most overlooked region of italy

"Italians only really discovered Puglia in the last five years, and now you are starting to see more tourists there. The dishes are very rustic: sausage and peppers, roasted potatoes. One of my grandmothers was from Puglia and she was not an innovative or 'good' cook; she served simple food that you couldn't mess up."

PUBLISHED BY CLARKSON POTTER, $35

CAVOLFIORI STUFATI AL POMODORO
the best cauliflower ever

PER 4 PERSONE

- 1 large head cauliflower
- 1 medium white onion
- ½ cup (125 milliliters) cubed hard cheese, rinds on (optional)
- ¼ cup (60 milliliters) extra-virgin olive oil
- 1 bunch fresh flat-leaf parsley, chopped

Salt and freshly ground pepper, QB (see Editor's Note)

- 2 cups (500 milliliters) tomato purée
- ½ cup (125 milliliters) water
- ½ cup (125 milliliters) freshly grated Parmigiano-Reggiano cheese

EDITOR'S NOTE

According to Rocco, QB, or *quanto basta,* is "a cooking philosophy that suggests that you use 'as much as you need.'"

EDITOR'S WINE CHOICE

Dry *frizzante* red: 2010 Francesco Vezzelli Grasparossa di Castelvetro Lambrusco

To many people, there's nothing very exciting about cauliflower. In fact, it always seems like an old auntie's dish. But when it's cooked a certain way, with some great cheese, I think that it reaches incredible heights. It cooks up to a luxurious silky texture.

Stewed cauliflower is a one-pot meal and so simple that your ten-year-old can make it. You can call him about forty-five minutes before you get home and let him know that "it's time to start cooking, son!" The hardest thing is cutting up the cauliflower, and that's not hard at all. The smaller the pieces, the faster this cooks.

Cut the cauliflower into small pieces and set aside.

Finely chop up your onion. Now look in your fridge. If you have chunks of tough Parmigiano or cheese that hasn't been properly wrapped, that's perfect! That's exactly what you want. Now is their time to shine. Cube up the tough cheese, rinds and all.

In a fairly large pot, heat up the olive oil and add your onions. Cook until they're translucent. This is your *soffritto,* or your flavor base. Throw in the chopped parsley and all your cauliflower. Give it all a good mix. Add a generous amount of salt and pepper, then add the puréed tomatoes and water. Mix again, lower your heat to medium, put the lid on and let it cook, checking on it every so often, for 40 minutes. Take it off the heat. (I like to give it a fairly rough mix and mash down any large pieces of cauliflower with the back of my spoon.) Now add the pieces of cheese and the grated Parmigiano. Mix it very well and let it rest for 10 to 15 minutes. It will thicken up. This tastes best served warm or at room temperature. Call me an old auntie, but cauliflower alone is one of my absolute favorites.

Consider tossing this cauliflower with pasta to make it more substantial.

PENNE ALLA TRAPANESE
penne trapani style

PER 4 PERSONE

- 1 pound (500 grams) penne
- 7 ounces (200 grams) almonds
- 1 large bunch fresh basil leaves
- 1 clove garlic
- 1 pound (500 grams) fresh tomatoes, peeled and seeded

Extra-virgin olive oil, QB
(see Editor's Note on page 202)

Salt and freshly ground pepper, QB

- 5 ounces (150 grams) Parmigiano-Reggiano or aged pecorino cheese, grated

EDITOR'S WINE CHOICE
Lively Sicilian white: 2010 Occhipinti SP68 Bianco

This dish has a cold, pesto-like sauce, made with a mortar and pestle, that is very typical of the western part of Sicily, in the area of Trapani. This is another example of the simplicity of Italian cooking. Even if I didn't give you exact measurements, I bet you'd still knock it out of the park. Note that some people roast their almonds before making this dish. But if they're fresh, there's no need.

If you're using a food processor, you could throw everything for the sauce in at once if you wanted to. But I recommend going old school and preparing one ingredient at a time. It's much more interesting, and you can see the pesto evolve. So, after putting the penne on to cook, start by using a cutting board and a mezzaluna to chop your almonds, basil and garlic into a coarse meal, and then put that into your mortar. Then go for your tomatoes: give them a good rough chop and add them. Now, add a little olive oil, some salt and pepper and, with the pestle, crush and mix everything together into a beautiful pesto. Finish the pesto with your grated cheese of choice and more olive oil if you need it. Taste as you go, so you can adjust the seasonings and find the right texture.

Once your penne is cooked, drain well, reserving a ladleful of cooking water. Put the pasta back in the pot with a little bit of the cooking water and your pesto, then mix to combine the sauce with the pasta, adding more cooking water as needed until you have the desired consistency.

The nutty crunch in this uncooked tomato sauce comes from almonds.

POLPETTE DI ZUCCHINE
zucchini balls

PER 4–6 PERSONE

FOR THE TOMATO SALAD

- 20   cherry tomatoes, halved
- 14   fresh basil leaves, torn
- 3   tablespoons (45 milliliters) extra-virgin olive oil

Salt and freshly ground pepper, QB (see Editor's Note on page 202)

FOR THE ZUCCHINI BALLS

- 3   large zucchini, chopped
- 1   cup (250 milliliters) cubed smoked scamorza cheese
- 1   cup (250 milliliters) cubed pecorino cheese
- 1   small bunch fresh mint leaves, finely chopped
- 2   eggs
- 1   cup (250 milliliters) bread crumbs, plus extra for coating

Salt and freshly ground pepper, QB
Flour, for dredging

- 1   cup (250 milliliters) extra-virgin olive oil

EDITOR'S WINE CHOICE
Light, lemony sparkling wine: NV Adriano Adami Garbèl Prosecco

These are wicked. The combination of zucchini and mint, blended with beautiful cheeses and then fried to a golden crust, is absolutely delicious!

Start by making the tomato salad. Toss the halved cherry tomatoes, basil, olive oil and salt and pepper together in a bowl. Set aside.

Boil the zucchini in salted water for 5 minutes. Drain, and when the zucchini is cool enough to handle, squeeze out the excess water.

In a mixing bowl, combine zucchini, the cheeses, mint, eggs, bread crumbs and salt and pepper. Mix well until ingredients are well combined. Roll the mixture into the shape and size of golf balls and then gently flatten with the palm of your hand. Lightly dredge them in flour, then in bread crumbs. Heat your olive oil in a frying pan, and when it's hot, put in the balls and fry until they're golden and crispy on both sides. Remove them to a plate covered with an absorbent paper towel to soak up any excess oil.

Serve the zucchini balls with a little of the tomato salad on top.

SPAGHETTI ALLA RAVELLESE

PER 4 PERSONE

- 1 pound spaghetti
- 4 large eggs, beaten
- ¾ cup milk
- 1 cup freshly grated Pecorino Romano cheese, plus more for serving
- ¾ cup extra-virgin olive oil
- 2 medium zucchini, thinly sliced crosswise
- 2 garlic cloves, crushed

Kosher salt and freshly ground pepper

EDITOR'S WINE CHOICE
Fruity Italian white: 2010 Terredora di Paolo Greco di Tufo

Zucchini grows in abundance in the southern Italian mountain town of Ravello, for which this vegetarian dish is named. Here, Rocco tosses sautéed zucchini and pasta in a silky carbonara-style sauce.

1. In a large pot of boiling salted water, cook the spaghetti until just done, about 12 minutes. Drain.

2. In a medium bowl, whisk the eggs with the milk and 1 cup of cheese.

3. In a very large skillet, heat the olive oil until shimmering. Add the zucchini and garlic and cook over high heat, stirring occasionally, until nicely browned, about 8 minutes. Discard the garlic and season the zucchini with salt and pepper. Add the spaghetti to the skillet and toss to combine. Add the egg mixture and cook over low heat, tossing vigorously, until the sauce is creamy and the pasta is coated, about 2 minutes. Season with salt and pepper. Transfer the pasta to bowls and serve right away, passing additional cheese at the table.

DAVID ROCCO ONLINE

davidrocco.com

🅵 David Rocco

🆃 DavidRoccosVita

Fried fideos for Mexican-style noodles, page 212

TRULY MEXICAN

roberto santibañez with jj goode
& shelley wiseman

why we love this book

Truly Mexican, by chef Roberto Santibañez of New York City's Fonda, is a master class on an essential building block of Mexican cuisine: sauces—namely, salsas, guacamoles, adobos and moles. You'll need to stock up on Mexican chiles and bring out the blender, but the end results are incredibly versatile, as in an adobo made with guajillos (page 220) that can be used as a marinade for meat, a braising liquid or a taco topping.

his childhood in mexico

"When I was growing up, the women in my family cooked from morning to evening. And they loved having me around. I remember peeling almonds with a cloth, picking out the stones from the rice and beans—the kitchen was like my playground. From pretty early on, I had a sense that I wanted to be a chef. So my parents said, 'If you want to cook, you have to go to a good cooking school.' When I graduated from high school, they sent me to the Cordon Bleu in Paris."

essential tools

"A blender. Another one: a blender. And a third one? A blender. To create smooth sauces, like for my Pork in Adobo (page 218), you must have a blender. A food processor will never, ever get the job done."

key mexican cooking technique

"The European way to roast is to first rub or drizzle food with oil. In Mexico, we dry roast—no oil, no nothing. You need to char the ingredient by itself to develop the right flavors. You can cook the vegetables and chiles for my Mexican-Style Noodles (page 212) in a toaster oven; you can roast almost anything in that little tray."

easiest recipe

"A tomato salsa made in the blender—a piece of garlic, a chile and a tomato, plus enough salt to brighten the flavors—is one of the most wonderful things."

PUBLISHED BY JOHN WILEY & SONS, $35

BLUE CHEESE GUACAMOLE

guacamole con queso azul

MAKES ABOUT 2½ CUPS
ACTIVE TIME: 20 MINUTES
START TO FINISH: 20 MINUTES

- 2 tablespoons finely chopped white onion
- 1 tablespoon minced fresh jalapeño or serrano chile, including seeds, or more to taste
- 1 teaspoon kosher salt, or ½ teaspoon fine salt
- ¼ cup chopped cilantro, divided
- 1 tablespoon freshly squeezed lime juice, or more to taste
- 1 large or 2 small ripe Mexican Hass avocados, halved and pitted
- ¼ cup coarsely chopped smoked almonds, divided
- 3 tablespoons crumbled blue cheese, divided

You might think I came up with this recipe just to make Diana Kennedy cringe. But blue cheese and avocado do make a truly delicious union that, as any fan of the Cobb salad understands, is not as odd as it sounds. I typically use the best stuff I can find at the cheese counter, such as Roquefort, Cabrales, or Danish Blue, but even the already crumbled blue cheese you find in a good grocery store will be delicious.

Mash the onion, chile, salt (the coarseness of kosher salt will help you make the paste), and half of the cilantro to a paste in a molcajete or mortar. You can also mince and mash the ingredients together on a cutting board with a large knife or a fork, and then transfer the paste to a bowl. Stir in the lime juice.

Score the flesh in the avocado halves in a crosshatch pattern (not through the skin) with a knife and then scoop it with a spoon into the mortar or bowl. Add the rest of the cilantro and most of the almonds and blue cheese, toss well, and mash coarsely with a pestle or fork. Season to taste with additional lime juice and salt.

Garnish with the rest of the almonds and blue cheese.

Serve it with tortilla chips.

This guacamole is best served right away.

Smoked almonds and blue cheese reinvent the classic recipe.

MEXICAN-STYLE NOODLES
fideos secos

SERVES 4 TO 6 AS A
MAIN COURSE, OR 8 TO 12
AS A FIRST COURSE
ACTIVE TIME: 1 HOUR
START TO FINISH: 1½ HOURS

FOR THE SAUCE

- ½ pound tomatoes (about 2 small)
- 2 dried árbol chiles, wiped clean and stemmed
- ¼ pound tomatillos (2 to 3), husked and rinsed
- 4 guajillo chiles, wiped clean, stemmed, slit open, seeded, and deveined
- 2 ancho chiles, wiped clean, stemmed, slit open, seeded, and deveined
- ½ cup finely chopped white onion
- 5 garlic cloves, peeled

One 1-inch piece canela (Mexican cinnamon)

- 1½ teaspoons cumin seeds
- 1 teaspoon dried oregano, preferably Mexican
- 1 teaspoon fine salt, or 2 teaspoons kosher salt
- ½ teaspoon sugar
- 5½ cups chicken stock

FOR THE NOODLES

- 1 pound fideo noodles or thin spaghetti, such as capellini or spaghettini
- ½ cup mild olive oil or vegetable oil
- 2 pasilla chiles, wiped clean and stemmed
- 10 large sprigs cilantro
- 6 large sprigs flat-leaf parsley
- 6 large sprigs mint

One 3-inch piece canela (Mexican cinnamon)

continued on page 214

It's almost an everyday thing for Mexicans to eat soups swimming with fideos, the thin little noodles that you also see in Spain. But this preparation is more like a pasta dish, or what Mexicans often call sopa seca, or "dry soup." The fabulous sauce made with anchos and guajillos is absorbed by the slippery little noodles, and the whole thing is crowned with toppings like salsa, avocado, cheese, and crema. You have to try this.

MAKE THE SAUCE Set the oven or toaster oven to broil and preheat. Alternatively, you can preheat the oven to 500°F. If you're using the oven broiler, position the rack 8 inches from the heat source. Core each tomato and cut a small "X" through the skin on the opposite end. Put the tomatoes, cored side up, árbol chiles, and tomatillos on a foil-lined baking pan, and roast, turning over the chiles frequently until they're brown with some blackened spots, about 8 minutes. Continue to roast the tomatoes and tomatillos until the tomatoes are blackened and cooked to the core, and the tomatillos turn a khaki-green color, turning the tomatillos over once halfway through, 20 to 30 minutes. Slip the skin from the tomatoes.

Soak the guajillo and ancho chiles along with the toasted árbol chiles in enough cold water to cover until they're softened, about 30 minutes. Drain and discard the soaking water.

Blend the chiles, tomatoes, tomatillos, onion, garlic, canela, cumin, oregano, salt, and sugar in the blender jar with 1½ cups of the chicken stock until the mixture is smooth, about 3 minutes. Strain through a medium-mesh sieve into a bowl, discarding any solids. Set the sauce aside.

PREPARE THE NOODLES Break the noodles (wrapped in a cloth so they don't scatter all over) into 2- to 3-inch pieces. If you have a very wide pot, break the noodles in half.

continued on page 214

Set out all
the garnishes
so guests
can add what
they like.

MEXICAN-STYLE NOODLES *continued*

FOR THE GARNISH

- 4 ounces queso fresco or ricotta salata, crumbled (1 cup)
- ½ cup chopped cilantro
- ½ cup Fresh Tomatillo Salsa (recipe follows)
- ¼ cup Mexican crema, crème fraîche, or sour cream, thinned slightly with water, if necessary, for drizzling
- 1 avocado, pitted, peeled, and thinly sliced
- 1 cup pork chicharrones, crumbled (see Editor's Note)

EDITOR'S NOTE
Pork chicharrones are fried pork rinds. They are available at many Mexican grocery stores.

EDITOR'S WINE CHOICE
Strawberry-inflected, zippy rosé: 2011 Quivira

Heat the oil in a wide 6- to 7-quart heavy pot set over medium-high heat until it shimmers. Fry the whole pasilla chiles in the oil, turning once or twice until puffed and crisp, about 1 minute total. Transfer to paper towels to drain. When cool, thinly slice the chiles crosswise and reserve them for garnish.

Working in about 4 batches, fry the noodles in the same oil, stirring and turning constantly with 2 flat-bottomed wooden spoons (or tongs) so they fry evenly, until they are a reddish-golden brown, about 2 minutes. Transfer the browned noodles to a large bowl lined with paper towels to drain.

Remove all but 2 tablespoons of the oil from the pot, if necessary, then carefully pour the sauce into the pot (it may splatter). Fry the sauce over medium heat, stirring frequently, until it thickens slightly, about 5 minutes. Stir in 4 cups of the chicken stock, then add the fried noodles, stirring briefly to coat them with sauce, and bring the liquid to a boil.

Tie the cilantro, parsley, mint, and canela into a bouquet with kitchen string and drop it into the pot. Reduce the heat to medium-low, cover the pot, and simmer the noodles until they are tender and have absorbed the sauce, about 10 minutes. Discard the bouquet of herbs and canela.

Serve the noodles in soup bowls topped with all the garnishes, including the fried pasilla chiles.

MAKE AHEAD The cooked noodles keep for up to three days in the refrigerator. Put them in a baking dish with a little chicken stock to moisten them, then cover with foil and rewarm them in a 350°F oven for 20 to 30 minutes.

MAKES 1½ CUPS
ACTIVE TIME: 15 MINUTES
START TO FINISH: 15 MINUTES

½ pound tomatillos (5 or 6), husked,
    rinsed, and coarsely chopped
½ cup chopped cilantro
2 fresh serrano or jalapeño chiles,
   coarsely chopped, including
   seeds, or more to taste
2 tablespoons chopped white onion
1 large garlic clove, peeled
¾ teaspoon fine salt, or
   1½ teaspoons kosher salt

FRESH TOMATILLO SALSA *salsa verde cruda*

Let me be dramatic for a second: I live for this salsa! Few things make me happier than going to my favorite taquerias in Mexico City, ordering tacos with carnitas, barbacoa, or other tasty braised meats, and spooning on salsa verde cruda. Really, though, I'll add it to almost anything that benefits from a bolt of tartness and spiciness. It always amazes me that a salsa that takes so little effort can deliver such tremendous flavor. You just toss tomatillos, such unassuming little fruits, along with a few other easy-to-find ingredients in the blender, puree, and you're done. Each time you make it, it'll get even better as you get a sense of the balance of flavors—tweaking the level of tomatillos' acidity with a little lime juice and adding just the right amount of salt to make it all sing.

Put the tomatillos in the blender jar first, then add the remaining ingredients. Blend until the salsa is very smooth (the tomatillo seeds will still be visible), at least a minute. Season to taste with additional chile and salt, and blend again.

This salsa tastes best no more than a few hours after you make it.

BLENDING STUBBORN TOMATILLOS It takes a minute or so for the blades of the blender jar to catch raw chopped tomatillos. Once they do, all the ingredients will be pulled toward them. Be patient, and do not add any water. If the tomatillos don't liquidize after a minute or so, stop the blender, prod them with a wooden spoon, and try to blend again.

CHICKEN IN CHUNKY TOMATILLO SAUCE
pollo entomatado

SERVES 6
ACTIVE TIME: 30 MINUTES (NOT
INCLUDING MAKING THE SALSA)
START TO FINISH: 3 HOURS (NOT
INCLUDING MAKING THE SALSA)

- 3 pounds chicken pieces
- ½ teaspoon fine salt, or 1 teaspoon kosher salt
- 1 teaspoon freshly ground black pepper
- 2 teaspoons dried oregano, preferably Mexican
- 1 tablespoon mild olive oil or vegetable oil
- 1 recipe Chunky Tomatillo Sauce (recipe follows)
- 1 cup water
- Distilled white vinegar to taste
- ½ cup chopped scallions
- 2 tablespoons chopped fresh epazote leaves (about 8; see Editor's Note)

EDITOR'S NOTE
Epazote, a pungent herb with pointed leaves, is available at Latin markets.

EDITOR'S WINE CHOICE
Watermelon-scented rosé: 2011 Castello di Ama

This easy, delicious braise makes a phenomenal dinner, whether you serve the tender, tangy, saucy chicken (duck or pork would be lovely, too) with tortillas and rice or crusty bread and potatoes. I strongly suggest you find epazote and use it here, but if you can't, just omit it.

Pat the chicken pieces dry, then rub them with the salt, pepper, and oregano. Marinate, covered and chilled, for at least 2 or up to 6 hours.

Heat the oil in a 5- to 6-quart wide heavy pot over medium-high heat until it shimmers. Brown the chicken pieces in batches without crowding the pot, turning occasionally, 8 to 10 minutes per batch.

Return all the chicken pieces to the pot, add the chunky tomatillo sauce and the water, and bring the liquid to a simmer. Cook, covered, over medium-low heat until the chicken is cooked through, about 30 minutes. Season to taste with vinegar and additional salt, and serve sprinkled with the scallions and epazote.

Serve it with corn tortillas and Mexican white rice.

MAKE AHEAD This dish keeps in the refrigerator for up to three days or in the freezer for up to one month.

CHUNKY TOMATILLO SAUCE *entomatado*

This sauce is as easy as chop, sauté, and simmer. The chunky, sweet-tart result is just the thing for cooking chicken or pork and reminds me of my dinners at home as a boy in Mexico City.

MAKES 4 CUPS
ACTIVE TIME: 30 MINUTES
START TO FINISH: 1 HOUR

- 3 tablespoons mild olive oil or vegetable oil
- 1 large white onion, sliced
- ½ teaspoon fine salt, or 1 teaspoon kosher salt
- 4 large garlic cloves, finely chopped
- ¼ cup chopped canned chipotles in adobo, including sauce
- ¼ cup grated piloncillo, or brown sugar (see Author's Note)
- 2 pounds tomatillos (20 to 24), husked, rinsed, and cut into eighths

One 5-inch piece canela (Mexican cinnamon)
- 1 large sprig epazote, optional (see Editor's Note on previous page)
- 1 tablespoon white distilled vinegar, or more to taste

Heat the oil in a 4- to 5-quart wide heavy pot over medium heat until it shimmers. Add the onion slices and the salt, and cook, stirring, until the onions are translucent, about 5 minutes. Add the garlic, chipotles in adobo, and piloncillo and cook, stirring, about 1 minute. Add the tomatillos, cinnamon, epazote, and vinegar. Stir and bring the mixture to a simmer. Cook, covered, over medium-low heat until the tomatillos have broken down but the sauce is still chunky and the liquid is slightly syrupy, about 30 minutes. Season to taste with additional salt and vinegar. Discard the epazote and cinnamon.

AUTHOR'S NOTE Piloncillo is a type of Mexican raw sugar that has a lovely molasses-like flavor and comes in a pestle-shape block. It is available at Mexican grocery stores or by mail order.

MAKE AHEAD This salsa keeps in the refrigerator for up to five days or in the freezer for up to one month.

PORK IN ADOBO
cerdo en adobo

SERVES 6
ACTIVE TIME: 45 MINUTES
(INCLUDES MAKING THE ADOBO)
START TO FINISH: 2¾ HOURS
(INCLUDES MAKING THE ADOBO)

- 2 pounds pork shoulder or other pork stewing meat, cut into 1½-inch cubes
- ½ teaspoon fine salt, or 1 teaspoon kosher salt
- 2 tablespoons mild olive oil or vegetable oil
- 1½ cups Basic Guajillo Adobo (recipe follows)
- 2 cups water or chicken stock, or more if necessary

Sugar and vinegar, if necessary

EDITOR'S WINE CHOICE
Juicy, fruit-forward Garnacha: 2010 Bodegas Borsao Monte Oton

As browned chunks of pork shoulder simmer away in chocolate-brown liquid, they virtually melt into some of the most tender, luscious bites you will ever eat. The sauce becomes equally impressive, even richer and silkier than it was when it first hit the pan. By the time the pork is done, the adobo will have acquired amazing depth of flavor. Make sure to tinker with the salt, sugar, and vinegar levels to reignite its spark.

Pat the pork dry and season it with the salt. Heat the oil in a 4- to 5-quart heavy pot over medium-high heat. Brown the pork, in two batches if necessary (you want to avoid crowding the pot, though a little crowding is OK in this case), turning occasionally, 8 to 10 minutes per batch.

Reduce the heat to medium and return all the pork to the pot. Carefully pour the adobo over the pork. If the adobo is in the blender, swish a little liquid around in the jar and add it to the pot. Simmer, stirring to coat the pork and fry the sauce, until the sauce is slightly thicker, about 5 minutes. Add the 2 cups of water or stock and return the sauce to a simmer.

Reduce the heat to low, cover the pot, and gently simmer the pork, adding a couple of tablespoons of water from time to time to maintain a silky texture (you don't want it to be gloppy), until the pork is fork-tender, 1½ to 2 hours. If you prefer, you can cook the pork, covered, in an ovenproof pot in a 350°F oven for the same length of time. Season to taste with sugar, vinegar, and additional salt.

Serve it with corn tortillas, rice, beans, or any other side dish you like. Or turn it into tacos, enchiladas, or tamales.

MAKE AHEAD Pork in adobo keeps in the refrigerator for up to five days or in the freezer for up to one month.

continued on page 220

PORK IN ADOBO *continued*

MAKES 1½ CUPS
ACTIVE TIME: 15 MINUTES
START TO FINISH: 45 MINUTES

- 3 ounces guajillo chiles (12), wiped clean, stemmed, slit open, seeded, and deveined
- ¾ cup water for blending, or more if necessary
- 2 garlic cloves, peeled
- 1½ teaspoons apple cider vinegar
- ¾ teaspoon fine salt, or 1½ teaspoons kosher salt
- ¾ teaspoon sugar

Rounded ¼ teaspoon ground cumin

BASIC GUAJILLO ADOBO *adobo de guajillo*

Depending on where they live, Mexican cooks build on this simple recipe by adding cloves or cinnamon or oregano, so feel free to tweak the recipe yourself by adding just a hint of spices—a clove or a few peppercorns, for instance. But first, try it at its most basic and see how just a few ingredients can add up to such great flavor. I love to marinate fish and shrimp in this adobo, but it's also delicious with meats like chicken and steak.

Heat a comal, griddle, or heavy skillet over medium-low heat, and toast the chiles 2 or 3 at a time, turning them over and pressing down on them with tongs frequently, until they're fragrant and their insides have changed color slightly, about 1 minute per batch. Soak the chiles in enough cold water to cover until they're soft, about 30 minutes. Drain and discard the soaking water.

Put the ¾ cup of fresh water in the blender jar with the chiles and the remaining ingredients. Blend until smooth, at least 3 minutes, adding a little more water if necessary to puree. If you'd like a silky texture, strain the adobo through a medium-mesh sieve.

Now you can use this highly flavored puree as a marinade for seafood and meat. Or turn it into a fabulous cooking liquid or sauce for eggs, beans, and enchiladas.

MAKE AHEAD This adobo keeps in the refrigerator for up to five days or in the freezer for up to one month.

STEWED FRANKFURTER TORTAS

MAKES 4 TORTAS

- 1 tablespoon extra-virgin olive oil
- 1 pound all-beef hot dogs, sliced crosswise into ¼-inch pieces
- 1 small white onion, halved lengthwise and thinly sliced crosswise
- 2 jalapeños, halved lengthwise and thinly sliced crosswise
- 2 garlic cloves, minced
- 2 bay leaves
- 1 large tomato, finely diced
- 1 chipotle in adobo sauce, minced

Kosher salt

- ½ cup refried beans
- 4 large Portuguese or kaiser rolls, split
- 2 tablespoons unsalted butter, softened
- ¼ cup mayonnaise
- 1 Mexican Hass avocado, thinly sliced

Santibañez revamps franks 'n' beans to fill these tortas *(Mexican sandwiches), adding flavor with jalapeño and chipotle chiles.*

1. In a large skillet, heat the olive oil until shimmering. Add the hot dogs, onion, jalapeños, garlic and bay leaves. Cook over moderately high heat, stirring occasionally, until the onions are softened and the hot dogs are slightly browned, about 10 minutes. Add the tomato and chipotle and cook over moderate heat, stirring occasionally, until the tomato is broken down and the mixture is slightly thickened, about 8 minutes. Season with salt. Discard the bay leaves.

2. In a microwavable bowl, microwave the refried beans at medium power until hot, about 1 minute.

3. Heat another large skillet. Brush the cut sides of the rolls with the butter and toast over moderate heat until golden brown. Transfer the rolls to a work surface and spread each with 1 tablespoon of the beans and ½ tablespoon of the mayonnaise. Spoon the hot dog mixture onto the bottoms of the buns and top with the sliced avocado. Close the sandwiches and serve right away.

MAKE AHEAD The stewed hot dogs can be refrigerated overnight. Reheat gently before proceeding.

ROBERTO SANTIBAÑEZ ONLINE

robertosantibanez.com

 Roberto Santibañez

MICHAEL'S GENUINE FOOD

michael schwartz & joann cianciulli

why we love this book

The first cookbook from Miami chef Michael Schwartz translates the straightforward and carefully sourced food of his acclaimed restaurant Michael's Genuine Food & Drink for the home cook. Schwartz's dishes don't adhere to one single flavor profile—there are Moroccan spices, Asian flavors, Latin ceviches and recipes as all-American as slow-roasted St. Louis ribs. Holding everything together is his attitude that cooking should be "all about practicality, flavor and time."

his hero chef

"When I was 22, I moved out to Los Angeles and got a job at Wolfgang Puck's Chinois on Main. Working for Wolfgang was a real eye-opener—different ingredients, different approach and different techniques than what I was used to. The Asian flavors were influential, helping me create dishes like Chile Chicken Wings (page 224), but Wolfgang's fearlessness in trying new things also helped shape my own style."

on sweet-and-savory dishes

"I love contrasts: hot and cold, crunchy and smooth, savory and sweet. Certain fruits are particularly good in savory dishes, like peaches, plums, persimmons and apricots. Apricots are especially terrific with gamey meats like lamb, a classic Moroccan combination that I use in my Roasted Sweet Onions Stuffed with Ground Lamb and Apricots (page 228)."

on florida produce

"The growing season in South Florida is completely backwards for ingredients like tomatoes, zucchini and corn; it starts in late November and extends through Easter. So our height of season is in the winter. In the summer, when it's too hot for those crops, we move on to mango, papaya and other tropical fruits. And then we're lucky to get tomatoes, zucchini and corn in the northern part of the state. Florida is the best of both worlds."

PUBLISHED BY CLARKSON POTTER, $35

CHILE CHICKEN WINGS
with creamy cucumbers

SERVES 4

- ½ cup sweet chile sauce, such as Mae Ploy
- 2 tablespoons tahini (sesame seed paste)
- 1 teaspoon rice vinegar
- 1 teaspoon soy sauce
- 1 teaspoon chopped garlic
- 1 teaspoon chopped fresh ginger
- 2 pounds chicken wings, preferably free-range

Canola oil, for deep-frying
Cilantro leaves
Sliced scallion
Creamy Cucumbers (recipe follows)

EDITOR'S WINE CHOICE
Dark cherry–scented, peppery
Malbec: 2010 Durigutti

These may resemble traditional Buffalo wings in appearance, but a blend of soy sauce, tahini, ginger, garlic, and Asian chile sauce (available at Asian markets) makes these wings major-killer. This sauce is bangin' and can be used on grilled anything. Instead of typical celery and blue cheese, a cool side of cucumbers, Greek-style yogurt, and fresh mint finishes this dish.

Combine the chile sauce, tahini, vinegar, soy, garlic, and ginger in a blender and process on high speed for 10 seconds. Set the chile sauce aside until ready to use or refrigerate for up to 1 week.

Cut off the chicken wing tips and discard. Split the wings in half at the joint to make wings and drumettes. Have your butcher do this if you want. Rinse the chicken wings and pat thoroughly dry.

Heat 3 inches of oil to 350°F in a countertop electric fryer or deep pot. If you don't have a deep-fry thermometer, a good way to test if the oil is hot enough is to stick the end of a wooden spoon or chopstick in it. If bubbles circle around the end, then you're good to go.

Carefully add the wings to the hot oil and fry in batches until they are crispy and float to the surface, 8 to 10 minutes. Transfer the wings to a large bowl. Add enough of the chile sauce to coat and toss well.

To serve, arrange the wings on a platter and garnish with cilantro and scallion. Serve immediately with the creamy cucumbers and the remaining chile sauce on the side for dipping.

BAKED CHILE CHICKEN WINGS
If you want to go the healthier route, you can bake instead of fry the wings.

Preheat the oven to 500°F. Put the rinsed and dried wings in a mixing bowl. Coat with 2 tablespoons canola oil and season with salt and pepper, tossing to coat. Arrange the wings in a baking pan large enough to hold them in one layer. Bake, flipping them over halfway through cooking, until crispy on both sides, 20 to 25 minutes. Serve as directed.

CREAMY CUCUMBERS

MAKES ABOUT 2 CUPS

- 1   English (hothouse) cucumber
- 1   tablespoon kosher salt
- ¼   cup Greek-style yogurt
- 2   tablespoons heavy cream
- 2   garlic cloves, minced
- 1   teaspoon chopped fresh mint

Juice of 1 lemon
- ¼   teaspoon freshly ground
      black pepper

Cut the cucumber in half lengthwise. Scoop out the seeds with a teaspoon. Slice the cucumber very thinly with a mandoline or a sharp knife. Put the cucumber in a medium stainless steel or glass bowl; add the salt and mix thoroughly to combine. Set aside for 10 to 15 minutes. Transfer the cucumbers to a colander and rinse thoroughly. Squeeze dry with your hands and then pat dry with paper towels.

Put the cucumbers back into the bowl and add the yogurt, cream, garlic, mint, and lemon juice. Toss to combine; season with the pepper. Refrigerate until ready to use or for up to 2 days.

PAN-ROASTED STRIPED BASS
with tunisian chickpea salad & yogurt sauce

SERVES 4

Two 15-ounce cans chickpeas, drained
    and rinsed
  ½ small red onion, finely chopped
  ½ English (hothouse) cucumber,
    cut lengthwise, seeded, and diced
  ¼ cup fresh cilantro leaves
  2 celery stalks and leafy tops,
    chopped
  ¼ teaspoon ground cumin
  ¼ cup tomato harissa (see Editor's
    Note) or drained canned
    fire-roasted crushed tomatoes
  ½ cup extra-virgin olive oil
  2 tablespoons champagne vinegar
Kosher salt and freshly ground
    black pepper
  2 tablespoons canola oil
Four 8-ounce striped bass fillets,
    skin on, about 1½ inches thick
Yogurt Sauce (recipe follows)

EDITOR'S NOTE
Schwartz makes his own tomato
harissa—tomatoes cooked with the
fiery North African chile paste—
and includes the recipe in *Michael's
Genuine Food.*

EDITOR'S WINE CHOICE
Zesty, full-bodied Pinot Gris: 2011
Mt. Difficulty Roaring Meg

MAKES ½ CUP

  ½ cup Greek-style yogurt
Juice of ½ lemon
  1 garlic clove, minced
  1 tablespoon extra-virgin olive oil
Kosher salt and freshly ground
    black pepper

This Mediterranean-inspired dish not only is light and healthy, but also has depth of flavor with a contrast of textures and temperatures. Most home cooks tell me they're intimidated by cooking fish with skin on; they find it tears or doesn't crisp up as it should. There are two keys to success: one is patience and the other is a well-seasoned cast-iron pan, preferably one that has gone through generations of use. The second alternative is to cheat and use a nonstick frying pan.

Put ½ cup of the chickpeas in a mixing bowl. Mash the beans with a fork or potato masher until they are smashed but still have some texture. Add the remaining chickpeas, the onion, cucumber, cilantro, celery, cumin, harissa, olive oil, and vinegar; season generously with salt and pepper. Set aside at room temperature, or cover and refrigerate overnight. Return to room temperature before serving.

Preheat the oven to 450°F.

Put a large cast-iron skillet or nonstick ovenproof skillet over medium-high heat and coat with the canola oil. Pat both sides of the fish dry with paper towels and season generously with salt and pepper. When the oil is shimmering, lay the fish skin side down in the pan. Sear for 4 to 5 minutes without moving the fillets. Transfer the pan to the oven and roast until the fish is opaque, 6 to 8 minutes. Remove the pan from the oven and carefully flip the fish over with a flat spatula, so the skin side is now up; it should be brown, crisp, and make a sound when you tap it. Let the fish sit in the hot pan for a minute to sear the bottom side.

To serve, pool 2 tablespoons of the yogurt sauce on each of 4 plates, place the fish skin side up on top of the sauce, and pile the chickpea salad next to it.

YOGURT SAUCE

In a small bowl, combine the yogurt, lemon juice, garlic, and oil; season with salt and pepper. Transfer the yogurt sauce to a container, cover, and refrigerate until ready to use, for up to 7 days.

The yogurt
sauce and
chickpea salad
would
be delicious
wrapped
in warm pita.

ROASTED SWEET ONIONS
stuffed with ground lamb & apricots

SERVES 4

- 4 medium Vidalia onions (about 3 pounds)
- 1½ cups chicken stock
- ½ cup dried apricots (about 16), cut into ¼-inch pieces
- 1 teaspoon finely grated lemon zest
- 5 tablespoons unsalted butter
- ½ pound ground lamb
- 1 teaspoon ground cinnamon
- 1 teaspoon ground cumin
- 1 teaspoon kosher salt
- ½ teaspoon freshly ground black pepper
- 3 or 4 shakes habañero hot sauce
- 2 tablespoons coarsely chopped fresh flat-leaf parsley
- 2 tablespoons coarsely chopped fresh mint
- 2 tablespoons fresh bread crumbs

Arugula leaves

EDITOR'S WINE CHOICE
Juicy, cinnamon-scented Syrah:
2009 Red Car Box Car

This Moroccan-inspired recipe is one of those dishes where less is more: a big, sweet onion stuffed with cinnamon- and cumin-scented ground lamb and plump apricots. While you may be tempted to put the whole spice cabinet in the lamb filling, the simple duo of cinnamon and cumin does the trick. The fruit plays off the rich gaminess of the lamb and the spices add a subtle background flavor to tie it all together. This stuffed onion is perfect for a weeknight dinner with a green salad and steamed basmati rice, or elegant enough to make as a starter for a dinner party. The best part is that you can do this all ahead of time and just pop the stuffed onions in the oven before dinner. Sweet!

Without peeling the onions, cut about 1 inch off the top of each and just enough off the bottoms so that the onions stand upright. Reserve the onion tops and discard the bottoms. Remove all but the outer two layers of each onion by scooping out the centers with a spoon or melon baller. Set the onion shells in a baking dish, along with the tops. Set aside. Finely chop the insides.

Preheat the oven to 400°F.

In a small pot, combine the stock, apricots, and zest over medium heat. Gently simmer until the apricots are plump and the liquid is reduced to ½ cup, roughly 10 minutes.

Melt 3 tablespoons of the butter in a skillet over medium-low heat. Stir in the chopped onions and cook until soft, about 12 minutes. Add the lamb, cinnamon, and cumin to the onions. Raise the heat to medium-high; season with the salt and pepper. Cook, continually stirring with a wooden spoon, until the lamb is crumbly, 7 to 8 minutes. Do not drain the rendered fat; you need it to keep the onions moist. Remove the pan from the heat. Stir in the apricot mixture with its liquid, hot sauce to taste, the parsley, and mint. Let cool slightly. The lamb filling can easily be prepared a day in advance, covered, and refrigerated.

Spoon the lamb mixture into the hollowed-out onions, pressing down with your hands to pack it in, and mound it over the onions. Sprinkle the bread crumbs on top and dot with the remaining 2 tablespoons butter. Cover the pan tightly with aluminum foil and bake for 30 minutes. Remove the foil and continue to bake for 10 minutes, until the bread crumbs are brown. Serve immediately with a few leaves of arugula on the side.

APRICOT-BOURBON-GLAZED GRILLED CHICKEN

SERVES 4

- ½ cup bourbon
- 1 tablespoon apricot preserves
- 1 teaspoon finely grated lemon zest
- 2 tablespoons fresh lemon juice
- 2 teaspoons honey
- ½ teaspoon finely chopped thyme
- 2 tablespoons extra-virgin olive oil, plus more for brushing

Kosher salt and freshly ground pepper

One 3½-pound chicken, backbone removed

Vegetable oil, for grilling

- 3 small apricots, halved and pitted
- 1 small red onion, cut through the root end into 6 wedges
- 3 cups packed baby arugula (3 ounces)
- ¼ cup smoked almonds, chopped
- 1 tablespoon champagne vinegar

EDITOR'S WINE CHOICE
Honeyed, peach-scented Chenin Blanc: 2010 Domaine du Closel La Jalousie Savennières

Schwartz glazes chicken with a combination of bourbon, apricot preserves, lemon and honey, which creates a delightfully sweet and crispy skin.

1. In a small saucepan, carefully simmer the bourbon over moderate heat until reduced to 3 tablespoons, about 5 minutes. Remove from the heat and stir in the apricot preserves, lemon zest, lemon juice, honey, thyme, 1 tablespoon of the olive oil, ½ teaspoon of salt and ¼ teaspoon of pepper. Let the marinade cool completely.

2. Pour all but 1 tablespoon of the marinade into a large resealable plastic bag. Add the chicken and turn to coat. Let marinate at room temperature for 30 minutes.

3. Light a grill and brush the grates with vegetable oil. Remove the chicken from the marinade and turn it skin side up; flatten the breastbone with the palm of your hand. Season the chicken with salt and pepper. Turn off the heat on half of the grill. Place the chicken breast side down over indirect heat and weight it down with a large cast-iron skillet. Grill the chicken until browned, 10 to 15 minutes. Flip the chicken and grill it directly over low heat until an instant-read thermometer inserted in the thickest part of a thigh registers 165°F, 15 to 20 minutes longer. Brush the chicken with the reserved marinade and transfer to a work surface. Let rest for 10 minutes.

4. Meanwhile, brush the apricots and onion with olive oil and season with salt and pepper. Grill over moderate heat until lightly charred and the onion wedges are just softened, about 10 minutes. Let cool slightly, then coarsely chop the apricots and onion.

5. In a bowl, combine the grilled apricots and onion with the arugula and almonds. Add the vinegar and the remaining 1 tablespoon of olive oil and toss to coat. Season with salt and pepper. Carve the chicken and serve alongside the salad.

MICHAEL SCHWARTZ ONLINE

michaelsgenuine.com

 Michael's Genuine Food & Drink

 @chefmschwartz

Ricotta doughnut holes with orange-scented dipping chocolate, page 232

DESSERTED

kate shaffer

why we love this book

Kate Shaffer runs one of America's most remote chocolate shops, Black Dinah Chocolatiers, on the tiny Maine island of Isle au Haut. The California-raised baker creates elegant truffles and clever updates of classic cakes, like her signature Black Dinah Chocolate Tiramisu (page 236), which replaces the traditional coffee-soaked ladyfingers with rum-doused chocolate sponge cake. Her debut book is an intimidation-free guide to working with what she calls "the most aggravating of ingredients": chocolate.

on island life

"Our nickname for Isle au Haut is 'lug-a-haut' because you have to carry everything up and down the dock. We order a thousand pounds of chocolate at a time, so that's a lot to lug. Plus, with only about 40 full-time residents on the island, the employment pool is limited. And then we have to cut all of our own wood to heat the café, kitchen and house. It's not your normal job or life."

her favorite flavors

"My inspirations come from what arrives at my front door. For instance, my favorite truffle flavor is our local goat cheese coated with dark chocolate; it's called Chèvre and Nib. Another traditional Maine-grown ingredient I like to use is pumpkin. It's not paired with chocolate very often, but I combine the two in my Pumpkin Cheesecake with Elderberry Glaze (page 238)."

most common mistakes

"If you mess up working with chocolate, there's usually a way to fix it. Just allow plenty of time to experiment, and be patient. Overheating the chocolate turns it lumpy, and if you get a little bit of water into the melted chocolate, it will seize up. In both cases, the chocolate can't be used for tempering [prepared to use for coating and dipping], but don't throw it away. It can be salvaged for baking or hot chocolate or a sauce."

PUBLISHED BY DOWN EAST BOOKS, $30

RICOTTA DOUGHNUT HOLES
with orange-scented dipping chocolate

MAKES ROUGHLY
30 TINY DOUGHNUTS

FOR THE DIPPING CHOCOLATE
- ¼ cup bittersweet chocolate, chopped
- ¼ cup Dutch-process cocoa
- 1 cup whole milk
- ½ cup strong brewed coffee
- 2 tablespoons granulated sugar
- ⅛ teaspoon freshly grated orange zest

FOR THE DOUGHNUTS
- 1 cup whole-milk ricotta cheese
- 2 large eggs, at room temperature
- ½ cup flour
- 1½ teaspoons baking powder
- ⅛ teaspoon salt
- ⅛ teaspoon ground ginger
- ¼ teaspoon freshly ground nutmeg
- ¼ teaspoon cinnamon
- 1 tablespoon honey
- ½ teaspoon vanilla extract

Safflower oil, for frying
Confectioners' sugar, for dusting

Steve and I spent most of 2006, the year before we opened Black Dinah Chocolatiers, researching the chocolate industry and trying to make ends meet. I was no longer employed by the Keeper's House, and we still had a lot of work to do on our business plan and product line. So, Steve spent the summer earning our "capital" by hiring himself out as a house painter and carpenter, and I sent flyers to everyone on the island that I was now available for private catering events.

As a side job, Steve and I dug a long-forgotten old children's playhouse out of the woods, and after subjecting it to a few minor renovations, set it in a little grassy patch where our long driveway meets the island's main road.

Every morning, I would stock the little stand with cinnamon rolls, cakes, muffins, cookies, and pies. On Sundays I baked bread. And on Saturdays I made doughnuts. I set out a large thermos of coffee, a few paper cups, and jars of sugar and cream. We stocked an ice chest full of bottled water and natural soda and put that out there, too. Steve found an old wooden folding chair at one of his project sites, and we set that up next to the stand, along with a copy of yesterday's paper. On the ground, next to the chair, we placed an inconspicuous coffee can: the universal symbol for the honor system. It was our very first café.

Though these days, our café is just a little farther down the driveway, the menu is much the same, and includes chairs to sit in and a copy of yesterday's paper. And we still offer doughnuts on Saturdays.

Place the chopped chocolate, cocoa, milk, coffee, sugar, and zest in a medium bowl, and set the bowl over a pot of simmering water. Allow the ingredients to melt together while you make the doughnuts.

To make the doughnuts, combine the ricotta and eggs in a large bowl. Beat in the flour, baking powder, salt, ginger, nutmeg, cinnamon, honey, and vanilla extract. Mix to form a smooth batter.

Pour 2 or 3 inches of oil into a cast-iron pot, and heat to 370°F. Drop the batter by teaspoonfuls into the hot oil, turning after a minute or so. Cook for another minute and then transfer to a pan lined with paper towels. Continue until you have fried all the batter.

After you have fried the doughnuts, whisk together the dipping chocolate ingredients until the sauce is smooth. If there are still some lumps, gently re-heat and whisk again over the simmering water.

Serve the doughnuts, four or five to a person, on dessert plates, and dust with confectioners' sugar. Accompany each plate with a small bowl of dipping chocolate.

BITTERSWEET CHOCOLATE CHUNK & CREAM CHEESE SCONES

MAKES 8

- 2 large egg yolks
- 1 cup heavy cream
- 1 teaspoon vanilla extract
- 3 cups flour
- ½ cup granulated sugar
- 4 teaspoons baking powder
- ½ teaspoon baking soda
- ½ teaspoon sea salt
- 8 tablespoons unsalted butter, cold
- 4 ounces cream cheese, cold
- 1 cup chopped bittersweet chocolate

I know I'm not supposed to say things like I'm going to say right now: There are no better scones on the planet than those made by Kyra Alex at Lily's Café across the water from us in Stonington [Maine]. They are truly magical, so if you ever find yourself in the neighborhood (perhaps next summer on your way to the Isle au Haut mailboat to come see us), you simply must stop at Lily's. She makes other good stuff, too (her Cold Chinese Noodles, and a tuna melt to die for), but the scones, well, I've already said it.

That said, the following recipe—developed in my kitchen over many, many years of trying to recreate something similar in texture to my favorites—ain't half bad. In fact, they've developed their own passionate following among certain of our café clientele.

The trick with this dough is not to overwork it. That may seem like a tall order when you see how dry and shaggy the dough is before you turn it out on the board. But all I can say is have faith. If you can manage to form it into a disc, get it cut, and transferred to the sheet pan without it completely falling apart, you will be rewarded with a gem of a scone.

Preheat the oven to 400°F.

In a glass measuring cup, whisk together the egg yolks and enough heavy cream to measure 1 cup. Stir in the vanilla extract. Set aside.

In a large mixing bowl, whisk together the flour, sugar, baking powder, baking soda, and salt.

Grate the butter directly into the dry ingredients, and mix in with your hands, rubbing gently.

Cut or tear the cream cheese into small chunks, and toss into the dry ingredients. Toss in the chocolate, and stir it all together.

Pour in the egg mixture and mix quickly with a large rubber spatula. Add more cream if needed, stirring briskly, with a few strokes after any addition. You should have a crumbly mixture that barely qualifies as dough at this point.

Turn the dough onto a cutting board and quickly knead together using a bench scraper to help you form the chunky mixture into a dough that barely holds together. Flatten the dough into a disc and cut into 8 triangles with a very sharp knife. Place the triangles onto two parchment-lined cookie sheets, four to a sheet, and sprinkle the tops with sugar.

Bake for 20 to 25 minutes. Rotate the sheets once during baking. The scones are done when they are lightly browned and just firm to the touch.

VARIATION Replace the chocolate with 1 cup of frozen Maine blueberries. You may need to increase cooking time a little.

BLACK DINAH CHOCOLATE TIRAMISU

SERVES 8 TO 10

FOR THE SOAKING SYRUP
- ½ cup granulated sugar
- ½ cup dark rum

FOR THE CAKE
- ⅔ cup flour (sift before measuring)
- ⅔ cup Dutch-process cocoa (sift before measuring)
- 8 tablespoons unsalted butter
- 1 tablespoon vanilla
- 8 large eggs
- 1⅓ cups granulated sugar

FOR THE FROSTING
- 16 ounces mascarpone cheese
- 2 cups heavy cream
- ¼ cup granulated sugar
- 1 teaspoon vanilla
- 1 tablespoon instant espresso powder

If I'm ever asked if I have a signature dessert, this cake is my answer. It consists of four feather-light layers of chocolate genoise, generously soaked with sweet rum syrup. The cake is then filled and covered with an espresso-spiked mascarpone cream, scattered with whole coffee beans, and dusted with cocoa. The cake made its debut, wrapped in a satiny sheet of chocolate and crowned with Nancy Calvert's fragrant late-summer roses, at an all-chocolate dinner I gave at the Keeper's House several years ago. A glorious conclusion to the meal, and an irrefutable showstopper. I have since scaled down the presentation, but the cake is no less delicious because of it.

To make the syrup, combine ½ cup of water and the sugar in a saucepan. Bring the mixture to a boil over medium heat and cook until all the sugar has dissolved. Remove from heat.

Allow the syrup to cool completely, and then add the rum and stir. Store the syrup in a glass jar or plastic squeeze bottle in the refrigerator.

To make the cake, grease by hand, or spray with vegetable oil, two 9-by-3-inch round cake pans. Line the cake pans with parchment paper.

Preheat the oven to 350°F.

Sift the flour and cocoa together. Re-sift three more times and set aside.

Melt the butter in a small saucepan, until it starts to bubble and a layer of foam forms on the surface. Scrape off the foam with a wide spoon and discard. Pour the melted butter into a medium-size bowl, being careful not to take the cloudy, white milk solids that remain at the bottom of the saucepan. Stir the vanilla into the clarified butter.

Meanwhile, have a pot of simmering water ready. Break the eggs into the bowl of your stand mixer, whisk in the sugar, and place the bowl over the simmering water. While stirring gently, heat the mixture until it is a little warmer than room temperature. Remove from heat and immediately begin to beat at high speed with the whisk attachment for 8 to 10 minutes. The mixture is ready when it falls in ribbons that hold their shape slightly when the whisk is lifted from the bowl.

Place the bowl that contains the clarified butter over the simmering pot of water, and leave it for a minute or two while you complete the next step.

Remove the mixing bowl from its stand, and sift the flour mixture onto the surface of the egg mixture in three additions, folding with a large rubber spatula between additions.

Remove the bowl of butter from the simmering pot, and pour roughly 2 cups of the batter into the butter. With a smaller spatula, fold the butter and batter together, and then return this mixture to the larger bowl of batter. Fold together.

Empty the batter into the cake pans, smoothing the top with an offset spatula. Bake for 20 to 30 minutes, or until the cake has completely come away from the sides of the pans.

Cool completely before removing the cake from the pans. To make the frosting, beat the cheese, cream, sugar, vanilla, and espresso powder in a stand mixer with the whisk attachment until the cream is smooth and spreadable. Try not to overbeat, as the mixture tends to get grainy and will eventually separate.

To assemble the cake, cut each layer in half so that you end up with four circular layers. Place one layer on your cake plate, and douse with the rum syrup (a plastic squeeze bottle works great for this). Allow the cake to soak up the syrup. Slather on a ½-inch layer of frosting, and top with the next layer. Douse this top layer with rum syrup, and then frost.

Repeat this process for each layer. You will probably not use all the syrup. It will keep in the refrigerator until your next project.

Cover the entire cake with frosting (if necessary, smooth out the sides of the cake by trimming with a long bread knife before frosting). Reserve a little frosting for eight "turbans" on top of the cake. Pipe these on with a pastry bag and a large star tip.

Toss a couple whole coffee beans onto the tip of each turban, and then, using a fine sieve, dust the entire cake lightly with cocoa powder. Refrigerate and serve the cake well-chilled, accompanied by something bubbly to drink.

PUMPKIN CHEESECAKE
with elderberry glaze & chocolate walnut crumb crust

SERVES 10 TO 12

FOR THE CRUST

1¼ cups chocolate wafer crumbs (if I don't have homemade from the café on hand, I use Nabisco)

⅓ cup finely ground walnuts

5 tablespoons unsalted butter, melted

¼ cup granulated sugar

FOR THE FILLING AND GLAZE

1 pound canned pumpkin

1½ pounds cream cheese

1 cup granulated sugar

½ teaspoon cinnamon

¼ teaspoon nutmeg

¼ teaspoon ground ginger

6 large eggs

2 tablespoons lemon juice

One ½-pint jar elderberry jelly

Confession: I am a life-long despiser of pumpkin pie. The only thing that would make me any less American is if I hated apple pie and baseball. Fortunately, I love apple pie, and, honestly, I don't know enough about baseball to either love or hate it. But pumpkin pie? I just can't get into it. And believe me, I've tried.

But I adore pumpkin. And Thanksgiving, the pumpkin pie holiday, is my favorite holiday of the year.

For the past five years, we've had a rotating Thanksgiving dinner on the island. Whoever hosts is responsible for the turkey, but beyond that, the dinner is a structured potluck, where guests bring the dishes that either are their specialty, or which define the holiday for them. Diana Santospago, the local innkeeper, always volunteers to help with the decorations, and the host house is transformed into a glittering cornucopia of apples, bittersweet, candles, and gourds.

Usually, as long as there's plenty of stuffing and gravy, I'm good. But this particular year, I got it into my head that I had to have a pumpkin dessert. So I volunteered to make the pie.

Needless to say, there was a lot of grumbling when, at dessert time, everyone realized that the pumpkin pie wasn't a pie at all, but a cheesecake. Then we all took our first bite. And just like that, we had a new Thanksgiving tradition.

If you're not lucky enough to know someone like islander Kathie Fiveash, who makes elderberry jelly from her garden, and you can't find it in your local grocery, feel free to substitute black currant— or even blueberry—jelly.

Preheat the oven to 350°F, and grease a 9-inch springform pan with butter. Place ¼ cup of the wafer crumbs in the pan and coat the entire inside of the pan, using the same method as you would to flour a buttered cake pan. Wrap the entire outside of the pan in several layers of commercial-quality plastic wrap.

continued on page 240

An unusually
generous
amount of fresh
lemon juice
gives this cake
a bright flavor.

PUMPKIN CHEESECAKE *continued*

Place the remaining 1 cup of chocolate wafer crumbs (and any excess from the pan), walnuts, melted butter, and sugar in a medium-size bowl and mix thoroughly. Press this mixture onto the bottom of the pan.

Next, make the filling. In a food processor, blend the pumpkin and cream cheese until smooth. Add the sugar, cinnamon, nutmeg, and ginger, and process. Add the eggs, two at a time, processing until smooth after each addition. Finally, mix in the lemon juice. Scrape this filling into the pan, level the top with an offset spatula, place the springform into a roasting pan large enough to hold it, and then pour boiling water into the roasting pan so that it comes halfway up the springform.

Bake for 1½ to 2 hours, removing the pan from the oven when there is just a small wiggly area in the middle.

Take the pan out of the water, and allow it to cool completely on a rack. Chill the cheesecake thoroughly.

When you are ready to serve it, remove it from the refrigerator and release the sides of the pan. Heat the elderberry jam gently in a small saucepan over a low flame. The point is not to heat it up, but to warm it enough that it becomes liquid. Pour the resulting glaze over the entire top of the cheesecake, leveling it out with an offset icing spatula.

PERSIAN LOVE CARAMEL SAUCE

MAKES ABOUT 1¾ CUPS

- 1 cup heavy cream
- 1 tablespoon loose hibiscus-rose tea (from about 2 tea bags)
- 1 cardamom pod, cracked
- ¾ cup sugar
- ½ cup light corn syrup
- ½ vanilla bean, split and seeds scraped
- 2 tablespoons unsalted butter
- 2 tablespoons honey
- ¼ teaspoon rose water (see Editor's Note)

Vanilla ice cream, for serving

EDITOR'S NOTE
Rose water is available at health food stores and specialty food shops.

Shaffer uses this fragrant caramel as a filling for special Valentine's Day chocolates at her shop. She likes to spoon any extra sauce over vanilla ice cream.

1. In a medium saucepan, bring the cream to a simmer over moderately low heat. Remove from the heat and add the tea and cardamom. Let steep for 30 minutes. Strain the cream through a fine-mesh sieve into a small saucepan. Keep warm over very low heat.

2. Wipe out the medium saucepan and add the sugar, corn syrup, the vanilla bean and seeds and 3 tablespoons of water. Insert a candy thermometer and simmer the mixture over moderately high heat until it reaches 292°F, about 7 minutes. Reduce the heat and stir in the warm cream, the butter and honey and cook over moderately low heat until the caramel reaches 220°F, 1 to 2 minutes.

3. Remove the vanilla bean from the caramel and stir in the rose water. Transfer to a heatproof container and let cool slightly. Serve the caramel sauce warm over vanilla ice cream.

MAKE AHEAD The caramel sauce can be refrigerated for up to 2 weeks. Reheat gently in a microwave before serving.

KATE SHAFFER ONLINE
blackdinahchocolatiers.com

[f] Black Dinah Chocolatiers

*Fiorentini with guanciale, tomato
and spicy pickled peppers, page 247*

THE MOZZA COOKBOOK

nancy silverton with matt molina & carolynn carreño

why we love this book

Neither dumbed-down nor too chef-y, Nancy Silverton's *Mozza Cookbook* smartly turns the spectacular Italian food of Los Angeles's Osteria Mozza and Pizzeria Mozza (both co-owned with Mario Batali and Joe Bastianich) into recipes that require care and time but not a lot of specialized gadgets or intricate techniques. Whether the dishes are Italian classics or her California-style updates (Nancy's Chopped Salad, page 244), Silverton's food is fresh and delicious.

how to cook like an italian

"The reason the food at Mozza is so flavorful is not because it's complicated, but because the flavors are layered. There are several steps and components to each dish. For instance, the basis of our Garganelli with Ragù Bolognese (page 250) is a long and slow-cooked *soffritto*—sautéed onions, celery and carrots—that takes a few hours to cook. The recipe is not hard, it just requires time management."

on fresh mozzarella

"The original inspiration for Mozza was this mozzarella bar in Rome called Obikà, where they treat the cheese like sushi, just serving it with simple accompaniments. I'm captivated with mozzarella and those fresh-milk cheeses because they are so mild—there are so many other ingredients that go with them. I don't think a Gorgonzola bar would work!"

her perfect italian meal

"My ultimate Italian feast would definitely be outdoors, because when I think of Italy, I think of being outside. Second of all, it would be room-temperature food, set out on platters with friends around one big table, with lots of red wine. There's nothing more uncomfortable to me, as a guest at someone's house, than when the host is in the kitchen the whole time. I think the person who prepared most of the food should enjoy it!"

PUBLISHED BY ALFRED A. KNOPF, $35

NANCY'S CHOPPED SALAD

**SERVES 4 AS A STARTER
OR 2 AS A MAIN COURSE**

Half of a small red onion (halved through
    the core)
1 small head iceberg lettuce
1 medium head radicchio
1 pint small sweet cherry tomatoes
    (such as Sun Golds or Sweet 100s),
    halved through the stem ends,
    or cherry tomatoes, quartered
Kosher salt
1½ cups cooked Ceci (recipe follows)
4 ounces aged provolone,
    sliced ⅛ inch thick and cut
    into ¼-inch-wide strips
4 ounces Genoa salami,
    sliced ⅛ inch thick and cut
    into ¼-inch-wide strips
5 peperoncini, stems cut off
    and discarded, thinly sliced
    (about ¼ cup)
½ cup Oregano Vinaigrette
    (recipe follows), plus more to taste
Juice of ½ lemon, plus more to taste
Dried oregano, for sprinkling (preferably
    Sicilian oregano on the branch)

AUTHOR'S WINE CHOICE
Orvieto Classico Superiore (Umbria)

I was introduced to the concept of a chopped salad in the 1970s at La Scala Boutique, a casual offshoot, now closed, of the Beverly Hills institution La Scala. The salad, which they call the Jean Leon Chopped Salad (it's now available at the original La Scala restaurant), is made of iceberg lettuce, salami, and mozzarella, all so finely chopped that you almost don't have to chew it, then topped with ceci, or chickpeas, and a tangy red wine vinaigrette. I was totally addicted to that salad. I've been making chopped salads ever since, always with La Scala's version in mind, but the one we serve at the Pizzeria with aged provolone and Sweet 100 tomatoes is my best yet.

Separate the layers of the onion, stack two or three layers on top of one another, and slice them lengthwise 1/16 inch thick. Repeat with the remaining onion layers. Place the onion slices in a small bowl of ice water and set them aside while you prepare the rest of the ingredients for the salad. Drain the onion and pat dry with paper towels before adding them to the salad.

Cut the iceberg in half through the core. Remove and discard the outer leaves from the head and remove and discard the core. Separate the lettuce leaves, stack two or three leaves on top of one another, and slice them lengthwise ¼ inch thick. Repeat with the remaining leaves and thinly slice the radicchio in the same way.

Cut the tomatoes in half, season them with salt, and toss gently to distribute the salt.

Combine the lettuce, radicchio, tomatoes, Ceci, provolone, salami, peperoncini, and onion slices in a large, wide bowl. Season with salt and toss to thoroughly combine the ingredients. Drizzle ½ cup of the vinaigrette and squeeze the lemon juice over the salad, then toss gently to coat the salad with the dressing. Taste for seasoning and add more salt, lemon juice, or vinaigrette if desired. Pile the salad on a large platter or divide it among individual plates, piling it like a mountain. Sprinkle the dried oregano on top and serve

continued on page 246

All the
meat, cheese
and beans
make this salad
a main-
course dish.

NANCY'S CHOPPED SALAD *continued*

MAKES 2 CUPS COOKED CECI

- 1 cup ceci (chickpeas), soaked overnight
- 2 tablespoons kosher salt
- ½ cup extra-virgin olive oil
- 1 large carrot, peeled and halved
- 1 celery rib, halved
- 1 dried arbol chile
- 16 garlic cloves
- ½ yellow Spanish onion, halved

AUTHOR'S NOTES

The key to good dried beans is to cook them long enough so that they become creamy. Many restaurants undercook their beans, and frankly I would rather have canned beans than beans that are dry and chalky.

The time will vary greatly depending on how long you soaked the beans and how old the beans are; the time could be anywhere from 1 hour to as long as 4.

CECI

These days it's almost old-fashioned to cook your own beans, even for restaurants. While canned are surprisingly good (I included many canned beans in recipes in my last book, A Twist of the Wrist*), homemade beans are so much better.*

Drain the ceci and put them in a medium saucepan with enough water to cover them by 1½ inches, salt, and the olive oil. Place the carrot, celery, chile, garlic, and onion in a doubled piece of cheesecloth and tie it into a closed bundle with kitchen twine. Add the bundle to the pot with the ceci and bring the water to a boil over high heat. Reduce the heat and simmer the ceci until they are very tender and creamy, about 2 hours, adding more water to the pot as needed but never covering them by more than an inch to an inch and a half. (Cooking them in just enough water yields richer-tasting, creamier beans than if you were to just boil them in tons of water.) Turn off the heat and allow the ceci to cool in the cooking liquid. Remove and discard the cheesecloth bundle. The ceci can be prepared to this point up to a week in advance. If you are using the ceci now, drain them, reserving the cooking liquid to use as a hearty, ceci-flavored base for vegetable soup. To use later, transfer the ceci and the cooking liquid to an airtight container and refrigerate until you are ready to use. Bring the ceci to room temperature and drain them before using.

OREGANO VINAIGRETTE

We put so much dried oregano in this vinaigrette that you might think it's a typo. It's not. Because the oregano is so prominent, look for sources such as Penzeys that specialize in dried herbs.

MAKES A LITTLE OVER 1 CUP

- 2½ tablespoons red wine vinegar
- 2 tablespoons dried oregano
- 1 tablespoon fresh lemon juice, plus more to taste
- 2 garlic cloves, 1 smashed and 1 grated or minced
- ½ teaspoon kosher salt, plus more to taste
- ¼ teaspoon freshly ground black pepper, plus more to taste
- 1½ cups extra-virgin olive oil

Combine the vinegar, oregano, lemon juice, smashed garlic, grated garlic, salt, and pepper in a medium bowl and whisk to combine the ingredients. Set the vinaigrette aside to rest for 5 minutes to marinate the oregano. Add the olive oil in a slow, thin stream, whisking constantly to combine. Taste for seasoning and add more salt, pepper, or lemon juice, if desired. Use the vinaigrette or transfer it to an airtight container and refrigerate it for up to three days. Bring the vinaigrette to room temperature, whisk to recombine the ingredients, and taste again for seasoning before using.

FIORENTINI

with guanciale, tomato & spicy pickled peppers

SERVES 4

Kosher salt

¼ cup extra-virgin olive oil

5 ounces *guanciale* or pancetta, cut into small dice

8 garlic cloves

2 cups *Passata di Pomodoro* (recipe follows) or tomato sauce

1 teaspoon sugar

12 large fresh basil leaves

12 ounces *fiorentini* or another artisanal pasta shape, such as *maccheroni alla chitarra*

½ cup thinly sliced fresh Italian parsley leaves

½ cup Spicy Pickled Peppers (recipe follows, or jarred), seeded and thinly sliced

¼ cup finishing-quality extra-virgin olive oil

Wedge of Parmigiano-Reggiano, for grating

AUTHOR'S WINE CHOICE
Lamezia Rosso (Calabria)

Matt got the inspiration for this dish from the Whole Hog Dinner that the restaurant Oliveto, in Oakland, hosts every year for chefs, food professionals, and friends from all over the world. One year they served pasta with cured pork, pickled peppers, and tomato sauce, which was so good that when we got back to Los Angeles, Matt decided to make his own version.

Fiorentini *means "Florentine," but here refers to a twisted short pasta shape made by Setar, an artisanal pasta producer in Napoli. If you can't find it, use another dried, artisanally produced pasta in its place, such as* maccheroni alla chitarra, *a big tube-shaped pasta from Napoli. The tubes collapse when they cook so they're like empty ravioli.*

Fill a pasta pot or a large stockpot with 6 quarts of water, add 6 tablespoons of kosher salt, and bring the water to a boil over high heat. If you are not using a pasta pot, place a colander in the sink or have a wire strainer handy to lift the pasta out of the water.

Combine the olive oil and *guanciale* in a large sauté pan over medium-high heat and cook until the *guanciale* is golden brown and crisp, about 3 minutes. Add the garlic, reduce the heat to medium, and cook for about 1 minute, until the garlic is light golden and fragrant, stirring constantly to prevent it from burning. Add the *passata,* sugar, and 1 teaspoon kosher salt and cook for about 1 minute, to dissolve the sugar and warm the sauce. Turn off the heat and add the basil while you cook the pasta.

Drop the pasta into the boiling water, stir to prevent it from sticking together, partially cover the pot so the water returns to a boil quickly and continues boiling, and cook the pasta, using the time indicated on the package as a guide, until it's al dente. About 1 minute before the pasta is done, place the sauce over high heat. Lift the pasta out of the cooking water, or reserve 1 cup of the water and drain the pasta, and immediately add it to the pan with the sauce. Cook the pasta with the sauce for 2 minutes, stirring with a rubber spatula to stain the pasta with the sauce, adding some of the reserved pasta water if the pasta is dry and sticky instead of slippery and glistening. Turn off the heat and stir in the parsley and peppers. Add the finishing-quality olive oil, stirring vigorously and shaking the pan to emulsify the sauce.

continued on page 248

FIORENTINI *continued*

Pile the pasta in the center of each of four plates, dividing it evenly, and spoon any sauce remaining in the pan over the pasta. Use a microplane or another fine grater to grate a light layer of Parmigiano-Reggiano over each plate, and serve.

PASSATA DI POMODORO

MAKES ABOUT 1 QUART

Two 28-ounce cans whole peeled plum tomatoes, including their juices (preferably San Marzano)

¼ cup extra-virgin olive oil

1 tablespoon sugar, plus more as desired

1 scant tablespoon kosher salt

1 heaping teaspoon freshly ground black pepper

Passata *comes from the word* passare, *which means "to pass" in Italian, and* passata di pomodoro, *often referred to as* passata, *is the name given to tomatoes that have been passed through a food mill, or through a gadget made especially for the task called a* passapomodoro, *or "tomato passer." Anyone who has ever successfully tried to grow tomatoes or who has ever visited a farmers' market in the late summer knows that when the time comes, you get all the tomatoes you could ever dream of—more than you could possibly eat or give away—and you get them all at once. During this time in the Italian countryside, they pass the tomatoes through the* passapomodoro, *which extracts the skin and seeds, and bottle the sauce that is extracted. A typical Italian larder might contain dozens of these bottles, which look like wine bottles and which allow cooks to use "fresh" tomato sauce year-round. Our* passata *is a little different from a traditional* passata *in that we cook it and season it to enhance the flavor, but it is still a very pure product.*

Pass the tomatoes, including their juices, through a food mill into a large bowl.

Heat the oil in a large sauté pan over medium-high heat until the oil is almost smoking and slides easily in the pan, 2 to 3 minutes. Add the tomato purée slowly as it will splatter when it hits the oil. Stir in the sugar, salt, and pepper, and cook until the sauce thickens slightly, about 30 minutes. Use the *passata* or set it aside to cool to room temperature, then transfer it to an airtight container and refrigerate for up to several days or freeze for up to several months.

SPICY PICKLED PEPPERS

MAKES 1 QUART

- 4 cups white wine vinegar
- 2 tablespoons honey
- 1 teaspoon juniper berries
- 1 teaspoon whole cloves
- 2 teaspoons black peppercorns
- 2 dried bay leaves
- ¾ pound Fresno chiles (red jalapeño peppers), rinsed, stems left on

We pickle Fresno chiles (also called red jalapeño peppers) for the pasta dish Fiorentini *with Guanciale, Tomato, and Spicy Pickled Peppers. It seemed silly to have you pickle just enough peppers for one dish, since they will keep, refrigerated, for at least several weeks and probably much longer. Slice the peppers and add them to grilled cheese or sliced meat sandwiches. If you can wait, the peppers are even better a few days after you make them.*

Combine the vinegar, honey, juniper berries, cloves, peppercorns, and bay leaves in a medium saucepan and bring the liquid to a simmer over high heat. Reduce the heat and simmer the brine for 10 minutes to meld the flavors. Add the chiles and increase the heat to high to return the brine to a boil. Reduce the heat and simmer the chiles until they soften slightly but still hold their shape, 4 to 6 minutes. Turn off the heat and set the chiles aside to cool in the brine. Use the chiles, or transfer them, along with the brining liquid, to an airtight container and refrigerate for up to several weeks.

GARGANELLI WITH RAGÙ BOLOGNESE

MAKES OVER 1 QUART OF
RAGÙ OR ENOUGH FOR MORE
THAN 16 SERVINGS; PASTA
WITH SAUCE SERVES 6

FOR THE RAGÙ BOLOGNESE

- 2 tablespoons extra-virgin olive oil
- 8 garlic cloves
- 2½ ounces pancetta, roughly chopped or ground
- 1 cup Soffritto (recipe follows)
- ½ of a 4.5-ounce tube (¼ cup plus 1 tablespoon) double-concentrated tomato paste
- 1 pound ground veal
- 1 pound ground pork
- 2 teaspoons kosher salt, plus more to taste
- ½ teaspoon freshly ground black pepper
- ¼ teaspoon freshly grated nutmeg
- 1 cup dry white wine
- 3 cups Basic Chicken Stock (recipe follows)
- ¾ cup whole milk

FOR FINISHING & SERVING THE PASTA

Kosher salt

- ¾ cup Basic Chicken Stock (recipe follows), plus more as needed or pasta-cooking water
- 3 teaspoons unsalted butter
- 12 ounces Garganelli (recipe follows)
- 6 tablespoons finishing-quality extra-virgin olive oil
- 3 tablespoons freshly grated Parmigiano-Reggiano, plus a wedge for grating
- 3 tablespoons freshly grated pecorino romano

AUTHOR'S WINE CHOICE

Sangiovese di Romagna
(Emilia-Romagna)

Prior to his working at Del Posto, Matt went to Italy with Mario [Batali] for a story for Gourmet. *The premise of the story was that Mario was taking his chefs and the general manager from Del Posto to Italy, specifically to the center of Emilia-Romagna, to show them what it was like to eat there. They ate sixty-two courses in five days and Matt had a lot of dishes to talk about, but the one he was most excited about was the ragù bolognese he had at Diana, a restaurant just outside the main piazza in Bologna. It was as if his eyes had just been opened. He called me right after that meal: "It was rich but delicate and with a touch of sweetness," he told me. When they got back to New York, while Matt was relegated to the soup station of the kitchen, Mark Ladner and Mark's team at Del Posto attempted to create a bolognese that captured the spirit of the one at Diana. When Matt tasted Mark's version, he called me again, excited: "They did it!" he said. "They nailed it." And that—the Del Posto version of the Diana bolognese—was what Matt was going for when we opened Mozza. Having eaten at Diana myself, I can also tell you that Matt nailed it. When making bolognese, the most important thing is to go slow. You never want the meat to cook directly against the pan, because you want to braise the meat, not brown it. The "secret" to it is the Soffritto, which takes several hours to make—so give yourself time. This is slow food!*

To make the ragù, combine the oil and garlic in the bowl of a miniature food processor fitted with a metal blade or the jar of a blender and purée. Add the pancetta and purée, stopping to scrape down the sides of the bowl or jar occasionally, until the ingredients form a homogenous paste. Transfer the pancetta-garlic paste to a large sauté pan and cook over medium heat until the fat from the pancetta is rendered, about 5 minutes, stirring constantly to prevent the garlic from browning. Stir in the Soffritto and cook for about 1 minute. Move the vegetables to create a bare spot in the pan, add the tomato paste to that spot, and cook for 1 minute, stirring, to caramelize the tomato paste slightly. Add the veal and pork; season with the salt, pepper, and nutmeg; and cook, stirring occasionally, until all the juices released from the meat have cooked off and the pan is almost dry, about 10 minutes. Add the wine, increase the

continued on page 252

The pasta
finishes cooking
in the ragù,
adding flavor.

GARGANELLI WITH RAGÙ BOLOGNESE *continued*

heat to medium high, and cook until the wine has evaporated and the pan is almost dry, about 10 minutes. Add the chicken stock, bring it to a simmer, reduce the heat, and simmer the meat with the stock for about 2 hours, stirring occasionally to prevent the meat from sticking to the bottom of the pan, until the stock has almost all cooked off but the pan is not completely dry. Add the milk and simmer until the ragù returns to a thick, saucy consistency, 30 to 40 minutes. Use the ragù, or allow it to cool to room temperature, transfer it to an airtight container, and refrigerate it for up to three days; freeze it for as long as three months. Warm the ragù over medium heat before serving, adding enough water to loosen it to a saucelike consistency.

To finish and serve the pasta, fill a pasta pot or large stockpot with 6 quarts of water, add 6 tablespoons of salt, and bring the water to a boil over high heat. If you are not using a pasta pot, place a colander in the sink or have a wire strainer handy for lifting the pasta out of the water.

While the water is coming to a boil, combine 1½ cups of the ragù, the chicken stock, and butter in a large sauté pan over medium heat. Stir the ingredients to combine and heat, stirring occasionally, until the butter is melted and the sauce is warmed through, adding more chicken stock, if necessary, to obtain a loose, sauce consistency. Turn off the heat while you cook the garganelli.

Remove the garganelli from the refrigerator or freezer and drop them into the boiling water. Stir to prevent the pasta from sticking together, partially cover the pot so the water returns to a boil quickly and continues boiling, and cook the pasta until it's al dente, about 2 minutes. About 1 minute before the pasta is done, place the sauce over high heat. Lift the pasta out of the cooking water, or reserve 1 cup of the water and drain the pasta, and immediately add it to the pan with the sauce. Cook the pasta with the sauce for 2 minutes, stirring gently with a rubber spatula so you don't tear the pasta, to stain the pasta with the sauce, adding some of the reserved pasta water if the pasta is dry and sticky instead of slippery and glistening. Turn off the heat and add the finishing-quality olive oil, stirring vigorously and shaking the pan to emulsify the sauce. Add the grated Parmigiano-Reggiano and pecorino romano and stir to combine.

Pile the garganelli in the center of each of six plates, dividing them evenly, and spoon any sauce remaining in the pan over the pasta. Use a microplane or another fine grater to grate a light layer of Parmigiano-Reggiano over each plate, and serve.

SOFFRITTO

Soffritto is a combination of sautéed onions, celery, and carrots, and it is the base of much Italian cooking. We start many of our dishes by sautéing these ingredients, and then we have this, a very dark soffritto, that we cook for four hours, after which the vegetables are transformed into a rich, thick paste. We make the soffritto in big batches and use it as a starting point for many of our ragùs. This soffritto might seem oily, but don't let that scare you as it's used to start dishes where olive oil would normally be used. At the restaurant, we chop the carrots and celery in a food processor, but we chop the onions by hand to avoid their becoming a watery purée.

MAKES ABOUT 3 CUPS

- 2 cups extra-virgin olive oil
- 2 pounds Spanish onions, finely chopped (about 7 cups)
- 1 pound carrots, peeled and finely chopped (about 3½ cups)
- 1 pound celery ribs, finely chopped (about 3¼ cups)

Heat the olive oil in a large sauté pan over medium-high heat until the oil is almost smoking and slides easily in the pan, 2 to 3 minutes. Add the onions and cook for about 20 minutes, stirring frequently, until they are tender and translucent. Add the carrots and celery, reduce the heat to medium, and cook the vegetables, stirring often, for about 3 hours, until the soffritto is a deep brown caramel color and the vegetables are almost melted. If the vegetables start to sizzle and stick to the bottom of the pot, reduce the heat to low and continue cooking. Use the soffritto or let it cool to room temperature, then transfer it to an airtight container and refrigerate for up to a week or freeze for up to several months.

continued on page 254

GARGANELLI WITH RAGÙ BOLOGNESE *continued*

MAKES ABOUT 2 QUARTS

- 5 pounds chicken feet and chicken wings
- 1 Spanish onion, quartered
- 1 large carrot, peeled and cut into large pieces
- 1 celery rib, cut into large pieces
- 1 tablespoon black peppercorns

MAKES 6 SERVINGS

Dry Dough (recipe follows)
Semolina, for dusting
All-purpose flour, for dusting

BASIC CHICKEN STOCK

This is a neutral chicken stock that doesn't contain any seasonings other than peppercorns. We keep it simple because we use it in a variety of dishes, each of which will contain its own seasonings. We go through an astonishing amount of this stock and as you cook from this book, you will, too.

Put the chicken in a tall stockpot (10 quarts) and fill the stockpot with 10 cups of water, or enough to cover the chicken liberally. Bring the water to a boil over high heat, skim off and discard the gray foam that rises to the top, and continue to boil until you have skimmed the foam two or three more times. Add the onion, carrot, celery, and peppercorns, reduce the heat, and simmer the stock for about 2 hours, until the water has reduced by half. Pour the stock through a fine-mesh strainer and discard the chicken and vegetables. Use the stock or set it aside to cool to room temperature. Transfer the stock to an airtight container, or several smaller containers, and refrigerate for up to several days or freeze for up to several months.

GARGANELLI

Garganelli, which comes from the word gargala, *meaning "trachea," are hollow ridged tubes, similar to penne. We prefer garganelli for our ragù bolognese over the more traditional tagliatelle because we like the way the small bits of sauce stick to the ridges on the outside and get tucked inside the tubes. Since garganelli are also a specialty of Bologna, we think that we haven't done too much injustice to tradition. To make this shape you'll want to have a thin plastic pen on hand. We remove the ink cartridge just to be safe, and you might want to do the same.*

Roll the dough out to the third thinnest setting on the pasta sheeter (number 6 using a KitchenAid attachment). Dust a baking sheet lightly with semolina and dust a work surface with flour. Lay one sheet of pasta on your work surface and use a long knife or straight-edged rolling pastry cutter to cut the edges straight. Use the knife or rolling cutter to cut each sheet into 1½-inch-wide strips and then into 1½-inch squares. Place the squares on the prepared baking sheet, dusting them with semolina to prevent them from sticking together.

MAKES 14 OUNCES

- 1½ cups all-purpose flour, plus more for dusting
- 12 extra-large egg yolks (16 ounces of yolks), whisked together in a medium bowl

Fold a clean, dry kitchen towel a few times to form a bed and place a ridged gnocchi or pasta board on the towel. Place one square on the board with the point facing the edge of the board. Pick up the pen and place it on the pasta at the point closest to you. Push down on the pen gently and roll it away from your body so the pasta wraps around the pen to form a tube with a ridged exterior. Slide the tube off the pen onto the prepared baking sheet and repeat, rolling the remaining pasta squares in the same way. Use the garganelli or cover the baking sheet with plastic wrap and refrigerate the pasta up to one day. To freeze, place the baking sheet in the freezer until the pasta is firm to the touch. Transfer the pasta to sealable plastic bags, or an airtight container, dusting off the excess semolina, and freeze for up to two weeks (any longer and the pasta will dry out and crack).

DRY DOUGH

We use dry dough to make the pastas that we serve with our ragùs. It gets shaped into maltagliati, *garganelli*, corzetti stampati, *and* tagliatelle, *as well as other short shapes. We call it dry dough because it feels dryer than our basic pasta dough since it is made with only egg yolks and no whites.*

Put the flour in the bowl of a standing mixer fitted with the paddle attachment and begin to run the machine at low speed. With the mixer running, add the egg yolks gradually, mixing until the dough comes together. Turn off the mixer and dust a flat work surface with flour. Turn the dough out onto the dusted surface, form it into a ball, and gently knead it for 20 to 25 minutes, until the ball begins to feel elastic and the surface of the dough feels smooth and silky. Wrap the dough in plastic wrap and refrigerate to rest for at least 45 minutes and up to overnight before sheeting it (any longer and the dough will discolor).

*Butter + Cinnamon
+ Sugar = Cake, page 268*

BAKING STYLE

lisa yockelson

why we love this book

At over 500 pages long, *Baking Style* is an exciting new source of inspiration for the serious baker looking to create refined, elegant versions of classic American cakes, cookies, bars and breads. Cookbook author Lisa Yockelson is a master of texture—her Craggy-Top Sour Cream Buns (page 264), for instance, are incredibly feathery and light—and her superdetailed recipes have consistently amazing results.

her first dessert

"I started baking brownies when I was seven years old with my grandmother's recipe. I would always hover over my grandmother and mother when they were baking and occasionally mess up their ingredients. I think that's why the recipes I generate are so approachable, because they come from my earliest taste memories. Though after all my endless tweaking, my brownies are nothing like my grand-mother's in texture or style."

essential baking tools

"In addition to accurate measuring tools, all bakers should own a freestanding heavy-duty mixer (with attachments); a finely serrated, stainless steel knife for cutting bar cookies, layer cakes and breads; and a set of nesting stainless steel mixing bowls."

baking stories

"I hope my book shows how to bake wonderful things, but it also tells the stories behind the recipes—the quirks, the anxieties and the great joy. The book was a 10-year project, but it really reflects my entire life."

her culinary icons

"I have a deep respect for Rose Levy Beranbaum and Flo Braker. Their cookbooks integrated the art, craft and chemistry of baking, bringing it to a very sophisticated level, and set new standards for the literature of baking."

PUBLISHED BY JOHN WILEY & SONS, $45

MOLASSES CRINKLES

SERVING: ABOUT 3 DOZEN
COOKIES

MOLASSES AND SPICE DOUGH

- 3 cups unsifted bleached all-purpose flour
- 2½ teaspoons baking soda
- ½ teaspoon baking powder
- ½ teaspoon salt
- 1 tablespoon ground ginger
- ¾ teaspoon ground cinnamon
- ½ teaspoon ground cloves
- ¼ teaspoon ground allspice
- ½ cup plus 2 tablespoons solid shortening
- 8 tablespoons (1 stick) unsalted butter, softened
- 1½ cups granulated sugar
- 1 large egg
- 1 large egg yolk
- 6 tablespoons light unsulphured molasses
- 2½ teaspoons vanilla extract
- ¾ cup coarsely chopped crystallized ginger

SUGAR AND SPICE ROLLING MIXTURE

- ¾ cup granulated sugar blended with ¼ teaspoon ground ginger and ⅛ teaspoon ground cloves

GINGER FINISH (OPTIONAL)

About ⅓ cup small crystallized ginger chunks

For the dough, sift the flour, baking soda, baking powder, salt, ginger, cinnamon, cloves, and allspice onto a sheet of waxed paper.

Cream the shortening and butter in the large bowl of a freestanding electric mixer on moderately low speed for 4 minutes. Add the sugar in 3 additions, beating on moderately low speed for 1 minute after each portion is added. Blend in the whole egg and egg yolk. Blend in the molasses and vanilla extract. On low speed, mix in the sifted ingredients in 3 additions, beating just until the flour particles are absorbed and blending in the crystallized ginger along with the last third of the sifted mixture. Scrape down the sides of the mixing bowl frequently with a rubber spatula to keep the dough even-textured.

Refrigerate the dough, covered with a sheet of food-safe plastic wrap, for 3 hours, or until moldable and rollable into balls. (The dough can be refrigerated overnight in the covered mixing bowl.)

Preheat the oven to 375°F.

Line several cookie sheets or rimmed sheet pans with lengths of ovenproof parchment paper.

Place the sugar and spice rolling mixture in a shallow bowl handy at your work surface.

Scoop up heaping 2-tablespoon-size mounds of dough and roll into balls. Roll each ball in the sugar mixture and place on the prepared baking pans, spacing them about 3 inches apart and arranging 9 mounds to a pan. Lightly press a chunk or two of crystallized ginger into the center of each ball, if you wish.

Bake the cookies in the preheated oven for 14 minutes, or until set. Let the cookies stand on the baking pans for 1 minute, then transfer them to cooling racks, using a wide offset metal spatula. Cool completely. Store in an airtight tin.

continued on page 260

Two kinds
of ginger—
ground and
candied—
add layers of
flavor.

MOLASSES CRINKLES *continued*

AUTHOR'S NOTES An all-butter dough can replace the butter/ shortening mix; use ½ pound plus 2 tablespoons (2 sticks plus 2 tablespoons) unsalted butter, softened.

For the sugar and spice rolling mixture, make sure you blend the mixture well so that the ground ginger and cloves are well distributed within it (to dispel tiny clumps of ginger or cloves, sift, then whisk, the sugar and spices).

Roll the balls of dough in the sugar mixture to coat the surfaces lightly, but evenly.

Never consume raw cookie dough.

MAKE AHEAD 2 days.

APPLE CAKE, MAPLE BUTTER GLAZE

SERVING: ONE 9-INCH CAKE, CREATING ABOUT 12 SLICES

SPICED APPLE BATTER

- 3 cups unsifted bleached all-purpose flour
- 1 teaspoon baking powder
- 1 teaspoon baking soda
- ¾ teaspoon salt
- 1¾ teaspoons ground cinnamon
- 1 teaspoon freshly grated nutmeg
- ½ teaspoon ground allspice
- ¼ teaspoon ground ginger
- 1½ cups granulated sugar
- ½ cup firmly packed dark brown sugar
- 3 large eggs
- 1 cup neutral vegetable oil (such as soybean or canola)
- 2 teaspoons vanilla extract
- 3½ cups peeled, cored, and coarsely shredded apples

Maple Butter Glaze (recipe follows)

Preheat the oven to 350°F.

Film the inside of a fluted 9-inch tube pan (4¼ inches deep, with a capacity of 11 cups) with nonstick flour-and-oil spray.

For the batter, sift the flour, baking powder, baking soda, salt, cinnamon, nutmeg, allspice, and ginger onto a sheet of waxed paper.

Place the granulated sugar, dark brown sugar, and eggs in the large bowl of a freestanding electric mixer and beat on moderate speed for 2 minutes. With the mixer running, add the oil in a thin, steady stream. Beat on moderate speed for 2 minutes. Blend in the vanilla extract and the apples. On low speed, add the sifted mixture in 2 additions, scraping down the sides of the mixing bowl thoroughly with a rubber spatula after each addition.

Pour and scrape the batter into the prepared baking pan. The batter will appear somewhat soupy.

Bake the cake in the preheated oven for 1 hour, or until risen, set, and a wooden pick inserted into the cake withdraws clean or with a few particles attached. The baked cake will pull away slightly from the sides of the baking pan.

Cool the cake in the pan on a rack for 10 minutes. Invert onto another cooling rack. Lift off the pan. Paint the warm glaze over the top and sides of the cake, using a soft pastry brush. Cool completely. Store in an airtight cake keeper.

AUTHOR'S NOTES Empire, Paula Red, Jonathan, or Granny Smith apples make a flavorsome cake; for the best texture, be sure to grate the apples on the coarse holes of a 4-sided box grater.

Nuts (either walnuts or pecans) would add a crunchy, autumnal counterpoint to the apples; 1 cup coarsely chopped nuts (ideally, lightly toasted before chopping) can be stirred into the batter after the apples are added.

continued on page 262

APPLE CAKE *continued*

Granulated sugar is used as the primary sweetening agent, along with ½ cup dark brown sugar for a light, caramel-flavored undertone.

A fluted tube pan that is 4¼ inches deep must be used in order to contain all of the batter and to bake properly.

Use a finely serrated knife to cut the cake.

MAKE AHEAD 2 days.

MAPLE BUTTER GLAZE

Place the maple syrup, butter, and salt in a small, heavy saucepan (preferably enameled cast iron). Set over moderately low heat and bring to the simmer, stirring occasionally. Simmer for 1 minute. Remove from the heat and stir in the apple brandy (if you are using it), return the saucepan to the heat, bring to the simmer, simmer for 1 minute, then remove from the heat. Pour the glaze into a heatproof bowl. Stir in the vanilla extract.

Use the glaze immediately to brush lavishly over the surface of the warm cake.

AUTHOR'S NOTES This simple glaze is a good one to remember for applying to the surface of fresh apple or pear butter cakes, or to cakes composed of dried fruit, especially those containing dates or raisins.

SERVING: ABOUT ¾ CUP

SWEET BUTTERY MAPLE COAT
⅔ cup pure maple syrup
4 tablespoons (½ stick) unsalted butter, cut into chunks
Pinch of salt
1 tablespoon apple brandy (such as Calvados, optional)
½ teaspoon vanilla extract

Shredded apples melt into this cake, keeping it tender and moist.

CRAGGY-TOP SOUR CREAM BUNS, VANILLA STREUSEL

SERVING: 16 BUNS

SOUR CREAM YEAST DOUGH

4½	teaspoons active dry yeast
¼	teaspoon granulated sugar
⅓	cup warm (105 to 110°F) water
1	cup sour cream
5	large egg yolks
1	tablespoon vanilla bean paste
1½	teaspoons vanilla extract
⅓	cup granulated sugar
4¼	cups unsifted bleached all-purpose flour
¾	teaspoon salt
½	pound (16 tablespoons or 2 sticks) cool unsalted butter, cut into teaspoon-size chunks

Vanilla Streusel (recipe follows)
Confectioners' sugar, for sprinkling over the baked buns

For the dough, stir together the yeast, the ¼ teaspoon granulated sugar, and the warm water in a heatproof measuring cup. Allow the mixture to stand until swollen, 6 to 7 minutes.

In the meantime, whisk the sour cream, egg yolks, vanilla bean paste, vanilla extract, and the ⅓ cup granulated sugar in a medium-size mixing bowl. Blend in the yeast mixture. Whisk 4 cups of the flour and the salt in a large mixing bowl. Drop in the butter chunks and, using a pastry blender or two round-bladed table knives, cut the fat into the flour mixture until reduced to large, irregularly sized flakes. Add the sour cream and yeast mixture and stir to combine. The dough will not come together at this point; there will be dry patches and moist sections.

Scrape the dough mixture, including all of the unincorporated flour, into the bowl of a heavy-duty freestanding electric mixer. Set the bowl in place and attach the dough hook. Beat on low speed for 2 minutes; the dough will be quite sticky. Stop the mixer and scrape down the sides of the mixing bowl and the dough hook. Beat the dough on moderate speed for 3 minutes. Add the remaining ¼ cup flour and beat for 6 minutes longer. Once or twice in the beating process, stop the mixer and scrape down the sides of the mixing bowl and the dough hook. At this point, the dough will be exceptionally smooth, silky, pull-y, but still somewhat moist—it will not clean the bottom or sides of the mixing bowl.

Turn the dough into a bowl heavily coated with softened unsalted butter, lightly turn to coat all sides in a film of butter, make several cuts in the dough with a pair of kitchen scissors, cover tightly with a sheet of food-safe plastic wrap, and let rise at room temperature for 1 hour and 45 minutes to 2 hours. During this time frame, the dough should just double in bulk. During this rise, make sure that the dough reaches, but does not exceed, the doubled-in-bulk stage.

Remove and discard the plastic wrap. Lightly compress the dough with your fingertips.

Transfer the compressed dough to a very lightly oiled double sheet of food-safe plastic wrap, enclose to wrap securely, and refrigerate the dough overnight, or for at least 12 hours. As the dough rises in the refrigerator, it will look like a fat, inflated pillow. After 4 hours of refrigeration, compress the dough lightly, rewrap it in lightly oiled plastic wrap, and return it to the refrigerator.

Film the inside of two 8-by-8-by-2-inch baking pans with softened unsalted butter. Dust the bottom of each pan with all-purpose flour, leaving the sides simply buttered.

To form the buns, remove the dough from the refrigerator. Remove and discard the plastic wrap. The cold dough will be pliable and moldable. Divide the dough in half, then cut each half into 8 even-size pieces. Flatten each piece into a patty measuring about 2 by 3½ inches. Arrange the sections of dough in the pans, spacing them in two rows of 4 patties each.

Cover each pan of buns with a sheet of lightly buttered food-safe plastic wrap and let rise at room temperature for 2 hours and 30 minutes. Remove the sheets of plastic wrap. Sprinkle the streusel mixture over the tops of the buns, dividing it evenly between the two pans. Lightly cover with plastic wrap. Let the pans of buns stand for 1 hour and 10 minutes to 1 hour and 20 minutes longer, or until quite puffy and a little more than doubled in bulk. The buns should rise to almost fill the pan, leaving about ¼ inch headspace.

Preheat the oven to 350°F in advance of baking.

Bake the buns in the preheated oven for 40 minutes, or until set and a medium golden color on top. The fully baked buns will pull away slightly from the edges of the baking pans. Let the buns cool in the pans on cooling racks. Carefully detach the buns with two small offset metal spatulas, taking care not to compress them, then remove them from the pan. Serve the buns freshly baked, their tops dusted with confectioners' sugar.

continued on page 266

SOUR CREAM BUNS *continued*

SERVING: ABOUT 2 CUPS

BUTTER CRUMBLE

 1 cup unsifted bleached
    all-purpose flour

Large pinch of salt

 ⅔ cup granulated sugar

 ⅓ cup firmly packed light
    brown sugar

 8 tablespoons (1 stick)
    cool unsalted butter, cut into
    tablespoon-size chunks

 1¼ teaspoons vanilla extract

AUTHOR'S NOTES Three leisurely rises (after mixing, during an over-night refrigeration, and once again after forming and topping) greatly enhance the flavor of the dough and stabilize its texture.

MAKE AHEAD Best on baking day; or freeze for 3 weeks, defrost, bundle in aluminum foil, and reheat in a preheated 300°F oven for 10 to 12 minutes.

VANILLA STREUSEL

Combine the flour, salt, granulated sugar, and light brown sugar in a medium-size mixing bowl. Scatter over the chunks of butter and, using a pastry blender or two round-bladed table knives, cut the fat into the flour until it is reduced to pieces about the size of large pearls. Sprinkle over the vanilla extract. Using your fingertips, crumble the mixture together until it clings in nuggets, large, small, and in between. The clumps will be moist and sandy-textured.

Use the streusel immediately, or turn it into a food-safe container, cover, and refrigerate.

MAKE AHEAD 2 days.

BUTTER + CINNAMON + SUGAR = CAKE

SERVING: ONE 9-INCH
CAKE, CREATING 16 SQUARES
OR 12 AMPLE FINGERS

CINNAMON BUTTER BATTER

2¾ cups unsifted bleached
     all-purpose flour
1¾ teaspoons baking powder
½ teaspoon salt
1 tablespoon ground cinnamon
½ pound (16 tablespoons or 2
     sticks) unsalted butter, softened
1 cup plus 3 tablespoons
     granulated sugar
3 large eggs
2 teaspoons vanilla extract
1 cup plus 2 tablespoons
     half-and-half

CINNAMON-SUGAR TOPPING

½ cup granulated sugar
     blended with 1 tablespoon
     ground cinnamon

Preheat the oven to 350°F.

Film the inside of a 9-by-9-by-2-inch pan with nonstick flour-and-oil spray.

For the batter, sift the flour, baking powder, salt, and cinnamon onto a sheet of waxed paper.

Cream the butter in the large bowl of a freestanding electric mixer on moderate speed for 3 minutes. Add the sugar in 2 additions, beating for 2 minutes after each portion is added. Beat in the eggs, one at a time, mixing only until incorporated. Blend in the vanilla extract. On low speed, alternately add the sifted mixture in 3 additions with the half-and-half in 2 additions, beginning and ending with the sifted mixture. Scrape down the sides of the mixing bowl with a rubber spatula to keep the batter even-textured. Beat the batter on moderately high speed for 30 seconds. The batter will be very creamy and moderately dense.

Spoon and scrape the batter into the prepared baking pan. Smooth the top with a rubber spatula.

Bake the cake in the preheated oven for 40 to 45 minutes, or until risen, set, and a wooden pick withdraws clean when inserted 1 to 2 inches from the center. Cool the cake in the pan on a cooling rack for 5 minutes. Sprinkle half of the cinnamon-sugar topping evenly over the surface of the cake. The first sprinkling will cause the surface to darken as it absorbs the mixture because the cake is emitting warmth. Let the cake rest for 30 minutes, then sprinkle the remaining cinnamon-sugar topping on the surface of the cake. The dual sprinklings at different cake temperatures will result in an interesting definition of taste and color. Serve the cake cut into squares or fingers directly from the pan. Lift out the pieces of cake, using a small offset metal spatula. Store in an airtight cake keeper.

AUTHOR'S NOTES Overbeating the mixture when the eggs are added may destabilize the cake as it bakes (risking an uneven rise), so be sure to beat the mixture just to incorporate each egg.

The fine, close-textured (some would call it "compact") crumb of the cake is ultra-buttery and creamy.

MAKE AHEAD 2 days.

BACON, ONION & GRUYÈRE SCONES

MAKES 8 SCONES

- 6 strips of bacon (about 5 ounces)
- 1½ sticks (6 ounces) cold unsalted butter, cubed
- 1 small onion, finely diced
- 1 cup buttermilk
- 1 large egg
- 3 cups all-purpose flour, plus more for dusting
- 2¼ teaspoons baking powder
- ½ teaspoon baking soda
- ½ teaspoon fine sea salt
- ½ teaspoon freshly ground black pepper
- 7 ounces Gruyère cheese, coarsely shredded (2 cups)

Yockelson's savory scones are rich with cheese and bacon, yet they're incredibly light and flaky in texture.

1. In a large skillet, cook the bacon over moderate heat, turning once, until crisp, about 7 minutes. Drain the bacon on paper towels and let cool completely, then finely chop.

2. In a small skillet, melt 2 tablespoons of the butter. Add the onion and cook over moderate heat, stirring occasionally, until golden brown and softened, about 8 minutes. Let cool completely.

3. Preheat the oven to 375°F and line a baking sheet with parchment paper. In a small bowl, whisk the buttermilk with the egg. In a large bowl, whisk the 3 cups of flour with the baking powder, baking soda, salt and pepper. Using a pastry blender or 2 knives, cut in the remaining 1 stick plus 2 tablespoons of butter until it resembles small peas. Pinch the pea-size bits into smaller flakes. Add the cheese and toss. Add the wet ingredients, bacon and onion and stir until evenly moistened.

4. Scrape the dough out onto a floured work surface and knead it gently just until it comes together. Cut the dough in half and pat into two 5½-inch disks, then cut each disk into 4 wedges. Arrange the scones 3 inches apart on the prepared baking sheet and bake for 25 to 35 minutes, until risen and golden brown. Transfer the scones to a rack and let cool for 30 minutes before serving.

LISA YOCKELSON ONLINE
bakingstylediary.com

INDEX

almonds

Apricot-Bourbon-Glazed Grilled
Chicken, 229
Blue Cheese Guacamole, 210, **211**
English Toffee, 194
Fish with Crispy Garlic & Almond Salad,
60, **61**
Israeli Couscous Salad, **10,** 31
Penne alla Trapanese
(Penne Trapani Style), 204, **205**
Romesco Sauce, 139
Spiced Almonds, 124

appetizers & starters

Blue Cheese Guacamole, 210, **211**
Chicken Cordon Bleu Meatballs, 99
Chicken Skewers, 132
Chile Chicken Wings with Creamy
Cucumbers, 224
Crispy Fresh Salmon Cakes, 143
Deviled Tomatoes, 88
Fresh Tomatillo Salsa, 215
Grilled Gözlemes, 64, **65**
Lemony Kale Caesar Salad, 142
Marinated Pepper Salad
with Pecorino, 176, **177**
Mini Buffalo Chicken Balls, 94, **95**
Nancy's Chopped Salad, 244, **245**
Petits Farcis, 148, **149**
Piquillo Pepper Jam, 132
Polpette di Zucchine (Zucchini Balls), 206
Roasted Sweet Onions Stuffed with
Ground Lamb & Apricots, **222,** 228
Roast Jerusalem Artichoke, Hazelnut
& Goat Cheese Salad, 72, **73**
Smoked Tomatoes with Ancho
Bread Crumbs & Creamy Cilantro
Vinaigrette, 85
Smoky Eggplant Dip, 43

Spiced Almonds, 124
Warm Leek & White Bean Salad with
Mustard Dressing, 70, **71**
Young Swiss Chard, Fennel & Parmesan
Salad, 121

apricots

Apricot-Bourbon-Glazed Grilled
Chicken, 229
Roasted Sweet Onions Stuffed
with Ground Lamb & Apricots,
222, 228
Artichokes & Tomato, an Italian Garden
Salsa of, Grilled Fish with, 62, **63**

arugula

Apricot-Bourbon-Glazed Grilled
Chicken, 229
Chicken Cutlet with American
Triple Cream Cheese, Southern
Ham & Arugula, 82, **83**
Fish with Crispy Garlic & Almond Salad,
60, **61**
Orecchiette with 'Nduja, 114, **115**
Asparagus, Gorgonzola & Hazelnut Risotto,
117

avocados

Blue Cheese Guacamole, 210, **211**
Stewed Frankfurter Tortas, 221

bacon

Bacon, Onion & Gruyère Scones, 269
Black-Eyed Pea & Kale Chili
with Monterey Jack Cheese, 36, **37**
Deviled Tomatoes, 88
Banana Bread with Nutty Streusel, 197

basil

Marinated Pepper Salad with
Pecorino, 176, **177**
Penne alla Trapanese (Penne Trapani
Style), 204, **205**

beans

Black-Eyed Pea & Kale Chili
with Monterey Jack Cheese, 36, **37**
Ceci, 246
Green Bean Salad with Mustard Seeds
& Tarragon, 178, **179**
Nancy's Chopped Salad, 244, **245**
Pan-Roasted Striped Bass with Tunisian
Chickpea Salad & Yogurt Sauce,
226, **227**
Stewed Frankfurter Tortas, 221
Summer Beans with a Spicy Lime Spritz,
14, **15**
Warm Leek & White Bean Salad with
Mustard Dressing, 70, **71**

beef. SEE ALSO *veal*

Bolognese Balls, **92, 98**
Grilled Gözlemes, 64, **65**
Korean Steak, 40, **41**
Korean-Style Short Ribs, 28, **29**
Quick Steaks with Green Olive Dressing
& Tomato Salad, 66, **67**
Roasted Beef Tenderloin with Mushroom
Ragout, **22,** 26
Sicilian Meatballs with Fresh Basil
Marinara, 140, **141**
Stewed Frankfurter Tortas, 221
Vietnamese Grilled Steak
& Cabbage Salad with Peanuts,
Cilantro & Chiles, 51, **53**
Wok-Tossed Beef with Kohlrabi, 160
Black-Eyed Pea & Kale Chili
with Monterey Jack Cheese, 36, **37**

blue cheese
Blue Cheese Guacamole, 210, **211**
Gorgonzola, Asparagus & Hazelnut Risotto, 117
Bourbon-Apricot-Glazed Grilled Chicken, 229

breads
Bacon, Onion & Gruyère Scones, 269
Banana Bread with Nutty Streusel, 197
Bittersweet Chocolate Chunk & Cream Cheese Scones, 234
Craggy-Top Sour Cream Buns, Vanilla Streusel, 264, **267**
Broccoli Velvet Puree, 184
Brownie Drops, One-Bowl, 110
Buns, Craggy-Top Sour Cream, Vanilla Streusel, 264, **267**
Burgers, Turkey, with Quick Barbecue Sauce, 169
Buttermilk Panna Cotta, **188**, 190

Cabbage Salad with Peanuts, Cilantro & Chiles & Vietnamese Grilled Steak, 51, **53**

cakes
Apple Cake, Maple Butter Glaze, 261, **263**
Black Dinah Chocolate Tiramisu, 236
Butter + Cinnamon + Sugar = Cake, **256,** 268
Chocolate Mashed Potato Cake, 108, **109**
Lemon Cloud Cake, 199
Sweet Potato Tea Cake with Brown Sugar–Rum Glaze, 57

candy
American Toffee, **195,** 196
Chocolate Caramels, 192
English Toffee, 194
Fleur de Sel Caramels, 191, **193**
Lemon Verbena or Bergamot Caramels, 192

caramels
Chocolate Caramels, 192
Fleur de Sel Caramels, 191, **193**
Lemon Verbena or Bergamot Caramels, 192
Caramel Sauce, Persian Love, 241

carrots
Roast Chicken with Preserved Lemons & Root Vegetables, 128, **129**
Soffritto, 253

cauliflower
Cavolfiori Stufati al Pomodoro (The Best Cauliflower Ever), 202, **203**
Cumin Seed Roasted Cauliflower with Salted Yogurt, Mint & Pomegranate Seeds, 46, **47**

cheese. SEE ALSO *cream cheese*
Bacon, Onion & Gruyère Scones, 269
Black Dinah Chocolate Tiramisu, 236
Black-Eyed Pea & Kale Chili with Monterey Jack Cheese, 36, **37**
Blue Cheese Guacamole, 210, **211**
Burned Ricotta Pie, 118, **119**
Cavolfiori Stufati al Pomodoro (The Best Cauliflower Ever), 202, **203**
Chicken Cordon Bleu Meatballs, 99
Chicken Cutlet with American Triple Cream Cheese, Southern Ham & Arugula, 82, **83**
Crusted Pumpkin Wedges with Sour Cream, 180, **181**

Deviled Tomatoes, 88
Gorgonzola, Asparagus & Hazelnut Risotto, 117
Grilled Gözlemes, 64, **65**
Hominy Salad, **86,** 89
Leek & Goat Cheese Speltotto, 77
Lemony Kale Caesar Salad, 142
Manicotti Baresi al Forno, 16, **17**
Marinated Pepper Salad with Pecorino, 176, **177**
Nancy's Chopped Salad, 244, **245**
Penne alla Trapanese (Penne Trapani Style), 204, **205**
Polpette di Zucchine (Zucchini Balls), 206
Ricotta Doughnut Holes with Orange-Scented Dipping Chocolate, **230,** 232
Roast Jerusalem Artichoke, Hazelnut & Goat Cheese Salad, 72, **73**
Sicilian Meatballs with Fresh Basil Marinara, 140, **141**
Spaghetti alla Ravellese, 207
Young Swiss Chard, Fennel & Parmesan Salad, 121
Cheesecake, Pumpkin, with Elderberry Glaze & Chocolate Walnut Crumb Crust, 238, **239**

chicken
Apricot-Bourbon-Glazed Grilled Chicken, 229
Baked Chicken Curry, 76
Baked Chile Chicken Wings, 224
Basic Chicken Stock, 254
Bone-In Chicken Breast with Soy Sauce, 168
Braised Chicken Thighs with Saffron, Green Olives & Mint, 21
Brown Chicken Stock, 18

INDEX

Chicken Cordon Bleu Meatballs, 99
Chicken Cutlet with American
    Triple Cream Cheese, Southern
    Ham & Arugula, 82, **83**
Chicken in Chunky Tomatillo Sauce, 216
Chicken Skewers, 132
Chicken Skin Tacos, 152
Chicken Stock, 164
Chile Chicken Wings with Creamy
    Cucumbers, 224
Hanoi Chicken & Vermicelli Noodle
    Soup, 162, **163**
Mini Buffalo Chicken Balls, 94, **95**
My Mother's Chicken Ragout, 187
Roast Chicken with Preserved Lemons
    & Root Vegetables, 128, **129**
Romesco Chicken Salad, 138
Spicy Ginger & Lemon Chicken, 186
Chicken Liver Ragù, Pappardelle with,
    112, 116
Chile Chicken Wings with Creamy
    Cucumbers, 224
chiles
    Basic Guajillo Adobo, 220
    Deviled Tomatoes, 88
    Fiorentini with Guanciale, Tomato
        & Spicy Pickled Peppers, **242,** 247
    Fresh Tomatillo Salsa, 215
    Mexican-Style Noodles, 212, **213**
    Smoked Chile Collard Greens, 80, **81**
    Spicy Pickled Peppers, 249
    Stewed Frankfurter Tortas, 221
Chili, Black-Eyed Pea & Kale, with Monterey
    Jack Cheese, 36, **37**
chocolate
    American Toffee, **195,** 196
    Bittersweet Chocolate Chunk
        & Cream Cheese Scones, 234
    Black Dinah Chocolate Tiramisu, 236
    Burned Ricotta Pie, 118, **119**
    Chocolate Caramels, 192
    Chocolate Cookie–Peanut Butter Pie,
        105, **107**
    Chocolate Mashed Potato Cake,
        108, **109**

Deep-Dish Chocolate Cream Pie, 84
English Toffee, 194
Light Chocolate Frosting, 108, **109**
Mallobars, **44,** 54, **55**
One-Bowl Brownie Drops, 110
Pumpkin Cheesecake with Elderberry
    Glaze & Chocolate Walnut Crumb
    Crust, 238, **239**
Red Velvet Cheesecake Bars, 111
Ricotta Doughnut Holes with Orange-
    Scented Dipping Chocolate, **230,** 232
cilantro
    Blue Cheese Guacamole, 210, **211**
    Fresh Tomatillo Salsa, 215
    Hanoi Chicken & Vermicelli Noodle
        Soup, 162, **163**
    Mexican-Style Noodles, 212, **213**
    Pan-Roasted Striped Bass with
        Tunisian Chickpea Salad & Yogurt
        Sauce, 226, **227**
    Silken Tofu & Pork Soup, **156,** 161
    Smoked Tomatoes with Ancho
        Bread Crumbs & Creamy Cilantro
        Vinaigrette, 85
    Vietnamese Grilled Steak
        & Cabbage Salad with Peanuts,
        Cilantro & Chiles, 51, **53**
Cinnamon + Butter + Sugar = Cake,
    256, 268
Collard Greens, Smoked Chile, 80, **81**
Cookie Crust, No-Bake, 106
cookies & bars
    Mallobars, **44,** 54, **55**
    Molasses Crinkles, 258, **259**
    One-Bowl Brownie Drops, 110
    Red Velvet Cheesecake Bars, 111
Couscous, Israeli, Salad, **10,** 31
Crab Rolls, Gulf Coast–Style, 91
cream cheese
    Bittersweet Chocolate Chunk
        & Cream Cheese Scones, 234
    Pumpkin Cheesecake with Elderberry
        Glaze & Chocolate Walnut Crumb
        Crust, 238, **239**
    Red Velvet Cheesecake Bars, 111

Crème Fraîche, Horseradish, 27
Cucumbers, Creamy, 225
Cumin Seed Roasted Cauliflower with
    Salted Yogurt, Mint & Pomegranate
    Seeds, 46, **47**
Curry, Baked Chicken, 76

D

desserts
    American Toffee, **195,** 196
    Apple Cake, Maple Butter Glaze,
        261, **263**
    Black Dinah Chocolate Tiramisu, 236
    Burned Ricotta Pie, 118, **119**
    Butter + Cinnamon + Sugar = Cake,
        256, 268
    Buttermilk Panna Cotta, **188,** 190
    Chocolate Caramels, 192
    Chocolate Cookie–Peanut Butter Pie,
        105, **107**
    Chocolate Mashed Potato Cake,
        108, **109**
    Deep-Dish Chocolate Cream Pie, 84
    English Toffee, 194
    Fleur de Sel Caramels, 191, **193**
    Lemon Cloud Cake, 199
    Lemon Verbena or Bergamot Caramels,
        192
    Mallobars, **44,** 54, **55**
    Molasses Crinkles, 258, **259**
    One-Bowl Brownie Drops, 110
    Persian Love Caramel Sauce, 241
    Pumpkin Cheesecake with
        Elderberry Glaze & Chocolate Walnut
        Crumb Crust, 238, **239**
    Red Velvet Cheesecake Bars, 111
    Ricotta Doughnut Holes with Orange-
        Scented Dipping Chocolate, **230,** 232
    Southern Belle Raspberry Pie, 102, **103**
    Sweet Potato Tea Cake with
        Brown Sugar–Rum Glaze, 57
dips & spreads
    Blue Cheese Guacamole, 210, **211**

Fresh Tomatillo Salsa, 215
Mayonnaise, 75, 153
Piquillo Pepper Jam, 133
Romesco Sauce, 139
Smoky Eggplant Dip, 43
Yogurt Sauce, 226
Doughnut Holes, Ricotta, with Orange-
Scented Dipping Chocolate, **230,** 232
doughs
Dry Dough, 255
Lattice Dough, 104
Sweet Pastry, 120
Duck with Peaches, Ginger & Lemon
Thyme, 38

E

eggplant
Grilled Eggplant Salad with Prawns, 165
Petits Farcis, 148, **149**
Smoky Eggplant Dip, 43
English Toffee, 194

F

fennel
Seared Saffron Albacore Tuna with
Fennel-Olive Tapenade, 136, **137**
Shrimp Scampi with Pernod & Fennel
Fronds, 48, **49**
Young Swiss Chard, Fennel & Parmesan
Salad, 121
fish. SEE ALSO *shellfish*
Crispy Fresh Salmon Cakes, 143
Fish with Crispy Garlic & Almond Salad,
60, **61**
Grilled Fish with an Italian Garden Salsa
of Artichokes & Tomato, 62, **63**
Halibut Steaks Grenoble-Style, 185
Pan-Roasted Striped Bass with
Tunisian Chickpea Salad & Yogurt
Sauce, 226, **227**
Salmon with Shiso Pesto, 170, **171**

Seared Saffron Albacore Tuna with
Fennel-Olive Tapenade, 136, **137**
Thrifty Fish Soup with Cheaty Rouille, 74
Yuan Yaki–Style Grilled Spanish
Mackerel, 173
Yukon Gold Soup with Smoked Fish
& Pumpernickel Croutons, 155
Ziti with Tuna & Salame Piccante, **12,** 20
Frankfurter, Stewed, Tortas, **221**
Frosting, Light Chocolate, 108, **109**
fruit. SEE SPECIFIC FRUITS

G

garlic
Baked Mushrooms with New (or Old!)
Garlic, 146, **147**
Fish with Crispy Garlic & Almond Salad,
60, **61**
Fried Garlic, 164
Garlic Oil, 164
Lamb Shanks with Leeks & Grapes,
18, **19**
Smoky Eggplant Dip, 43
ginger
Duck with Peaches, Ginger & Lemon
Thyme, 38
Molasses Crinkles, 258, **259**
Spicy Ginger & Lemon Chicken, 186
Yuan Yaki–Style Grilled Spanish
Mackerel, 173
Glaze, Maple Butter, 262
goat cheese
Leek & Goat Cheese Speltotto, 77
Roast Jerusalem Artichoke, Hazelnut
& Goat Cheese Salad, 72, **73**
Gorgonzola, Asparagus & Hazelnut Risotto,
117
grains
Gorgonzola, Asparagus & Hazelnut
Risotto, 117
Leek & Goat Cheese Speltotto, 77
Grapefruit Butter, Scallops with, 34
Grapes & Leeks, Lamb Shanks with, 18, **19**

green beans
Green Bean Salad with Mustard Seeds
& Tarragon, 178, **179**
Summer Beans with a Spicy Lime
Spritz, 14, **15**
greens
Apricot-Bourbon-Glazed Grilled
Chicken, 229
Black-Eyed Pea & Kale Chili with
Monterey Jack Cheese, 36, **37**
Fish with Crispy Garlic & Almond Salad,
60, **61**
Grilled Gözlemes, 64, **65**
Lemony Kale Caesar Salad, 142
Marinated Pepper Salad with Pecorino,
176, **177**
Nancy's Chopped Salad, 244, **245**
Orecchiette with 'Nduja, 114, **115**
Smoked Chile Collard Greens, 80, **81**
Young Swiss Chard,
Fennel & Parmesan Salad, 121
grilled dishes
Apricot-Bourbon-Glazed Grilled
Chicken, 229
Bone-In Chicken Breast with Soy Sauce,
168
Chicken Skewers, 132
Fish with Crispy Garlic & Almond Salad,
60, **61**
Grilled Eggplant Salad with Prawns, 165
Grilled Fish with an Italian Garden
Salsa of Artichokes & Tomato, 62, **63**
Grilled Gözlemes, 64, **65**
Korean Steak, 40, **41**
Lamb & Pita Salad, 24, **25**
Pork Chops with Yuzu-Miso Marinade,
166, 172
Quick Steaks with Green Olive Dressing
& Tomato Salad, 66, **67**
Salmon with Shiso Pesto, 170, **171**
Smoked Tomatoes with Ancho
Bread Crumbs & Creamy Cilantro
Vinaigrette, 85
Turkey Burger with Quick Barbecue
Sauce, 169

Vietnamese Grilled Steak
& Cabbage Salad with Peanuts,
Cilantro & Chiles, 51, **53**
Yuan Yaki–Style Grilled Spanish
Mackerel, 173
Gruyère, Bacon & Onion Scones, 269
Guacamole, Blue Cheese, 210, **211**
Guanciale, Tomato & Spicy Pickled
Peppers, Fiorentini with, **242,** 247

H

Halibut Steaks Grenoble-Style, 185
ham
Chicken Cordon Bleu Meatballs, 99
Chicken Cutlet with American
Triple Cream Cheese, Southern
Ham & Arugula, 82, **83**
Manicotti Baresi al Forno, 16, **17**
Harissa Powder, 125
hazelnuts
Gorgonzola, Asparagus & Hazelnut
Risotto, 117
Roast Jerusalem Artichoke, Hazelnut
& Goat Cheese Salad, 72, **73**
herbs. SEE ALSO SPECIFIC HERBS
Purée de Fines Herbes, 153
Hominy Salad, **86,** 89
horseradish
Horseradish Crème Fraîche, 27
Smashed Turnips with
Fresh Horseradish, 96, **97**

I

Israeli Couscous Salad, **10,** 31

J

Jam, Piquillo Pepper, 133
Jerusalem Artichoke, Roast, Hazelnut
& Goat Cheese Salad, 72, **73**

K

kale
Black-Eyed Pea & Kale Chili
with Monterey Jack Cheese, 36, **37**
Lemony Kale Caesar Salad, 142
Kohlrabi, Wok-Tossed Beef with, 160
Korean Steak, 40, **41**
Korean-Style Short Ribs, 28, **29**

L

lamb
Lamb & Pita Salad, 24, **25**
Lamb Shanks with Leeks & Grapes,
18, **19**
Manicotti Baresi al Forno, 16, **17**
Roasted Sweet Onions Stuffed with
Ground Lamb & Apricots, **222,** 228
leeks
Crispy Fresh Salmon Cakes, 143
Lamb Shanks with Leeks & Grapes,
18, **19**
Leek & Goat Cheese Speltotto, 77
Warm Leek & White Bean Salad with
Mustard Dressing, 70, **71**
Lemongrass, Honey & Soy, Oven-Browned
Spareribs with, 30
lemons
Duck with Peaches, Ginger & Lemon
Thyme, 38
Lemon Cloud Cake, 199
Lemony Kale Caesar Salad, 142
Roast Chicken with Preserved Lemons
& Root Vegetables, 128, **129**
Spicy Ginger & Lemon Chicken, 186
Lemon Verbena or Bergamot Caramels,
192
lettuce
Fish with Crispy Garlic & Almond
Salad, 60, **61**
Lamb & Pita Salad, 24, **25**
Nancy's Chopped Salad, 244, **245**

Warm Leek & White Bean Salad with
Mustard Dressing, 70, **71**
Lime Spritz, Spicy, Summer Beans with a,
14, **15**
Liver, Chicken, Ragù, Pappardelle with,
112, 116

M

Mallobars, **44,** 54, **55**
Maple Butter Glaze, 262
Mayonnaise, 75, 153
meat. SEE *beef; lamb; pork; veal*
meatballs
Bolognese Balls, **92,** 98
Chicken Cordon Bleu Meatballs, 99
Mini Buffalo Chicken Balls, 94, **95**
Sicilian Meatballs with Fresh Basil
Marinara, 140, **141**
Mexican-Style Noodles, 212, **213**
mint
Braised Chicken Thighs with Saffron,
Green Olives & Mint, 21
Cumin Seed Roasted Cauliflower with
Salted Yogurt, Mint & Pomegranate
Seeds, 46, **47**
Fish with Crispy Garlic & Almond Salad,
60, **61**
Hanoi Chicken & Vermicelli Noodle
Soup, 162, **163**
Lamb & Pita Salad, 24, **25**
Polpette di Zucchine (Zucchini Balls), 206
Miso-Yuzu Marinade, Pork Chops with,
166, 172
Molasses Crinkles, 258, **259**
mushrooms
Baked Mushrooms with New (or Old!)
Garlic, 146, **147**
Roasted Beef Tenderloin with Mushroom
Ragout, **22,** 26
mussels
Mouclade, 150, **151**
Mustard Dressing, Warm Leek & White
Bean Salad with, 70, **71**

N

'Nduja, Orecchiette with, 114, **115**
noodles
Hanoi Chicken & Vermicelli Noodle
Soup, 162, **163**
Mexican-Style Noodles, 212, **213**
nuts. SEE ALSO *almonds*
American Toffee, **195,** 196
Banana Bread with Nutty Streusel, 197
Chocolate Cookie–Peanut Butter Pie,
105, **107**
Gorgonzola, Asparagus & Hazelnut
Risotto, 117
One-Bowl Brownie Drops, 110
Roast Jerusalem Artichoke, Hazelnut
& Goat Cheese Salad, 72, **73**

O

Oil, Garlic, 164
olives
Braised Chicken Thighs with Saffron,
Green Olives & Mint, 21
Grilled Fish with an Italian Garden Salsa
of Artichokes & Tomato, 62, **63**
Israeli Couscous Salad, **10,** 31
Quick Steaks with Green Olive Dressing
& Tomato Salad, 66, **67**
Seared Saffron Albacore Tuna with
Fennel-Olive Tapenade, 136, **137**
onions
Bacon, Onion & Gruyère Scones, 269
Deviled Tomatoes, 88
Petits Farcis, 148, **149**
Roasted Sweet Onions Stuffed with
Ground Lamb & Apricots, **222,** 228
Soffritto, 253
oranges
Israeli Couscous Salad, **10,** 31
Ricotta Doughnut Holes with Orange-
Scented Dipping Chocolate, **230,** 232
Oregano Vinaigrette, 246

P

Panna Cotta, Buttermilk, **188,** 190
parmesan cheese
Cavolfiori Stufati al Pomodoro
(The Best Cauliflower Ever), 202, **203**
Crusted Pumpkin Wedges with Sour
Cream, 180, **181**
Lemony Kale Caesar Salad, 142
Penne alla Trapanese
(Penne Trapani Style), 204, **205**
Sicilian Meatballs with
Fresh Basil Marinara, 140, **141**
Young Swiss Chard, Fennel & Parmesan
Salad, 121
pasta & noodles
Fiorentini with Guanciale, Tomato
& Spicy Pickled Peppers, 242, **247**
Garganelli with Ragù Bolognese,
250, **251**
Hanoi Chicken & Vermicelli Noodle
Soup, 162, **163**
Manicotti Baresi al Forno, 16, **17**
Mexican-Style Noodles, 212, **213**
Orecchiette with 'Nduja, 114, **115**
Pappardelle with Chicken Liver Ragù,
112, 116
Penne alla Trapanese
(Penne Trapani Style), 204, **205**
Spaghetti alla Ravellese, 207
Ziti with Tuna & Salame Piccante,
12, 20
Peaches, Ginger & Lemon Thyme, Duck
with, 38
peanuts & peanut butter
American Toffee, **195,** 196
Chocolate Cookie–Peanut Butter Pie,
105, **107**
Vietnamese Grilled Steak
& Cabbage Salad with Peanuts,
Cilantro & Chiles, 51, **53**
peas
Green Bean Salad with Mustard Seeds
& Tarragon, 178, **179**

pecans
Banana Bread with Nutty Streusel, 197
pecorino cheese
Manicotti Baresi al Forno, 16, **17**
Marinated Pepper Salad with Pecorino,
176, **177**
Polpette di Zucchine (Zucchini Balls), 206
Spaghetti alla Ravellese, 207
peppers. SEE ALSO *chiles*
Deviled Tomatoes, 88
Marinated Pepper Salad with Pecorino,
176, **177**
Petits Farcis, 148, **149**
Piquillo Pepper Jam, 133
Romesco Sauce, 139
Spicy Pickled Peppers, 249
Pesto, Shiso, Salmon with, 170, **171**
Pickled Peppers, Spicy, 249
pies
Burned Ricotta Pie, 118, **119**
Chocolate Cookie–Peanut Butter Pie,
105, **107**
Deep-Dish Chocolate Cream Pie, 84
Southern Belle Raspberry Pie, 102, **103**
Piquillo Pepper Jam, 133
Pomegranate Seeds, Salted Yogurt
& Mint, Cumin Seed Roasted Cauliflower
with, 46, **47**
pork. SEE ALSO *bacon; ham*
Bolognese Balls, **92,** 98
Fiorentini with Guanciale, Tomato
& Spicy Pickled Peppers, **242,** 247
Garganelli with Ragù Bolognese,
250, **251**
Hanoi Chicken & Vermicelli Noodle
Soup, 162, **163**
Oven-Browned Spareribs with
Lemongrass, Honey & Soy, 30
Petits Farcis, 148, **149**
Pork Chops with Yuzu-Miso Marinade,
166, 172
Pork in Adobo, 218, **219**
Pork Terrine, 164
Schnitzel of Pork, 154
Silken Tofu & Pork Soup, **156,** 161

potatoes
Chicken Skin Tacos, 152
Chocolate Mashed Potato Cake, 108, **109**
My Mother's Chicken Ragout, 187
Salt-Roasted Potatoes, 122, **126**
Thrifty Fish Soup with Cheaty Rouille, 74
Yukon Gold Soup with Smoked Fish & Pumpernickel Croutons, 155

poultry. SEE ALSO **chicken**
Duck with Peaches, Ginger & Lemon Thyme, 38
Turkey Burger with Quick Barbecue Sauce, 169

Prawns, Grilled Eggplant Salad with, 165
Prunes, Spiced, 131

pumpkin
Crusted Pumpkin Wedges with Sour Cream, 180, **181**
Pumpkin Cheesecake with Elderberry Glaze & Chocolate Walnut Crumb Crust, 238, **239**

R

Ragout, My Mother's Chicken, 187
Raspberry Pie, Southern Belle, 102, **103**
Red Velvet Cheesecake Bars, 111

rice. SEE **risotto**

ricotta cheese
Burned Ricotta Pie, 118, **119**
Manicotti Baresi al Forno, 16, **17**
Ricotta Doughnut Holes with Orange-Scented Dipping Chocolate, **230,** 232
Risotto, Gorgonzola, Asparagus & Hazelnut, 117
Romesco Chicken Salad, 138
Romesco Sauce, 139

rum
Black Dinah Chocolate Tiramisu, 236
Sweet Potato Tea Cake with Brown Sugar–Rum Glaze, 57

S

salads
Fish with Crispy Garlic & Almond Salad, 60, **61**
Green Bean Salad with Mustard Seeds & Tarragon, 178, **179**
Grilled Eggplant Salad with Prawns, 165
Hominy Salad, **86, 89**
Israeli Couscous Salad, **10,** 31
Lamb & Pita Salad, 24, **25**
Lemony Kale Caesar Salad, 142
Marinated Pepper Salad with Pecorino, 176, **177**
Nancy's Chopped Salad, 244, **245**
Quick Steaks with Green Olive Dressing & Tomato Salad, 66, **67**
Roast Jerusalem Artichoke, Hazelnut & Goat Cheese Salad, 72, **73**
Romesco Chicken Salad, 138
Vietnamese Grilled Steak & Cabbage Salad with Peanuts, Cilantro & Chiles, 51, **53**
Warm Leek & White Bean Salad with Mustard Dressing, 70, **71**
Young Swiss Chard, Fennel & Parmesan Salad, 121

salami
Nancy's Chopped Salad, 244, **245**
Ziti with Tuna & Salame Piccante, **12,** 20

salmon
Crispy Fresh Salmon Cakes, 143
Salmon with Shiso Pesto, 170, **171**

salsas
Chunky Tomatillo Sauce, 217
Fresh Tomatillo Salsa, 215
Grilled Fish with an Italian Garden Salsa of Artichokes & Tomato, 62, **63**

Salt-Roasted Potatoes, **122,** 126

sandwiches & burgers
Gulf Coast–Style Crab Rolls, 91
Stewed Frankfurter Tortas, 221
Turkey Burger with Quick Barbecue Sauce, 169

sauces
Basic Guajillo Adobo, 220
Chunky Tomatillo Sauce, 217
Horseradish Crème Fraîche, 27
Passata di Pomodoro, 248
Persian Love Caramel Sauce, 241
Romesco Sauce, 139
Yogurt Sauce, 226

sausage
Orecchiette with 'Nduja, 114, **115**
Petits Farcis, 148, **149**
Sausage Dinner, 90
Ziti with Tuna & Salame Piccante, **12,** 20

Scallops with Grapefruit Butter, 34
Schnitzel of Pork, 154

scones
Bacon, Onion & Gruyère Scones, 269
Bittersweet Chocolate Chunk & Cream Cheese Scones, 234

seafood. SEE **fish; shellfish**

shellfish
Grilled Eggplant Salad with Prawns, 165
Gulf Coast–Style Crab Rolls, 91
Mouclade, 150, **151**
Sautéed Jumbo Shrimp, 158, **159**
Scallops with Grapefruit Butter, 34
Shrimp Scampi with Pernod & Fennel Fronds, 48, **49**
Thrifty Fish Soup with Cheaty Rouille, 74

Shiso Pesto, Salmon with, 170, **171**

shrimp
Grilled Eggplant Salad with Prawns, 165
Sautéed Jumbo Shrimp, 158, **159**
Shrimp Scampi with Pernod & Fennel Fronds, 48, **49**

Soffritto, 253

soups & stocks
Basic Chicken Stock, 254
Brown Chicken Stock, 18
Chicken Stock, 164
Hanoi Chicken & Vermicelli Noodle Soup, 162, **163**

Silken Tofu & Pork Soup, **156,** 161
Thrifty Fish Soup with Cheaty Rouille, 74
Yukon Gold Soup with Smoked Fish
    & Pumpernickel Croutons, 155

sour cream
Craggy-Top Sour Cream Buns, Vanilla
    Streusel, 264, **267**
Crusted Pumpkin Wedges with Sour
    Cream, 180, **181**
Spanish Mackerel, Yuan Yaki–Style Grilled,
    173
Speltotto, Leek & Goat Cheese, 77

spinach
Grilled Gözlemes, 64, **65**

squash
Crusted Pumpkin Wedges
    with Sour Cream, 180, **181**
Petits Farcis, 148, **149**
Polpette di Zucchine (Zucchini Balls),
    206
Pumpkin Cheesecake with
    Elderberry Glaze & Chocolate Walnut
    Crumb Crust, 238, **239**
Spaghetti alla Ravellese, 207

starters. SEE *appetizers & starters*
Striped Bass, Pan-Roasted, with
    Tunisian Chickpea Salad & Yogurt
    Sauce, 226, **227**
Sweet Potato Tea Cake with Brown Sugar–
    Rum Glaze, 57
Swiss Chard, Young, Fennel & Parmesan
    Salad, 121

Tacos, Chicken Skin, 152
Tiramisu, Black Dinah Chocolate, 236
toffee
American Toffee, **195,** 196
English Toffee, 194
Tofu, Silken, & Pork Soup, **156,** 161
tomatillos
Chunky Tomatillo Sauce, 217
Fresh Tomatillo Salsa, 215

tomatoes
Baked Chicken Curry, 76
Cavolfiori Stufati al Pomodoro
    (The Best Cauliflower Ever), 202, **203**
Deviled Tomatoes, 88
Fiorentini with Guanciale, Tomato
    & Spicy Pickled Peppers, **242,** 247
Grilled Fish with an Italian Garden Salsa
    of Artichokes & Tomato, 62, **63**
Hominy Salad, **86,** 89
Mexican-Style Noodles, 212, **213**
Nancy's Chopped Salad, 244, **245**
Orecchiette with 'Nduja, 114, **115**
Passata di Pomodoro, 248
Penne alla Trapanese
    (Penne Trapani Style), 204, **205**
Petits Farcis, 148, **149**
Polpette di Zucchine (Zucchini Balls), 206
Quick Steaks with Green Olive Dressing
    & Tomato Salad, 66, **67**
Sicilian Meatballs with Fresh Basil
    Marinara, 140, **141**
Smoked Tomatoes with Ancho
    Bread Crumbs & Creamy Cilantro
    Vinaigrette, 85

tuna
Seared Saffron Albacore Tuna with
    Fennel-Olive Tapenade, 136, **137**
Ziti with Tuna & Salame Piccante, **12,** 20
Turkey Burger with Quick Barbecue Sauce,
    169

turnips
Roast Chicken with Preserved Lemons
    & Root Vegetables, 128, **129**
Smashed Turnips with Fresh
    Horseradish, 96, **97**

Vanilla Streusel, 266
veal
Garganelli with Ragù Bolognese, 250, **251**
Manicotti Baresi al Forno, 16, **17**
Petits Farcis, 148, **149**

vegetables. SEE ALSO SPECIFIC VEGETABLES
Petits Farcis, 148, **149**
Roast Chicken with Preserved Lemons
    & Root Vegetables, 128, **129**
Soffritto, 253
Vietnamese Grilled Steak & Cabbage Salad
    with Peanuts, Cilantro & Chiles, 51, **53**
Vinaigrette, Oregano, 246

walnuts
One-Bowl Brownie Drops, 110
Pumpkin Cheesecake with Elderberry
    Glaze & Chocolate Walnut Crumb
    Crust, 238, **239**
Wok-Tossed Beef with Kohlrabi, 160

yogurt
Creamy Cucumbers, 225
Cumin Seed Roasted Cauliflower
    with Salted Yogurt, Mint
    & Pomegranate Seeds, 46, **47**
Yogurt Sauce, 226
Yuzu-Miso Marinade, Pork Chops with,
    166, 172

zucchini
Petits Farcis, 148, **149**
Polpette di Zucchine (Zucchini Balls), 206
Spaghetti alla Ravellese, 207

CREDITS

MOLTO BATALI
*simple family meals from
my home to yours*

Four recipes, four interior photos, book cover from
Molto Batali by Mario Batali. Copyright © 2011 by
Mario Batali, LLC. Reprinted by permission of Harper
Collins Publishers. Photography by Quentin Bacon.

THE COOK & THE BUTCHER

Recipes from *The Cook & the Butcher* by Brigit
Binns. Conceived and produced by Weldon Owen,
Inc., in collaboration with Williams-Sonoma, Inc.
Copyright © 2011 Weldon Owen, Inc., and Williams-
Sonoma, Inc. Photographs by Kate Sears.

AMERICAN FLAVOR

Four recipes, three interior photos, book cover from
American Flavor by Andrew Carmellini and Gwen
Hyman. Copyright © 2011 by Andrew Carmellini and
Gwen Hyman. Reprinted by permission of Harper
Collins Publishers. Photography by Quentin Bacon.

COOK THIS NOW
*120 easy & delectable dishes you
can't wait to make*

From the book *Cook This Now: 120 Easy and
Delectable Dishes You Can't Wait to Make* by Melissa
Clark. Photographs by Andrew Scrivani. Cover
photograph by Matthew Benson. Copyright © 2011
Melissa Clark, Inc. Published by Hyperion. Available
wherever books are sold. All rights reserved.

MY GRILL
outdoor cooking australian style

From *My Grill* by Pete Evans. Text copyright ©
2009 by Peter Evans. First published in 2009 by
Murdoch Books Australia. Published in the United
States in 2011 by Weldon Owen. Photography copyright © 2009 by Anson Smart.

RIVER COTTAGE EVERY DAY

Recipes from *River Cottage Every Day* by Hugh
Fearnley-Whittingstall, copyright © 2009 by Hugh
Fearnley-Whittingstall. Jacket cover copyright ©
2009 by Ten Speed Press. Used by permission of
Ten Speed Press, an imprint of the Crown Publishing
Group, a division of Random House, Inc. Photography
copyright © 2009 by Simon Wheeler.

BOBBY FLAY'S BAR AMERICAIN COOKBOOK
celebrate america's great flavors

Recipes from *Bobby Flay's Bar Americain Cookbook:
Celebrate America's Great Flavors* by Bobby Flay
with Stephanie Banyas and Sally Jackson, copyright
© 2011 by Boy Meets Grill, Inc. Jacket cover copyright © 2011 by Clarkson Potter. Used by permission
of Clarkson Potter/Publishers, an imprint of the
Crown Publishing Group, a division of Random House,
Inc. Photographs copyright © 2011 by Ben Fink.

A SOUTHERLY COURSE
recipes & stories from close to home

Recipes from *A Southerly Course: Recipes &
Stories from Close to Home* by Martha Hall Foose,
copyright © 2011 by Martha Foose. Jacket cover
copyright © 2011 by Clarkson Potter/Publishers.
Used by permission of Clarkson Potter/Publishers,
an imprint of the Crown Publishing Group, a division
of Random House, Inc. Photographs copyright
© 2011 by Chris Granger.

THE MEATBALL SHOP COOKBOOK

Book cover and recipes from *The Meatball Shop
Cookbook* by Daniel Holzman and Michael Chernow
with Lauren Deen. Text copyright © 2011 by Daniel
Holzman and Michael Chernow. Book cover copyright © 2011 by Ballantine Books. Used by permission
of Ballantine Books, a division of Random House,
Inc. Photographs copyright © 2011 by John Kernick.

DESSERTS FROM THE FAMOUS LOVELESS CAFE
*simple southern pies, puddings,
cakes & cobblers from nashville's
landmark restaurant*

Excerpted from *Desserts from the Famous Loveless
Cafe*. Copyright © 2011 by Alisa Huntsman and
Loveless Cafe, LLC. Used by permission of Artisan,
a division of Workman Publishing Co., Inc., New
York. All rights reserved. Photographs copyright ©
2011 by Karen Mordechai.

BOCCA COOKBOOK

Recipes from *Bocca Cookbook* by Jacob Kenedy.
Text copyright © 2011 by Jacob Kenedy. Used by
permission of Bloomsbury Publishing Plc. Photography copyright © 2011 by Howard Sooley.

MOURAD: NEW MOROCCAN

Excerpted from *Mourad: New Moroccan*. Copyright
© 2011 by Mourad Lahlou. Used by permission of
Artisan, a division of Workman Publishing Co., Inc.,
New York. All rights reserved. Photographs copyright
© 2011 by Deborah Jones.

BI-RITE MARKET'S EAT GOOD FOOD
*a grocer's guide to shopping, cooking
& creating community through food*

Recipes from *Bi-Rite Market's Eat Good Food:
A Grocer's Guide to Shopping, Cooking, and Creating
Community through Food* by Sam Mogannam and
Dabney Gough, copyright © 2011 by Bi-Rite Market,
Inc. Jacket cover copyright © 2011 by Ten Speed
Press. Used by permission of Ten Speed Press, an
imprint of the Crown Publishing Group, a division
of Random House, Inc. Photographs copyright ©
2011 by France Ruffenach.